W9-BCO-449

COMPUTE!'s
Quick & Easy
Guide to
OS/2

Ted Crooks

COMPUTE! Books Publications

Editor: Robert Bixby

Printed in the United States of America

10 9 8 7 6 5 4 3 2

ISBN 0-87455-137-4

COMPUTE! Books, Post Office Box 5406, Greensboro, North Carolina 27403, (919) 275-9809, is a Capital Cities/ABC, Inc. company and is not associated with any manufacturer of personal computers. IBM is a registered trademark and OS/2 is a trademark of International Business Machines Corporation. Microsoft and MS-DOS are registered trademarks of Microsoft Corporation.

Contents

Foreword

OS/2 is the fast, powerful multitasking operating system that seems to have accomplished the impossible. It's the most up-to-date operating system in the world, the operating system computers will be using well into the next decade. Yet it's still compatible with DOS 1.1, the very first operating system for the IBM PC.

COMPUTE!'s Quick and Easy Guide to OS/2 unleashes all the power within OS/2. It includes a full explanation of OS/2 commands, a review of the uses of directories and files, and a how-to section packed with valuable information. And *COMPUTE!'s Quick and Easy Guide to OS/2* assumes no technical knowledge of the system or the computer that runs it, so even novice computer users will master OS/2 in no time.

If you've worked with MS-DOS in the past, you'll recognize the names of some of OS/2's commands, but OS/2 is more than a new version of MS-DOS. It has features, commands, and abilities undreamed of in MS-DOS.

But with power comes complexity. Some commands work in *protected mode*, the multitasking system that can run many complex operations in the background without your even being aware of them. Other commands work only in *real mode*, the mode that emulates DOS so convincingly that few DOS-based programs will know the difference. Some commands can be used with both modes. Interchanging OS/2's real and protected modes can result in fouled-up printouts and general confusion. *COMPUTE!'s Quick and Easy Guide to OS/2* will unsnarl the complexity with clear and concise explanations—it'll have you up and running right away.

Whether you're just beginning to use a computer or you're upgrading from MS-DOS, *COMPUTE!'s Quick and Easy Guide to OS/2* is the reference you need. It will ease your progress from novice to power user. And, as a power user, you'll use it as a handy reference to the commands you'll need to make OS/2 perform for you.

Introduction
How to Use This Book

This book was written to give you the information you need about the OS/2 operating system when you need it and in a form you can use to get the most from OS/2.

To do this job, COMPUTE!'s *Quick and Easy Guide to OS/2* is organized so that you may use it in several ways.

- If you want to learn about OS/2 in an orderly manner, treat this as if it were a school textbook and read it from beginning to end.
- If you want to get started with OS/2 right away, use Chapter 7 to lead you through the tasks you want to perform. As you read that chapter, if you find a command you want to know more about, look it up in the command reference in Chapter 6. If the text brings up concepts with which you are not familiar, look them up in Chapter 2.

The how-to chapter takes a narrow view of the task at hand and is very brief. Each command reference section is very specific (and very thorough) when discussing a command. The concepts discussed in Chapter 2 give you the broad, general background you'll need to put commands and tasks into perspective.

If You Have DOS Experience
If you have a background in using either MS-DOS or PC-DOS, you'll find that OS/2 is similar at its face but different in its internal workings. The differences you'll need to understand first have to do with OS/2's ability to run multiple programs at once (multitasking). These differences are discussed in Chapter 3, "Programs and Processes."

As you use OS/2, you may find that ideas and techniques that were hazy and seemingly unimportant to you while using DOS are more important in using OS/2. To develop into a power user, you'll have to understand some things better, like the way files are handled, how programs get started, and OS/2's use of special system files. *COMPUTE!'s Quick and Easy Guide to OS/2* thoroughly discusses these matters as well as the other things you'll need to know to take full advantage of OS/2.

Deciding How Much You Need or Want to Know

When you dip into this book, you should first make a conscious decision about how much you want to know right away. If it's late and a deadline is approaching, you probably just want to get from point A to point B without knowing much about how you did it. At times like these, you will rely mostly on the how-to chapter.

If you're doing something for the first time and know you'll be doing similar things frequently, you'll probably want to look at the command reference in Chapter 6 to read about the commands you will be using. This will give you ideas about better ways to do the job and how to handle exceptions.

When you have time to invest in improving your overall productivity, use the concepts part of this book to build your understanding. Time invested in this way pays off well in greater capability, less frustration and problems avoided.

Not only will different parts of this book be of interest at different times, but different material will be of interest as your skill and understanding increase. For example, in your first uses of command references, you probably won't be concerned with all the material presented. Some of it will seem too far afield from what you want to get done. But later, when the commands are more familiar, their details, exceptions, and nuances will become important to you. Those details and nuances also become critical when something doesn't work as you expect it to.

Chapter 1
System Requirements and Recommendations

Chapter 1
System Requirements and Recommendations

It makes no sense to use OS/2 where computer capacity is limited. If you are short on memory or disk capacity, DOS is a better choice than OS/2. The following features are needed to run OS/2 well:

- Intel 80286 or 80386 central microprocessor or compatible
- A minimum of 2 megabytes RAM recommended
- Twenty megabytes hard disk storage
- A 1.2 megabyte 5¼-inch floppy disk drive
- A 1.44 megabyte 3½-inch floppy disk drive
- A "standard" display system

OS/2 may be heavily customized by hardware manufacturers who offer a version of it to work with their systems. As a result of such customization, some of the preceding features may be altered slightly. Particularly, the requirement that you have a floppy disk drive only exists because the drives listed can read the OS/2 distribution disks. There is no reason a different type of floppy drive, smaller or larger, or even no floppy drive at all, would not be adequate if the distributor of OS/2 provides a way to get it into your system.

An 80286 or 80386 processor is fundamental to the way OS/2 works. This requirement isn't likely to change. However, it's possible that an 80386-only version of OS/2 will be offered in the future. Currently, OS/2 cannot use the full capabilities of the 80386 processor. In fact, it probably will never take full advantage of this processor's more advanced features. But it's reasonable that OS/2 will be enhanced to handle the 32-bit operations so beneficial to some applications built specifically for the 80386 processor. In the first release, OS/2 will step on such programs when it switches from one task to another. This is likely to be remedied.

3

As for RAM, OS/2 is anything but compact. It uses memory intensively. Two megabytes is a good start for an efficient and fully functional system, but four megabytes is better, six is better still, and so on. If you run a number of concurrent tasks and find system operation slowing as you add additional programs in additional sessions, more memory will probably significantly speed up operation.

If you aren't used to a multitasking operating system, it will probably take a few months of use before you start using many programs at once. It's difficult to keep track of what they're all doing until you've had some practice. As you accumulate practice and start using more concurrent operations, you'll begin to tax the memory system more heavily. That's when you might find decreased speed as you add programs. If the system becomes unacceptably slow, you will have good reason to add additional memory.

For a start, you'll probably find two megabytes adequate, but expect to grow to four or six megabytes when your program library grows and you become an experienced, heavy user of the system.

The continued growth of memory requirements for programs will probably continue for a long time. For example, today's word processors are considerably fancier than the early microcomputer word processors. But the core features of today's word processors—entering and editing text—are not much different. In the meantime, the memory requirements for typical word processors have increased more than tenfold in the past six years. There are four major reasons for the increase:

- First, the easiest way to increase the speed of operation of a program involves trading memory for speed. In most programming situations, the more memory you use, the faster the program will run—and there's always competitive pressure for a faster program.
- Second, there's a trend toward lower memory costs. As trade issues intervene, RAM chip prices may go up and down a bit, but the clear, long-term trend is always toward less expensive memory.

- Third, there's a trend toward fancy user interfaces. Pretty icons, point-and-shoot menus, what-you-see-is-what-you-get displays, and quick, elaborate help facilities eat memory in large gulps. Some of these techniques involve bit-by-bit display images rather than character-by-character images—this change alone can multiply display-handling memory requirements 100 times.
- Finally, there's the self-fulfilling prophecy phenomenon. If users start buying more memory to run bigger programs, developers see that more memory is generally available, so they write programs that take more memory, so users buy even more memory, and so on.

One result of this memory inflation in the DOS world is that too many programs use memory wastefully. In OS/2, this waste is even less acceptable. In DOS, if you have 640K available, there is little reason an application program shouldn't use most of it. If it doesn't use the memory, the extra RAM will probably go to waste. But with OS/2, there's usually another program running that could make use of any leftover RAM. Program size has become an issue, but it probably won't become enough of an issue to make developers work hard at using memory efficiently.

Display systems are an area where considerable innovation is underway by many vendors. It is also an area where the de facto standard setter—IBM—has not exhibited much innovation. As a result, there are many nonstandard display systems in use, and there are some good reasons for using them. Under DOS, this presented compatibility problems, but many of these problems could be solved through the use of relatively simple software drivers that coexisted with DOS.

DOS itself doesn't pay much attention to the display system. It relies on software provided by the computer builder or by the display device supplier to perform the limited range of display services needed by DOS. OS/2, on the other hand, must take nearly full control of the display system in order to switch screens between applications and to provide all the display services needed by applications, without allowing the applications to deal directly with the display hardware.

In real (DOS) mode, OS/2 gives up and allows application programs to get at the display device directly. The developers had little choice but to do so, if existing DOS programs are to work properly.

In protected mode, OS/2 provides services to programs that allow a wide range of display controls. In order to do this, OS/2 must be customized to deal with the display installed. In the first release, device drivers that allow OS/2 to deal with display hardware are provided for only the standard IBM display adapters: the monochrome display adapter (MDA), the color/graphics adapter (CGA), the enhanced graphics adapter (EGA), and the display adapters built into the higher models of the PS/2 line (VGA). You don't need to tell OS/2 which you are using because the installation program and OS/2 figure this out automatically.

If you have another type of display adapter, OS/2 cannot work with it unless it's compatible with one of the IBM standards or unless you provide a software device driver to help OS/2 deal with the display. If you have a nonstandard display that isn't compatible with an IBM display, make a lot of noise at the manufacturer of the adaptor until an OS/2 device driver for the display is made available. It isn't easy to write one of these device drivers, but all of the necessary tools and specifications are available from Microsoft.

If you have an IBM-compatible display adapter from another supplier that also offers features beyond ordinary IBM-style operations, you won't be able to use these features in protected mode. You'll be able to use them in real mode as you did in DOS, but there's a good chance that OS/2 will not be able to get the display back to normal when you switch from real to protected mode. You will have to use your real mode programs to get the display back to a standard setup before OS/2 can use it properly in protected mode. This is most likely to be a problem for EGA adapters that offer extra capability over the IBM standard (as most do).

Even with the plain IBM EGA, it's possible to set the adapter in real mode so OS/2 can't use it properly in protected mode. The EGA has hundreds of possible configurations, and, once set, there is no way for OS/2 or any other program to figure out precisely what the settings are or how to make them right.

When OS/2 can't figure out how the display adapter was set in real mode, it can't reset it for a protected mode session when you switch screens. In fact, OS/2 can't even figure out that there's a problem as you look at a scrambled screen. The EGA most definitely was not designed with multitasking in mind.

When OS/2 Makes Sense

OS/2 is designed to run multiple programs simultaneously for one human operator. No doubt you will see products designed to use OS/2 on one machine to serve several users, but such systems will never provide the full capabilities of a multiuser system until Microsoft changes some of the basic methods used in OS/2—and they say they won't do that. OS/2 doesn't change the one-user-one-computer rule of DOS (although you can place several OS/2 computers and their users on a network to share a file system and to send messages to each other).

The DOS file system used by OS/2 doesn't keep enough information about the ownership and privacy of files to support good multiuser operations. The DOS file system will probably be replaced in a later version of OS/2, but still other aspects of OS/2 will tend to keep it a multitasking, single-user operating system until Microsoft decides to write a major revision of OS/2.

As long as OS/2 retains the file system it inherited from DOS, there will be problems with multiuser schemes.

The file system is based on the File Allocation Table indexing scheme (a personal invention of Bill Gates, founder of Microsoft). It's too susceptible to physical damage for use in situations where high reliability is required. One not-too-unlikely hardware failure can easily wipe out an entire file system. One power failure at the wrong time can wipe out an entire database. This is not the stuff of which heavily used production systems for day-in-day-out reliability are made.

The DOS file system might be made to work, but in the long run, the answer will have to be a more sophisticated file indexing and location system (which Microsoft will probably provide). But OS/2 does very well what it was intended to do. It's an excellent single-user system. It provides the basis for topnotch personal productivity tools and other advanced programs. The point is to use OS/2 for what it was intended—a basis for effective, skillful use of an advanced personal computer.

When to Use Unix or Xenix Instead of DOS or OS/2

Unix is a popular multiuser operating system used to control a wide variety of large and small computers. It's specifically designed to support several users on one computer. Normally, each user has a terminal with display and keyboard hardware and no computer. The computing is all done on the central, shared computer.

This can offer a lower cost per user, but it often means that each user does not have as much available computer power as with a one-person-one-computer arrangement. The result can be slower operation.

It's possible to have the best of both worlds by supplying each user with his or her own computer which can also tap the resources of the central computer through Unix. However, this tends to get a bit expensive and also introduces some complexity to the software required. There's one major advantage to multiuser systems like Unix. They are ideal for shared database systems where many people need to access the same information in central files at the same time. This can be done with single-user operating systems and networks along with some specialized database software, but the software for such systems is not yet as mature as that for straight multiuser database systems.

Microsoft is in an interesting situation when it comes to the multiuser versus single-user dilemma. In addition to the single-user OS/2 system, Microsoft produces Xenix, which is a specialized version of Unix. Its position has been that OS/2 will continue to be a single-user system and Xenix will be remain its multiuser offering. But, as the software available for OS/2 grows, and as more and more people become accustomed to OS/2, there will be pressure to expand it to encompass multiuser operation. If so expanded, OS/2 will be very similar to Xenix. It remains to be seen if Microsoft can resist the temptation and keep both systems alive and well. The decision to use Unix or Xenix instead of OS/2 will depend upon the allowable cost per user and the need for a centralized database with concurrent access by multiple users.

When to Use DOS Instead

Microsoft and IBM would be happy to see all DOS users who have the right hardware move to OS/2. This won't happen for a while. DOS will continue to be the operating system of choice for a period of time. If you generally use a computer for one task—such as word processing—there's little reason for you to invest in the extra hardware to run OS/2 efficiently. DOS requires much less from the computer for a given task.

If you won't benefit from combining multiple programs toward common goals, there's little reason to go beyond DOS. Some years from now, your choice will probably narrow. As OS/2 becomes more common, the best software available will tend to be exclusively for OS/2 or its future variants. Ultimately, you won't be able to get the best tools for a DOS system. At that point, it'll be wise to leave DOS for a more modern system with greater capability. But, by that time (if current trends continue), the cost of the necessary hardware to run a more elaborate system will have been greatly reduced and your reasons for not going beyond DOS will consequently diminish. If you have a computer that doesn't use an 80286 or 80386 processor, you don't have the option of OS/2. You will be spared making a decision until you have to decide upon a new computer.

Chapter 2
OS/2 Concepts

Chapter 2
OS/2 Concepts

A *file* contains information which may be saved and retrieved. If you save information in a file, OS/2 will keep track of the order of the information, the date the file was saved or last changed, and the length of the file. What the file *means* or what's in it is your responsibility to remember. Generally, the content of the file doesn't mean anything to OS/2—it's just a block of bits to be stored together under a name you specify. And bits are just little magnetic fields on a metal disk, or electricity in a wire, or electric charges in a memory capacitor. OS/2's job is to keep the bits together, to make sure they are not inadvertently changed, and to keep track of the name and deliver the bits back again when you ask for them by name.

OS/2 expects some special files to contain certain patterns of bits, but only to the extent that the system won't work right if the patterns are not found. For example, if you tell OS/2 that your most recent letter to your mother is a program, it will try to execute the bits in the letter as if they were specially coded instructions. That won't work, and OS/2 will tell you so. In fact, to help avoid this, program files can only have special names, and before OS/2 tries to use a file as a program, it checks for certain standard numbers near the beginning of the file. If it doesn't find these numbers, it quits trying to use the file as a program and issues an error message.

ASCII Files

The difference between files that contain programs and other types of files is in how the files are *encoded*. The letter to Mom is coded in *ASCII* characters. ASCII (American Standard Code for Information Interchange) is just the name used in computer circles for a standard coding scheme. That coding scheme says, for example, that an *A* is coded with the bit pattern 01000001. There is no *A* in the file containing Mom's letter, just the bit pattern 01000001. The *A* becomes visible when you *input* the file to a program which is built to accept ASCII codes. That program can then send the code to your display circuits. There, in the display hardware, the code is turned into dots on the screen which humans recognize as the letter *A*.

Many coding schemes are used in files. ASCII is the most common for text. The hardware in your display, printer, and keyboard all works with modified ASCII codes. But the processor—the main controller of your computer—doesn't use ASCII codes. The processor manipulates signals based upon the instructions sent to it. These instructions are in a unique, special code called *machine language*. All processors in computers patterned after the IBM PC, AT, and PS/2 machines use very similar machine language codes. (But Apple computers and many others don't.)

Program Files—Briefly

Files which are going to be *executed* or run as programs must be encoded in machine language. Machine language is also called *executable* code, *object* code, and *binary* code. Files which contain machine language are called *executable* files, *program* files, *object modules*, *.EXE* files, or *.COM* files. OS/2 only lets you run or execute a file that has a name ending in .EXE or .COM. In fact, executable files contain machine language encoded instructions as well as other information that is used by OS/2 to get the program started.

For instance, .EXE files contain numbers indicating how much memory the program needs and those standard numbers which identify the file as an .EXE file. Similar to .EXE files are .COM files, but .COM files have less extra information and can only be run by that part of OS/2 which acts like a version of DOS.

Binary Files

Besides ASCII and machine language codes, many other codes are used in files on your system. For example, programs that work with files of numbers often code those numbers in one of many different binary coding schemes. In one scheme, 2 is encoded as 00000010. In ASCII, it's 00110010. You can quickly realize that two programs which share a numeric data file had better use the same coding scheme, or things just won't add up right.

Files of Extended ASCII Codes

Even programs which use ASCII encoding often extend the code with special characters. For example, many word processing programs store carriage returns at the end of a line in two different ways. Carriage returns entered by the operator are "hard" carriage returns, and those entered automatically by the program to keep a line on the page or screen are "soft" carriage returns. ASCII only has one code for carriage returns, so the programmers of the word processing program make up a new, nonstandard code for soft carriage returns. Some word processing programs use hundreds of these special codes. Since your display hardware and printer were built for standard ASCII codes (more or less), these special characters make funny marks or cause strange behavior. If you try to display a file created by a word processing program without using that same program to translate the codes, you usually will see some sensible letters interspersed with the gibberish of untranslated special characters.

Directories—Files of Files

A group of files which reside together is called a *directory*. A directory is actually a file which contains a list of other files. Each element of a directory contains a filename, the file's length, the date it was last changed, a code for where the file begins on the surface of the storage disk, and markers to indicate several "file attributes." One of these attributes, if marked on, says: "this file is a directory." So a directory is a specially marked file which lists more files or directories.

In an outline, you might have a sentence labeled III.A.3.b.iii. In OS/2, this same label would be typed using the backslash character (\ ) to divide heading levels—like this:

III \ A \ 3 \ b \ ii

But you can do better than that. For example, you might do something like

concepts \ files \ names \ abbrevs \ dot_dot

which is the label for an upcoming part of this book. It's in the concepts section and is about "files," about "names" for files, about abbreviations for names, and, in particular, about an abbreviation named "dot-dot." At each step along this chain of directories, there would be other directories and files. For example, there's concepts \ programs which is a directory, and there's concepts \ draft1 which is a file—not a directory. Concepts \ draft1 contains the ASCII codes of the letters typed in for the beginning of the concepts section. Part of the structure might look like what's shown in Table 2-1.

Table 2-1. An Example Directory Structure

Note: Directories are shown in all uppercase; filenames are in all lowercase.

Directory or File	Meaning
BOOK	the top directory about the book
BOOK \ INTRO	the directory containing the introduction
BOOK \ INTRO \ USAGE	first part of introduction
book \ intro \ usage \ draft1	ASCII file—first draft of first part of introduction
BOOK \ INTRO \ WHYOS2	directory for second part of introduction
book \ intro \ whyos2 \ draft1	ASCII file—first draft of this section
book \ intro \ whyos2 \ draft2	ASCII file—second draft
BOOK \ HARDWARE	empty directory—work to be done here
BOOK \ CONCEPTS	directory for concept part of book
book \ concepts \ draft1	ASCII file—draft of first part of "concepts"
BOOK \ CONCEPTS \ FILES	
book \ concepts \ files \ notes	ASCII file—notes on files section
book \ concepts \ files \ draft1	ASCII file—draft of this section
book \ concepts \ files \ draft2	ASCII file—another draft
BOOK \ CONCEPTS \ FILES \ NAMES	directory for filename concepts
book \ concepts \ files \ names \ draft1	ASCII file—draft of this section
BOOK \ CONCEPTS \ FILES \ NAMES \ ABBREVS	directory about abbreviations of filenames
book \ concepts \ files \ names \ abbrevs \ draft1	ASCII file
book \ concepts \ files \ names \ abbrevs \ draft2	ASCII file
book \ concepts \ files \ names \ abbrevs \ figures	ASCII file

In reality, a directory structure of this complexity might carry hundreds of files. We've only shown some of the ASCII files for the sake of brevity. In addition, there would be other directories at the level of the "book" directory which would contain programs and system files needed by OS/2, as well as files about other projects. An actual listing of the entire directory structure for a heavily used OS/2 disk might take 10 or 20 pages.

Directory Trees

Often, this kind of directory structure is likened to a tree. If you take the tree analogy seriously, you can think of directories as branches or twigs and files as leaves. (Notice that, since any directory can contain ordinary files, there may be leaves on any branch.) Also, you will probably think of your tree as being upside-down. In an outline, you look "down" from the general to the specific. If you think of down as meaning more specific or detailed, your directory tree grows down from the trunk to the branches.

There is a long tradition in computer science of imagining trees which grow from the trunk down to the leaves. True to the burrowing tree tradition, the designers of OS/2 have officially named only one directory: the *root* directory. Just so you can tell who has read the manual and who has not, you're supposed to write the name of this directory as \ and read it aloud as "the root directory." Abbreviating "the root directory" to \ saves a good bit of typing, but it requires that you remember that *the root directory* is denoted by \.

The root directory is the only directory on a disk which is not a subdirectory to any other directory. It's the start, the top, the all-inclusive directory for the disk which carries it.

Now that we have insulted horticulture with inverted trees, on to genealogy. Every file is a *child* of some directory. Every directory, except the root directory, also has one *parent*. Two directories with the same parent are *siblings*.

The root directory has children but no parent. All other files and directories have one and only one parent. Whenever a directory is deleted, all its descendants are deleted as well.

(Note the potential for mass destruction if your accounting directory were deleted—OS/2 won't let you do this in one step.) Since the name of a file or directory is stored in its parent directory, if the parent is deleted, the child loses its identity.

Is there only one family tree of files per computer? No. Each disk contains a tree of files and directories. It may be a tree with no branches or leaves, but it still has a root. Each disk holds its own tree as does each hard disk. The difference is disks hibernate when they're on the shelf—their family remains dormant. Since the disk in a hard disk drive usually cannot be removed, its family of files is ready for action whenever the computer is active.

Is there communication between trees? Yes, by cloning and adoption. When you copy from one disk to another, the copied branch of the family is *cloned*, and that clone is adopted by a directory in the recipient family. The adoption is egalitarian—the cloned files and directories do not know they are clones and their new parent takes them as its own. The same applies to copies from a disk to itself. When a file or a directory and its children are copied from one place in the tree to another, the new copy has no further attachment to the original. It happens to contain the same pattern of bits, but OS/2 doesn't remember this fact.

Volumes

Disks are not the only places where a tree of files can exist. A tape drive can be installed to work the same way. Also, a part of the computer's electronic memory is often set aside and used as a *ramdisk* or *virtual disk* to hold directories and files. Much of the time, when we speak of files and directories, it doesn't matter whether the material is on disk, tape, or in memory. In such cases, we do not talk about the disk, we talk about the *volume*.

A *volume* is a physical unit which contains a root directory and its descendants. In the case of a removable disk or tape, the volume is the removable storage medium, not the drive which reads and writes on the volume. Drives do not store information, volumes do. Drives write or read information to or from volumes. A batch of volumes is sometimes called *storage* media, *magnetic* media or just *media*—especially in mail-order adds for tapes and disk.

File Attributes

You'll remember that directories are actually special files which list other files and directories. Also, recall that the way OS/2 can tell a directory from a file is that the parent directory contains a listing for that child directory. That listing, in turn, contains a *file attribute* mark saying the child is a directory. File attribute marks can specify other types of special files as well as directories.

Volume Labels. There is another special type of directory entry used to keep track of volumes. It's called a *volume label* or just a *label*. If one of the files listed in a directory is marked as being a label, it does not refer to any other file or directory. It's a name for the entire volume. There is no file, special or otherwise, attached to a volume label. Normally there is at most one label for a volume, and it's in the root directory of the volume. If there is more than one label, or if a label is found in a directory other than the root directory, something has gone wrong.

OS/2 occasionally reads a volume label to check that the volume it expects is actually installed in the drive where OS/2 expects it. This helps keep OS/2 from doing disastrous things when you swap the volumes in a drive without telling OS/2 about it. You should use volume labels, too. If every volume in your collection has a meaningful volume label, you can keep track of your data more easily. You should get in the habit of using volume labels and making sure that they are also shown on the paper label attached to each volume.

Since a label is meant to stay with its volume, deleting all the entries in a root directory will not normally delete the volume label. Also, copying a root directory from one volume to another will not copy the label. The facilities in OS/2 for deletion and copying are smart enough to ignore labels. (But the DISKCOPY command does copy volume labels, along with everything else on a disk.)

Read-Only File Attribute. There are other file attributes in addition to the directory attribute and label attribute. (You might find it handy to think "mark" when you see the word *attribute*.) There is the *read-only attribute*.

A file which is marked as *read-only* will not be changed by OS/2 without asking you for confirmation. (But OS/2 will allow a read-only file to be renamed without warning or complaint.) Usually OS/2 doesn't ask politely, it just tells you it cannot change a read-only file and stops the operation you requested. It's then up to you to remove the read-only mark and then repeat the command which will modify that file. Usually, after you modify a read-only file, you'll want to mark it read-only again. (See the command reference for the ATTRIB command for more about the read-only attribute.)

Hidden File Attribute. There is also a file attribute for *hidden files*. OS/2 keeps hidden files a secret. You cannot mark a file as hidden with OS/2, but some programs make hidden files, and you'll probably buy some utility program which can mark files as hidden or not. Hidden files do not appear in directory listings. The COPY command will not copy them, but if you copy to a file that is marked hidden, the hidden file will be deleted and a new, unhidden file will receive the copy. The COPY command just doesn't know the hidden file is there at all and steals its name for the newly copied file. Usually, hidden files are also marked read-only to prevent such invisible destruction.

System File Attribute. *System files*, that is files with the system attribute, are treated just like hidden files. The reason for having both hidden and system attributes probably has to do with planned additions to DOS or OS/2. Microsoft doesn't say why. The most basic parts of OS/2, used when OS/2 is putting itself together upon starting, are stored in files marked read-only, hidden, and system. That's so you don't mess around with them.

Archive Attribute. So far, all of the file attributes we have discussed are ones which the operator must in some way tell OS/2 to set. They are never set automatically by OS/2. For example, OS/2 never changes a file into a directory. You must create it as a directory from the beginning.

There is one automatic file attribute. Whenever you create or change a file, a file attribute called the *archive* attribute is turned on. It is turned off when you use the BACKUP or XCOPY commands to make a copy of the file. (You can also turn it off directly with the ATTRIB command. More on these commands later.) The purpose of this file attribute is to make it easy for you to make backup copies of groups of files. Backup copies are safety copies made to protect against the time when your hardware fails or you goof and destroy valuable information.

The BACKUP and XCOPY commands can be used to make copies of all files which have changed since they were last backed up. These commands use the archive attribute to determine if a file has changed and to mark the fact that a safety copy of a file has been made. In general, if the archive attribute of a file is on, it means there is no current safety copy of the file.

Remember that these file attributes are not stored in the file itself. They're stored in the directory which names the file. This is one reason why every file or directory except the root directory must have a parent directory. The parent is where all the information about the file or directory is stored—including its name. In addition to the file attributes, each entry in a directory also includes the date and time the subject file was created or last changed. This date and time are automatically updated by OS/2 whenever a file is altered or might have been altered. (It is not updated for directories—it remains the date and time the directory was created.) Each directory entry also contains the length of the file and the location where the file begins on the volume.

Filenames

What you have read about directories is OS/2's way of remembering files. All this is done so you can conveniently find the file you want among the thousands that may exist on a volume. Now it's time to look at how to refer OS/2 to a file of our choosing. Referring to files is one of the most common tasks in using OS/2. To make things convenient (but more confusing), OS/2 provides a variety of ways to specify a file or group of files.

Drive Designation and Default Drive

Let's say your computer has two floppy disk drives and two hard disk drives. By the way the drives are plugged into the computer, each is designated by a letter. Typically, your two floppy disk drives are called drive A and drive B. Your two hard disks are probably C and D. Note that these are the names of the drives, not the volumes in them. To point out a file to OS/2, you first must tell it which drive contains the volume holding the file. Since A, B, C, and D can also be directories or filenames, OS/2 recognizes a colon (:) as a special character referring to a drive. A: refers to your first floppy drive, B: is your second floppy drive, C: is your first hard disk, and D: is your second hard disk. H: refers to a drive you don't have, and OS/2 will normally tell you so if you try to direct it to that drive.

So, when naming a file for OS/2, first tell it which drive can access the file. This is communicated with a drive letter followed with a colon—this is the first part of a filename. Usually OS/2 does not notice the name of the volume in the specified drive. If the drive has a removable medium, it's normally the operator's job to make sure the right volume is in the drive.

You can often avoid a bit of typing by relying on the default drive. At all times, OS/2 knows the current default drive. It's normally identified in the prompt OS/2 puts on the screen when it's ready for a command. If the volume containing the file you want is in the default drive, then not mentioning a drive letter or colon is the same as indicating the letter for the default drive followed by a colon.

Path Names

Once you have pointed OS/2 to the right drive for the file you want, you aren't finished. You need to tell it which directory contains our file. You'll remember that the root directory is special: It's the only directory that doesn't have a parent, and all files and directories on a volume are descendants of it.

That's why you start with the root directory when you name a directory. Tell OS/2 the names of each of the ancestors of the desired directory in the order they follow from the root directory. For example, the steps OS/2 would follow to find C: \COMPUTER \MICROS \IBM \PS2 are shown in Table 2-2.

Table 2-2. Finding C: \ COMPUTER \ MICROS \ IBM \ PS2

1. This file search is to be conducted on the volume in drive C:.
2. Start at the root directory. (Notice the first directory name starts with \ . That's the root directory.)
3. In the root directory, find a directory named COMPUTER.
4. In the COMPUTER directory, find a directory named MICROS.
5. In the MICROS directory, find a directory named IBM.
6. In the IBM directory, find an entry (either a file or directory) named PS2.

The name C: \COMPUTER \MICROS \IBM \PS2 is actually a small program to tell OS/2 how to hunt for the desired directory. Notice in step 6 that OS/2 cannot tell from the filename whether PS2 is a file or a directory. When OS/2 finds PS2, it immediately discovers that it is a directory, but it has to look it up first. OS/2 can determine that COMPUTER, MICROS and IBM should be directories before finding them because the name implies that they have children: Only directories can have children.

Given the step-by-step character of directory specifications, it's natural to call one a *path* or *path name*. But be careful. The PATH command and the *current command path* are two different things.

Main Name and Extension

All directory entries allow 11 characters for the name of the child file or directory. There is an implied period or dot in these names. At most, 8 characters may precede the period and 3 may follow it. A name may not contain any spaces, and it must have at least one character before the period. By tradition, the three characters after the period are called the *extension* and are used to denote what kind of coding and information format is used in the file. The extension doesn't have to be three characters. It may be one, two, or none; but if you don't use any, the period is not usually typed at all.

Remember that filenames ending with .COM and .EXE identify files that contain machine language codes packaged with other information in a COM or EXE file format. Other extensions, like .DOC for document or .WKS for worksheet, are common. Some programs require that the files they use have specific extensions. Most programs presume that the files they work with have some standard extension unless you specify otherwise. The eight, or fewer, characters before the period are sometimes called the *main name* and generally can be of your choice. In Microsoft's OS/2 literature, they define a main name as a *filename*, but nobody else does. After all, many files in a tree may have the same main name, each with a different path and extension, so Microsoft's filename doesn't uniquely name a file.

Once you have led OS/2 to the directory containing the file you want, you then specify the name of the file itself. For example, once OS/2 has found the PS2 directory, the following tells OS/2 to locate bugs.doc within that directory:

c: \ computer \ micros \ ibm \ ps2 \ bugs.doc

By convention, directory names are not given extensions. This isn't a rule, it's just a general practice. There is no reason you can't create a directory named \ COMPUTER.DIR. You can even name a directory \ COMPUTER.EXE. This shouldn't confuse OS/2. Even if you tell OS/2 to execute the directory COMPUTER.EXE as a program, it wouldn't try to run it as a program. It would give a somewhat different error message than it would if COMPUTER.EXE were a file that wasn't really a program. OS/2 might not get confused, but you probably will. It's best to go along with the crowd and not give directory names extensions unless there is some compelling reason to do so. Always avoid misleading or confusing directory names or extensions. COMPUTER.EXE is not a good choice for a directory name.

Note that no place within a filename, not in the drive letter, not in directory names, and not in the main name, does OS/2 care about capitalization. In names, *a* and *A* mean exactly the same. In this text, directories will be capitalized and filenames will not, in order to better distinguish between them.

Default Directories

Take the command

type c: \computer \micros \ibm \ps2 \bugs.doc

This command will copy the contents of the file bugs.doc to your screen. This may seem like a lot of typing just to read a document. The designers of OS/2 recognize that the command line often requires long strings of very specific characters, and they have provided some abbreviations to make working with OS/2 simpler and quicker.

Recall that the default drive is the one drive to which OS/2 will refer if you don't tell it some other drive. There is always exactly one default drive, but there are usually several default directories. OS/2 keeps track of a default directory for each drive that contains a volume. If you specify a filename that doesn't include the root directory (one that doesn't begin with \ immediately after any drive designation) OS/2 will start searching for the file in the current default directory of the drive you specify.

For example, here's how OS/2 would search for c:ps2 \bugs.doc when the current directory for drive C: is \COMPUTER \MICROS \IBM.

1. This file search is to be conducted on the volume in drive C:.
2. In the current default directory for drive C: (which is \COMPUTER \MICROS \IBM), look for a directory named PS2.
3. In the PS2 directory, find an entry (either a file or a directory) with the name bugs.doc.

Note that it's critical that c:ps2 \bugs.doc is different from c: \ps2 \bugs.doc. The first \ in c: \ps2 \bugs.doc tells OS/2 to start searching at the root directory. The absence of this first backslash in c:ps2 \bugs.doc tells OS/2 to start with the default directory for drive C:.

The name ps2 \bugs.doc certainly is shorter than \computer \micros \ibm \ps2 \bugs.doc. Not only is it less to type, it's less for OS/2 to do. OS/2 already knows where the default directory is, so it doesn't have to perform the searches for the COMPUTER, MICROS, and IBM directories. It should get to the file more quickly, but you probably won't be able to see the difference. Names that don't start with \ (for the root directory), are called *relative filenames* because they're relative to the current default settings. Names that reference the root directory are called *absolute filenames* because they begin at an absolute starting point (the root) and don't depend upon any default settings. Since you can quickly change the default drive and default directories, you will most often deal with relative filenames for convenience.

In the last example, if C were the default drive and the default directory for drive C: were \ COMPUTER \ MICROS \ IBM \ PS2, then the only name you would need is bugs.doc. In practice, names like bugs.doc, which rely on the default drive and its default directory, are the most common names actually typed in OS/2 commands. Even so, always remember that bugs.doc means c: \ computer \ micro \ ibm \ ps2 \ bugs.doc and is only an abbreviation. Forgetting what shortened filenames really mean and not understanding file naming in the first place are main causes of most errors and operator disasters in using microcomputers.

There is a default directory for each drive with a volume in place, but OS/2 literature often talks about *THE default directory*. When mentioned without any reference to a drive, *the default directory* means the default directory for the current default drive. As with relative filenames, you will have problems if you forget that this is just shorthand for *the default directory of the default drive*. Just to add a little more confusion, *the current directory* and *the working directory* also mean the same thing: the default directory of the default drive.

Working with Groups of Files

Many OS/2 commands can deal with groups of files. For example, when you are copying files, you will often want to copy several at once. To simplify this process, OS/2 offers a variety of ways to refer to a group of files rather than to one at a time. The most obvious example is when you tell a command to work on a directory rather than a single file. Remember that OS/2 can quickly tell that a name refers to a directory rather than a single file. Many OS/2 commands will accept a directory name and will then operate on all files in the directory. A few, like XCOPY, will even work on the directory, its children, and all of its more distant descendants in one run of the command.

Ambiguous filenames. There is another type of filename that can be used as a name for a group of files. This type of name is called an *ambiguous filename*. As you might guess, an ambiguous filename doesn't name a particular file. It names a file or files whose names match some pattern. For example, the name *.doc refers to all files in the current directory which have the extension .doc. To find files with a name like this, OS/2 uses a simple character-matching scheme. In this scheme, * matches any string of characters in a filename except a period. Similarly, ? matches any single character except a period. OS/2 doesn't go to great lengths to apply this matching business. For example, *e.* does the same as *.*: The *e* gets lost in the shuffle. In general, any characters that follow a star in the main name or in the extension are ignored. If you use F*E*.*, you will get the same result as for f*.*: all files in the current directory that begin with an *f*.

The part of an ambiguous filename that includes * or ? is often called a *file pattern*. It is used by OS/2 as a pattern or template against which to match filenames.

You can sensibly use * and ? in filenames that include a path of directories leading to the desired directory, but OS/2 will properly interpret * and ? only in the last part of a complex filename. For example, micros \ ibm \ ps2 \ b*.??? will work properly, but micros \ i?m \ ps2 \ bugs.doc won't. Nor will micros \ ibm \ ps* \ bugs.doc be handled properly.

Table 2-3. Examples of Ambiguous Filename Matches

Pattern:	*.elf	e*.elf	elf.*	el*.*
File				
dragon.bst	no	no	no	no
unicorn.bst	no	no	no	no
elf	no	no	match	match
eof	no	no	no	no
elf.elf	match	match	match	match
elvin.elf	match	match	no	match
imp.elf	match	no	no	no

puck.bad	no	no	no	no
goblin.bad	no	no	no	no
Pattern:	*.b*	?????n.b*	*.b?t	e?f.*
File				
dragon.bst	match	match	match	no
unicorn.bst	match	no	match	no
elf	no	no	no	match
eof	no	no	no	match
elf.elf	no	no	no	match
elvin.elf	no	no	no	no
imp.elf	no	no	no	no
puck.bad	match	no	no	no
goblin.bad	match	match	no	no

For convenience in speaking, * is usually called a *star*. (*Asterisk* can be a mouthful when spouting characters as someone types them.)

What if no files match? Then the command given has no effect. If 100 files match, 100 files are acted upon by the command *if* the command can deal with ambiguous filenames. Some commands can and others can't. In the command reference section of this book, it will be made clear which are which.

Dot and dot-dot. Probably the most commonly used ambiguous filename is *.*. This refers to all the files in the current directory. There is an even shorter way to say this:

.

If you use the DIR command to look at the contents of a directory, you will see an entry for files named . and .. which are called *dot* and *dot-dot* files. In fact, *dot* is a directory's name for itself. In a sense, a directory contains itself—at least to the extent that it contains dot and the date and time the dot was created. (This date and time are not updated when the directory is changed as they are for ordinary files.)

Dot-dot is a short name for the parent of the current directory. For example, if C: \ COMPUTER \ MICROS \ IBM is the current directory, then using . for a filename would be the same as typing C: \ COMPUTER \ MICROS \ IBM. Using ..

would be the same as typing C: \ COMPUTER \ MICROS.

Remember that dot and dot-dot each refer to an entire directory of files, not just one file. You cannot delete dot and dot-dot from a directory. They are part of the directory itself. Notice that a root directory does not contain dot and dot-dot. You can still use dot when the current directory is a root directory, but you can't use dot-dot because the root has no parent.

Dot and dot-dot in searches. When used in the path portion of a filename, dot and dot-dot have a slightly different meaning. While OS/2 is searching for a file according to the path in a filename, it acts as if it temporarily resets the current directory to the directory it is searching. Dot is useless as part of a path. Its effect is to keep you where you are.

Using dot-dot tells the computer to *go up one directory* to the parent of the directory you are now searching. In searches from the root, dot-dot is not very useful, but for relative filenames like .. \ .. \ FILE.DOC, dot-dot is a handy way of typing the names of parents and grandparents. Get used to using dot and dot-dot—they're handy. For example, the command DIR .. will list all the directories that are siblings of the current directory, along with all the files in the current directory's parent.

Filenames as Devices

In OS/2, there are a few filenames that don't refer to files. They refer to *devices* like the screen, keyboard, printer, and serial ports. To keep things simple, the designers of OS/2 generally let you treat devices as if they were files. You can copy files to and from devices. In fact, along with device names, there is a phantom device directory called DEV. It doesn't exist on your disk (and shouldn't—don't make a directory by this name). But, if you prefix a device name with \ DEV \, it will perform as if the prefix had not been attached.

One peculiarity about devices is that some can only output, some can only input, and a few do both. It makes sense that OS/2 wouldn't let you wait for input from your console screen. It makes equal sense that it would expect input from the keyboard. For that reason, the SCREEN$ device can only be used to accept input. The devices you may have occasion to use in OS/2 are listed in Table 2-4.

Table 2-4. Devices Used in OS/2

Value	Meaning
KBD$	Your console keyboard. Input only.
SCREEN$	Your console screen. Output only.
CON	Console. On input, it refers to KBD$, on output, SCREEN$.
PRN	Your current printer. Output only.
LPT1	Printer 1. Output only.
LPT2	Printer 2. Output only.
LPT3	Printer 3. Output only.
NUL	Eats input and does nothing with it. On output, it always acts like an empty file.

In addition, there are the devices CLOCK$ and POINTER$, which you won't use. You should never use these names for files.

Naming Tips

Here are a few guidelines for using OS/2's file system: If a directory has 20 or 30 files, it's probably time to split it into two directories or start using a child directory before adding many more files. You lose the descriptive power of directories if they contain too many files.

Sometimes you can't avoid a long list of files in a directory. Too many commercial programs are built with massive directories in mind. If you start getting hundreds of files in a directory, performance will suffer, as OS/2 works harder to find files in large directories.

If you're managing directories well, you won't need ambiguous filenames often. Try to build your directories around the files you will use at about the same time. Since relative filenames are easier, faster, and less error-prone, try to make your directories such that the files you are likely to use at about the same time are in the same or neighboring directories.

Stay out of the root directory of hard disks. OS/2 uses it for some critical files you should not alter or copy. You should never have a personal data file in the root directory of a hard disk. Make all the directories you need in the root, but keep your files out of it. Also, the root directory is the only directory that has a fixed limit on the number of entries it can hold.

Avoid a fancy system of file extensions. Don't expect three characters to tell you everything you need to know about the format and coding of a file. Use directories to categorize files instead. If a file doesn't need an extension, don't use one. They take time to type and often don't tell you much. Many editors and word processors make safety copies of files with the extension .BAK. If you can't tell what a file is without seeing its extension, you won't be able to tell what the .BAK file is about. Now we'll discuss some reference material and examples about files, their names, and the rules governing them.

Rules for Filenames

The following characters are legal for use in filenames:

A–Z	_
a–z	@
0–9	{
$	}
%	!
'	#
'	(
-	)

Some programs may succeed in creating filenames containing other characters—even invisible ones that will not be shown in a directory display. Avoid such names. You may not be able to use the DELETE or RENAME commands on them because their name contains an odd or illegal character. The _ character (called *underscore, underline, underbar,* or just *bar*) is not allowed by the documentation for OS/2, but it works and is useful as an alias for a space. For example, the name read_me is commonly used for disk files that update documentation. Some programs will not work properly with names containing characters other than letters and numerals.

The colon. The colon is only allowed as the second character of the filename, following valid drive designation letter (as in C: or A:).

The period. The period is only allowed as one of the last four characters of a name, or part of a name ending with \. The period must be preceded by a character other than \ or :.

Filename lengths. See Table 2-5, "Parts of a Filename," following. Note that an entire name plus path may not exceed 64 characters. If you have a file with a full name of over 64 characters, like:

c: \ directy1 \ directy2 \ directy3 \ directy4 \ directy5 \ directy6 \ directy7 \ file.f

you may still reference the name by making C: \ DIRECTY1 \ DIRECTY2 \ DIRECTY3 \ DIRECTY4 the default directory and using the relative filename c:directy5 \ directy6 \ directy7 \ file.f.

In general, you should not allow your directory structure to nest so deeply.

Table 2-5. Parts of a Filename

Filename:
c: \ computer \ micros \ ibm \ ps2 \ bugs.doc

Part	Name
c:	Drive designation
\	Root directory designation
\ computer \ micros \ ibm \ ps2	Path
\ computer \ micros \ ibm \ ps2 \ bugs.doc	Path name
bugs.doc	Filename{1}
bugs;	Filename{2}
.doc	Extension{3}

{1} Filename as defined in some places in OS/2 manuals.
{2} Filename as defined elsewhere in OS/2 manuals.
{3} Sometimes called *filename extension.*

Figure 2-6. Example Family of Files

Names in caps refer to directories, others refer to files.
Not all files and directories are shown.

c: \
C: \ PROGRAMS
C: \ COMPUTER
C: \ COMPUTER \ MINIS
C: \ COMPUTER \ MINIS \ DEC
C: \ COMPUTER \ MINIS \ DEC \ VAX

c: \ computer \ minis \ dec \ vax \ bugs.doc	not the same as c: \ computer \ micros \ ibm \ ps2 \ bugs.doc
c: \ computer \ minis \ dec \ vax \ bugs.bak	backup copy of c: \ computer \ minis \ dec \ vax \ bugs.doc

C: \ COMPUTER \ MINIS \ IBM
C: \ COMPUTER \ MICROS
C: \ COMPUTER \ MICROS \ APPLE
C: \ COMPUTER \ MICROS \ APPLE \ MAC
C: \ COMPUTER \ MICROS \ APPLE \ IIE
C: \ COMPUTER \ MICROS \ COMPAQ
C: \ COMPUTER \ MICROS \ COMPAQ \ PROT
C: \ COMPUTER \ MICROS \ COMPAQ \ DESK
C: \ COMPUTER \ MICROS \ IBM

c: \ computer \ micros \ ibm \ bugs.doc	
c: \ computer \ micros \ ibm \ 12-31-87.not	a year-end note?

C: \ COMPUTER \ MIRCOS \ IBM \ XT
C: \ COMPUTER \ MICROS \ IBM \ AT
C: \ COMPUTER \ MICROS \ IBM \ PS2

c: \ computer \ micros \ ibm \ ps2 \ bugs.doc	a word processing document?
c: \ computer \ micros \ ibm \ ps2 \ bugs.bak	backup copy of c: \ computer \ micros \ ibm \ ps2 \ bugs.bak
c: \ computer \ micros \ ibm \ ps2 \ features	
c: \ computer \ micros \ ibm \ ps2 \ speed.doc	a document about speed of PS2's
c: \ computer \ micros \ ibm \ ps2 \ speed.wks	a worksheet with speed calculations
c: \ computer \ micros \ ibm \ ps2 \ speed.dbf	a database file with speed-test results
c: \ computer \ micros \ ibm \ ps2 \ speed.ndx	an index to the database file
c: \ computer \ micros \ ibm \ ps2 \ speed.exe	a program that tests speed
c: \ computer \ micros \ ibm \ ps2 \ spend.doc	a document about prices
c: \ computer \ micros \ ibm \ ps2 \ spud.doc	a document about potatoes

C: \ COMPUTER \ MICROS \ TANDY

D: \	the root directory of the volume in drive D:.

D: \ COMPUTER
D: \ COMPUTER \ MICROS

D: \ COMPUTER \ MICROS \ IBM
D: \ COMPUTER \ MICROS \ IBM \ PS2
d: \ computer \ micros \ ibm \ ps2 \ bugs
d: \ computer \ micros \ ibm \ ps2 \ bugs.doc   not the same file as c: \ computer
                                                 \ micros \ ibm \ ps2 \ bugs.doc

d: \ computer \ micros \ ibm \ ps2 \ bugs.bak
D: \ COMPUTER \ MICROS \ APPLE

The current default drive is C:.
The current default directory for drive C: is \ COMPUTER \ MICROS \ IBM \ PS2.
The current default directory for drive D: is \ COMPUTER \ MICROS \ IBM \ PS2.

Observations About Example File Tree

1. *These names refer to the same file*
   c: \ computer \ micros \ ibm \ ps2 \ bugs.doc
   c:bugs.doc
   bugs.doc
   b*.doc
   ????.doc
   b???.d*
   b*.d*
   b*.d??
   c: \ computer \ micros \ ibm \ ps2 \ b*.d??

2. *These names refer to different files (different drives)*
   c: \ computer \ micros \ ibm \ ps2 \ bugs.doc
   d: \ computer \ micros \ ibm \ ps2 \ bugs.doc

3. *These names refer to different files (different drives, note default drive is C:)*
   d:bugs.doc
   bugs.doc

4. *These names refer to different files (same drive, but different directories)*

   bugs.doc   this is c: \ computer \ micros
                                             \ ibm \ ps2 \ bugs.doc.

   \ bugs.doc   this file doesn't exist; it would
                                             be in the root directory

   c: \ bugs.doc   this file doesn't exist; it would
                                             be in the root directory

   .. \ .. \ .. \ minis \ dec \ vax \ bugs.doc   this is: c: \ computer \ minis
                                             \ dec \ vax \ bugs.doc

   .. \ bugs.doc   this is c: \ computer \ micros
                                             \ ibm \ bugs.doc

5. *Thes files match speed.*:*

   c: \ computer \ micros \ ibm \ ps2 \ speed.doc
   c: \ computer \ micros \ ibm \ ps2 \ speed.wks
   c: \ computer \ micros \ ibm \ ps2 \ speed.dbf
   c: \ computer \ micros \ ibm \ ps2 \ speed.ndx
   c: \ computer \ micros \ ibm \ ps2 \ speed.exe

6. *These files match "s*.*"*

   c: \ computer \ micros \ ibm \ ps2 \ speed.doc
   c: \ computer \ micros \ ibm \ ps2 \ speed.wks
   c: \ computer \ micros \ ibm \ ps2 \ speed.dbf
   c: \ computer \ micros \ ibm \ ps2 \ speed.ndx
   c: \ computer \ micros \ ibm \ ps2 \ speed.exe
   c: \ computer \ micros \ ibm \ ps2 \ spend.doc
   c: \ computer \ micros \ ibm \ ps2 \ spud.doc

7. *These files match sp??d.**

   c: \ computer \ micros \ ibm \ ps2 \ speed.doc
   c: \ computer \ micros \ ibm \ ps2 \ speed.wks
   c: \ computer \ micros \ ibm \ ps2 \ speed.dbf
   c: \ computer \ micros \ ibm \ ps2 \ speed.ndx
   c: \ computer \ micros \ ibm \ ps2 \ speed.exe
   c: \ computer \ micros \ ibm \ ps2 \ spend.doc
   But not c: \ computer \ micros \ ibm \ ps2 \ spud.doc. The file must have
   two characters between *sp* and *d.*

8. *These files match *.d??*

   c: \ computer \ micros \ ibm \ ps2 \ bugs.doc
   c: \ computer \ micros \ ibm \ ps2 \ speed.doc
   c: \ computer \ micros \ ibm \ ps2 \ speed.dbf
   Note that c: \ computer \ micros \ ibm \ bugs.doc is not included. It's in a different directory.

9. *These files are included in .:*

   c: \ computer \ micros \ ibm \ ps2 \ bugs.doc
   c: \ computer \ micros \ ibm \ ps2 \ bugs.bak
   c: \ computer \ micros \ ibm \ ps2 \ features
   c: \ computer \ micros \ ibm \ ps2 \ speed.doc
   c: \ computer \ micros \ ibm \ ps2 \ speed.wks
   c: \ computer \ micros \ ibm \ ps2 \ speed.dbf
   c: \ computer \ micros \ ibm \ ps2 \ speed.ndx
   c: \ computer \ micros \ ibm \ ps2 \ speed.exe

c: \computer \micros \ibm \ps2 \spend.doc
c: \computer \micros \ibm \ps2 \spud.doc
All the files in the current default directory of the default drive.

10. *These files are included in ..:*

c: \computer \micros \ibm \bugs.doc
c: \computer \micros \ibm \12-31-87.not
All the files in the parent directory of the current default directory of the default drive.

11. *These are filename translations:*

bugs.doc	= c: \computer \micros \ibm \ps2 \bugs.doc
. \bugs.doc	= c: \computer \micros \ibm \ps2 \bugs.doc
\bugs.doc	= c: \bugs.doc
.. \bugs.doc	= c: \computer \micros \ibm \bugs.doc
.. \.. \ibm \bugs.doc	= c: \computer \micros \ibm \bugs.doc

Chapter 3
Programs and Processes

Chapter 3
Programs and Processes

The term *process* in the computer world has much the same meaning as it does in ordinary life. A process is a connected chain of events. Each event causes one or more other events to occur, and so on, until the process is complete.

With most computers, including those running OS/2, a single process is begun when power is first applied to the hardware. This first process is the *boot* process. The job of the boot process is to copy the instructions for other processes from permanent disk storage to RAM storage where the instructions can be used. It then directs the hardware to take instructions from these newly loaded series of instructions.

The boot process creates and initiates other processes. The act of creating a new process is often called *spawning* a new process. The spawned process is usually called a *child process* or a *subprocess*. And, as you might guess, the spawning process is a *parent process*.

When the instructions required to control a process are loaded into RAM and the hardware is set to run those instructions, a new process has been *dispatched*. At any moment, the computer is executing instructions that are a part of one process or another. Even if the computer is apparently doing nothing or just seems to be going in circles, it's still executing instructions. And, since instructions form a chain of events, they are part of a process.

Trying to tell one process from another can get a bit hazy. Since all processes trace their ancestry back to the boot process, they are all branches of the same historical tree. There is one particularly gnarly point on the tree of processes where most branches get started. In OS/2, this is the *program selector*.

The program selector is a program for starting processes. After starting the system, the program selector's screen is usually the first screen you see that allows you to do anything.

Before reaching the program selector, the boot process is normally on autopilot as you wait for the process to finish.

When the program selector screen is displayed, you can pick a program to run. When you do this, the program selector spawns a process controlled by the program you have selected. The program runs, you use it, and the program ends. When it ends, control of the hardware is passed back to the program selector, and you can start over again.

What Is a Session?

OS/2 has its own terminology for this tangle of processes. Processes that begin and end at the program selector (or began with the START command) are called *sessions*.

Note that a single session may involve multiple programs successively controlling the process until it ends and returns to the program selector. When a session process spawns subprocesses of its own, these are normally called *threads*. The difference is that each session has a *virtual screen* of its own, but individual threads do not.

Since OS/2 is a multitasking operating system, multiple processes can coexist. Still, at any one time, one process has control of the hardware, but not necessarily for very long. The way OS/2 and other *timesharing* systems work is to jump quickly from process to process, executing a bit of one, then a bit of the next. You can control how often OS/2 jumps from one process to another, but it is normally about once each quarter of a second. By hopping around like this, OS/2 gives the appearance that it's doing several tasks simultaneously.

From the perspective of human time, for which the second is normally the smallest division of time, OS/2 is running multiple processes simultaneously. But, from the perspective of computer time, for which terms like nanoseconds and picoseconds (billionths and trillionths of seconds) have been coined, OS/2 is working on one process for many milliseconds at a time. It occasionally changes the process on which it's working. To the computer, it represents a leisurely pace, like the progression of the seasons. To the operator, it appears that everything is happening at once.

Recall the earlier mention of a virtual screen. If OS/2 is working on several processes apparently simultaneously, the display screen could become messy as each process sends characters, squiggles and error messages to the screen unaware that other programs are doing the same. To keep this jumble straight, each major process or session is given its own screen.

The best way to do this would be to have five or ten display screens on your desk, each showing output from a different session. Microsoft and IBM weren't sure you would buy so many monitors or have such a big desk, so they settled for building OS/2 to keep a copy of a virtual screen for each running session.

At any time, only one of these virtual screens is displayed on your real screen. With a keystroke, you can switch which virtual screen is shown on the real screen at any time (or you can jump to the program selector and select a particular session's screen). When you switch virtual screens, you also switch the keyboard and mouse along with it.

When you see the output from a session on the screen, you can be fairly certain that any typing or mouse-mashing will provide input to the session from which the screen came.

Let's review for a moment. A process is a chain of events. Events in a computer are controlled by instructions, so a process is also a chain of computer instructions, each leading to the next. All processes trace their origin back to the single boot process that begins when the computer is started. Therefore, all processes are really branches of one all-subsuming process.

But how do programs fit in?

Programs and Sessions

A *program* is a package of computer instructions. As such, when a program runs, it controls a process. However, when a program stops, it may invoke another program that continues where the first left off. The chain of events is unbroken, so there are two programs, each involved in a single process.

Remember that a program is just a way of packaging instructions. There's often contention among programmers as to whether a particular job should be done by one program or a chain of two or several programs. It's a question of packaging and programming style.

OS/2 gives programmers a new packaging question to argue about. Many programs have to be built to handle more than one activity nearly simultaneously. At its simplest, this might include displaying text and watching for keystrokes—two activities often easily combined in programs.

On a more complex level, one might write a spreadsheet program to recalculate cell values and accept new keyboard input to cells at the same time. A programmer may decide to do this entirely as a part of the spreadsheet program. If so, he or she has to provide a way to jump rapidly between the parts of the program that do these very different jobs. This isn't always easy. Furthermore, the jumping must be done efficiently or the system may spend most of its time performing the jumps and perform very little real work on either task between jumps.

Programs and Threads

With OS/2, programmers are provided with another alternative. One program can spawn multiple threads. Each thread is treated as a separate process by OS/2. That means each thread is put on OS/2's list of processes between which to share computer time.

As a result, OS/2 will cause the threads to run nearly simultaneously without jumping around within the program. The programmer still has to cause the threads to be created and killed as appropriate, and must program how the different threads from one program will communicate and share information, but OS/2 offers some helpful utilities to assist.

Threads don't get the full treatment given to sessions. All the threads in one session share a common virtual screen. As a result, they must be built so they won't conflict in their screen and keyboard use, and they must not collide on other parts of the computer's hardware. In short, they must be cooperative children of a single-parent process.

Detached Processes

But that's not all the options OS/2 offers to organizing processes. Besides sessions and threads, you can create processes that have no virtual screen attached. Such processes are *detached processes*. They run like a session and get their fair share of computer time, but they cannot access the screen or keyboard. You can't even select them from the program selector or stop them with a command. Once you start a detached process, it's on its own and you can have no further communication with it. (See the DETACH command in the command reference section.)

You might see some effects of the detached process in files or printing. Detached programs can read, write, delete, and create files. Surprisingly, there are many good jobs for detached processes. Any time you want to run an ordinary OS/2 command and send its result to a file, it's a good candidate to run as a detached process.

The benefit of a detached process is that you don't have to wait for the process to complete before going on to other commands. The detriment is that it isn't always easy to tell when it's finished. And, if the command stops to wait for a keystroke, it can wait forever because it will never get one: It can't read the keyboard.

Special facilities for detached processes. Just as there are threads to enhance sessions, OS/2 offers some special facilities for detached processes. You are probably familiar with *pop-up, memory-resident,* or *terminate-and-stay-resident* programs in MS-DOS. These are all names for the same type of program. These programs sit in memory and take over the computer and screen when some special *hot key* keyboard combination is pressed. Such memory-resident programs are wasteful of computer resources, especially in a multitasking system like OS/2. Instead, a detached process in OS/2 can be made to act like a DOS memory-resident program.

Detached processes can create a pop-up screen that will appear over the current virtual screen when the pop-up is activated. In addition, OS/2 provides a way for processes to *eavesdrop* on keyboard or mouse input. Eavesdropping requires the creation of a special-purpose program fragment called a *monitor*. A detached process can create and install a monitor and, when certain keys are pressed, invoke a pop-up screen to give the detached process a way to communicate with the user. The net effect is similar to that of a memory-resident DOS program, but computer resources are not tied up lying dormant as they are for DOS memory-resident programs.

Here's the rub with detached programs, pop-ups, and monitors: The program running in detached mode must be designed to do so. Most programs are not so designed and will seem to disappear if run as detached processes. But they don't really disappear. They lurk around in the computer, using its resources to no good end. The only certain way to remove them is by rebooting the computer.

Batch Files

Batch files are literally scripts for OS/2 to follow. They are ordinary text files that contain OS/2 commands. Batch files are usually used for four types of operations:

• Causing OS/2 to run certain commands automatically when it starts for the first time or when it starts a session.
• Starting programs that require setup commands before running or that require a long and inconvenient command line.
• Executing frequent or difficult sequences of commands.
• Implementing new commands that are more convenient for you or are more capable than the standard OS/2 commands.

If you want to become a more capable computer user, one of the best investments of your time is to spend it learning to build and make effective use of batch files. Besides simple sequences of commands, batch files allow limited testing of the current situation and can respond to different situations with different commands.

Batch files are the quick and easy way to program. But, being quick and easy, they don't offer the flexibility and detailed control of regular programming languages, but they can do many things with a few commands. There is much more about batch files in this book, but for now, suffice it to say that entering the name of a batch file as an OS/2 command causes it to execute instructions from the batch file rather than the keyboard until the batch file is finished.

You can use batch files just as you would use programs. You can start a session with a batch file as its first command. You can use a batch file to start another session. You can run a batch file as a detached process. But, batch files cannot create or deal with threads or pop-ups, except as these might be created by programs started with a batch file.

Historical Necessity: Real and Protected Modes

OS/2 didn't come out of nowhere. It's a child of MS-DOS (also known as PC-DOS when IBM is the vendor). MS-DOS 1.1, the first version of DOS to see wide use, was very similar to CP/M 80, one of the pioneering operating systems for personal computers. (CP/M 80 in turn owed much to earlier operating systems from Digital Equipment, the minicomputer pioneer.)

With the introduction of MS-DOS 2.0, DOS made a sharp turn. It was clearly descended from the Unix operating system developed at Bell Laboratories, again, primarily for use on Digital Equipment minicomputers. (Unix's lineage even goes back to the GE, and later the Honeywell, Multics operating system—one of the first timesharing systems.)

MS-DOS 2.0 was built with an eye toward market practicality. Though much different from MS-DOS 1.1 internally, it retained enough from DOS 1.1 to allow it to run programs written for 1.1. Programs written for DOS 1.1 couldn't use all the facilities of DOS 2.0, but they were able to perform the same tasks they had under DOS 1.1 with few problems. It's rare to see an unrevised DOS 1.1 program in use nowadays, but when DOS 2.0 was released, those were the only programs available. The compatibility of DOS 2.0 with 1.1 was crucial to its initial market acceptance.

Now, with OS/2, yet another generation of the operating system appears on the scene. Early versions of OS/2 implemented more Unix ideas and some entirely new ways of doing things. OS/2 owes some of its structure to the IBM mainframe operating system VM (Virtual Machine), IBM's term for virtual screens or consoles.

Later versions of OS/2, which incorporate more Microsoft *Windows* technology, owe much in spirit and use to the Apple MacIntosh, which itself is derived from work at the Xerox Palo Alto Research Center (PARC) on its Star machine.

Later OS/2 versions may also draw on IBM's sophisticated mainframe database system *DB2* (which is as much like dBase II as freight trains are like motor scooters).

OS/2 has a lineage. Its lineage is important for two reasons. First, operating system designers learned a long time ago to use what works. They rely heavily on concepts developed in earlier systems. Designers often add a few concepts of their own, but they are prudent not to throw out too much of what has proven successful.

Second, there is the immediate practical need for programs to run under OS/2, and MS-DOS has by far the most varied and successful program library in history. Microsoft has a good record for learning from its successes and has been very careful to make new versions of MS-DOS compatible with programs written under older versions.

But OS/2 is multitasking and MS-DOS is not. That's a big difference for operating systems, especially given the bizarre nature of the Intel 80286 processor OS/2 was designed to use. There wasn't a way to make OS/2 run ordinary DOS programs without major compromises in the system's capabilities. The result is one of computer history's most glaring *kludges*.

A kludge (rhymes with *huge*) is an ugly thing stuck onto a program or computer that doesn't fit the rest of the system. Kludges are usually distracting, inelegant, and quirky but practical necessities.

OS/2's kludge goes by the names *real mode, DOS mode, DOS compatibility mode,* and the *DOS Box.* OS/2's multitasking system is called *protected mode.*

Real mode is actually a separate operating system (though it uses some of the protected mode facilities). It's more or less compatible with MS-DOS 3.3. Without real mode, you couldn't run any MS-DOS programs under OS/2. As it is, most DOS programs perform acceptably in real mode. DOS and OS/2 are so different that Microsoft's ability to make real mode emulate DOS so well is an impressive accomplishment.

As a user, you should consider real mode an interim inconvenience. Plan on eventually switching away from DOS programs to programs written with OS/2 in mind. (Or get rid of OS/2 and go back to using DOS alone.) But, when you begin using OS/2, you'll probably have no choice, either because you can't afford to replace all of your DOS programs or because the programs you need are not yet available for protected mode.

Real Mode

Real mode is not a process, program, or session. It is a unique thing in OS/2, unlike any other. You can switch between protected mode and real mode as if real mode were just another protected session, but it isn't. There's only one real mode process at any time, just as there is normally only one process in DOS at any time.

The commands used in real mode sometimes have the same names as commands in protected mode, and sometimes they don't. When they have the same name, they appear to do about the same thing. Often the tasks use different techniques in real and protected modes.

Since protected mode processes don't deal directly with hardware input and output facilities, they continue to run when real mode is invoked. While you are looking at the real mode screen, OS/2 may be briefly running a program in a protected mode session. However, since real mode programs deal directly with the screen and other input/output devices, they cannot be allowed to continue to run while a protected mode session screen is displayed. Doing so would frequently result in the real mode program interfering with the protected mode screen.

The main point at this juncture is that real and protected modes are more separate and different than they might appear.

A Program's Runtime Environment and Hardware Independence

A major part of an operating system is the *environment* it provides for the programs that run under the operating system. This is where you'll find a big difference between real and protected modes. The *runtime environment* is the way a program sees the computer: assumptions it can safely make about the computer hardware and operating system services available at the time the program runs.

Take the screen display as an example. Many different hardware display systems are available for PC machines. They differ radically in capabilities and in the way those capabilities are controlled. Not only are there many different hardware systems, there are also different modes of operation for many of those systems. In each different mode of operation, the display system is controlled differently. It is not unusual for a programmer to be asked to develop programs that can cope with 20 or more display control methods, and that's a compromise reflecting only the more popular display systems available.

Since the primary impediment to advancing computer technology and cost reduction is software—not hardware—development, it would be nice if the programmer could write one set of display-controlling code that would work with all available options.

That's one of the main reasons for an operating system: to make hardware differences *transparent* to programs. In other words, the operating system should make the program's runtime environment accommodating enough that the program doesn't need to know about the display hardware. The program should call on the operating system to perform all hardware-dependent display control activities.

Unfortunately, it isn't that simple. If the display hardware is made transparent to programs, usually some speed of operation will be lost. Since the operating system, applications programs, and display devices are all built by different companies, there is no guarantee that the operating system will support the latest and greatest display device from an obscure hardware manufacturer. Making *standard device interfaces* makes programming easier, but that tends to add a greater burden of corporate politics to hardware innovation.

When it comes to display devices, the designers of DOS punted. They provided a minimum set of display control functions in a standard interface for programmers to use. But these display control functions are slow. Furthermore, they offer no way to use any of the more advanced display capabilities available. For this reason, any commercial DOS program that involves intensive user interaction will directly control the display hardware and bypass the operating system's display control components.

Programs are more complex because they have to work differently with different display systems, but the performance achieved is generally good. In OS/2, this cannot be tolerated. Since virtual screens are used, the operating system must be able to control the display hardware to save and restore different images created in different modes of operation. So OS/2 makes much more elaborate and better performing display control services available to programs.

That's fine for programmers, but when you see a new type of display system, the odds that it will fully function under OS/2 are not very good yet. Display makers know this and generally try to make their systems act like popular standard display systems. When they do, they usually have to disable some of the unique capabilities that make the new systems attractive.

With the advent of Microsoft's Presentation Manager for graphics applications, some of these problems will be reduced by forcing the hardware makers to supply programming that controls their own display in a standard way, as with *Windows* today. Unfortunately, the people who make the most innovative display systems seem to have a hard time making the best display control software.

We could hold forth at length about the oddities of display control and compatibility, but the bottom line is that OS/2 controls the display in protected mode, and the application program controls the display in real mode. (That's why a DOS program in real mode can alter the display settings so that OS/2 shows gibberish when protected mode screens are selected. The only way around this is to make sure the DOS program controlling the screen returns it to a display mode sympathetic to OS/2 before switching to a protected mode virtual screen.)

In protected mode, OS/2 is called upon by programs to control the display, keyboard, mouse, printers, and serial ports

49

using standard commands that are largely the same regardless of the real hardware attached to the computer. These hardware control services are part of the environment in which protected mode programs run.

In real mode, these services are not available or are greatly reduced, so they aren't part of a program's runtime environment. The program must sense and deal more directly with the hardware attached. Real mode programs are less insulated from the hardware. Their runtime environment is more hardware-dependent than the environment provided to protected mode programs.

Pre-Runtime Communications with Programs

There are several other aspects to a program's runtime environment which are important to how a program is built and functions.

The command line. Most programs, including OS/2 external commands (which are simply programs), are started with a command that contains more than just an indication of which program to run. Usually the command line allows for the naming of one or more files and several coded options which either tell the program what to do or feed it information about how it is to be done.

In both real and protected modes, OS/2 provides every program with a copy of the part of the command that started the program. Usually, this is all of the command line you typed or all of the command OS/2 read from a batch file. But a running program may be given only a part of the entire command line, since a command line can contain more than one command or option for OS/2.

A copy of the command line becomes a part of the runtime environment created and maintained by OS/2. A programmer can safely assume that OS/2 will have a copy of the command line available to a program when the program is run. To get this copy, the programmer must call a particular OS/2 function to deliver the command line copy.

Environment variables. In addition to the command line, OS/2 makes a copy of all current *environment variables* available to each program. Environment variables are simply strings of characters. They begin with a variable name followed by an equal sign and a string of characters, which end with a special, invisible character. With these strings of characters, you can set the value of an environment variable. A program can read that value and act accordingly.

Environment variables are generally used to save information about the state of the computer system and as an alternative to long, complex command lines.

Environment variables are simple, but they have a quirk. The copy of environment variables provided to a program is made when the program is run. The copy is not updated if an environment variable is changed outside the program. The program can change its own copy of the environment variables, but it isn't allowed to change the copies given to other programs. When one program invokes another, that is, when a parent spawns a child, a copy of the parent program's environment is made for the child program. In this way, child processes *inherit* environment variables from the parent process, but the children cannot make changes in the parent's copy of the environment variables.

This system is simple and effective, but people are often confused when changes to an environment variable disappear with the child program that made the changes.

Environment variables are created, set, and destroyed by you or a batch file using the SET command. The OS/2 commands PATH, PROMPT, DPATH, and (in a funny way) APPEND all set environment variables that are used not only by ordinary programs, but by the OS/2 command interpreter program (discussed below) and by the OS/2 file-access functions used by programs to find and open files.

Environment variables work essentially the same for real and protected modes. In protected mode, each session has its own environment variables, which are kept separately from those for other sessions.

The file system as part of the runtime environment.
Besides the command line and environment variables, a program may sense and alter much about the file system.

All files on your system and the OS/2 functions needed to access and alter these files are available to programs. The current disk drive and the current directory for each installed drive are particularly convenient to a program.

Changes to default directories don't behave like changes to environment variables: When a program changes default directories, the change persists after the program and its subprograms are finished.

Each session in protected mode and the single real mode session may have different default directories. Since all programs see the same file system, programs can communicate between each other, between sessions and even between real and protected modes by altering files. Within protected mode, OS/2 offers more efficient communication services that behave somewhat like files but are more temporary in nature.

To pass information between protected mode programs and real mode programs, the only answer is for one program to write and close a file which is subsequently read by the other program.

Standard files as part of the runtime environment. When a program uses a file, it must first find the file by name; then it must open it. If the file is for output and doesn't already exist, the program must create the file, a process that also opens the file. You open and create files by calling the operating system to do the necessary work.

After a file is opened in a program, it's no longer referred to by name. Thereafter, the program refers to the file by a special number called a *file handle* or *file ID*.

When one program invokes another as a child process, the files open in the parent process are inherited by the child process. The child process need not know the names of the files. It only needs to know the file handle or file ID. One simple but powerful trick performed by both DOS and OS/2 is to open several standard files before running a program. Thereafter, the program need not open these files, but instead can refer to them by handle. In fact, the program never knows the real names of these files. Traditionally, these files are referred to as

- File ID 0, *stdin* for standard input.
- File ID 1, *stdout* for standard output.
- File ID 2, *stderr* for standard error output.

• File ID 3, *stdaux* for standard auxiliary input and output.
• File ID 4, *stdprn* for standard printer output.

Normally, stdout is opened for output to the console screen as is stderr, stdin is opened for input from the keyboard, stdaux is opened for input and output to a serial port, and stdprn is opened for output to LPT1, the first printer. However, with commands from the keyboard or a batch file, you can change the assignment of these files. You can send stdout to a file. Or you can assign stdin to read a file instead of the keyboard, and so on. If the program is designed to use these standard files, you can *redirect* its input and output to patch the program into a chain of programs, each getting its input from a prior program's output.

OS/2's protected mode has elaborated on this idea from DOS (originally from Unix). Instead of stdin, stdout, stderr, stdaux, and stdprn, OS/2 assigns stdin, stdout, stderr, and seven other handles referred to only by number.

Now up to ten standard files are available, all of which can be redirected to named files or programs.

Dynamic linking as part of the runtime environment. In protected mode, OS/2 offers hundreds of different services that can be called upon by a program. To make each service available to a program, OS/2 must have a chunk of machine instructions ready to run. This code will carry out the service called upon by a program.

There are so many services and alternate ways of doing similar things, it's unlikely that all the programs running at a given time will take advantage of all the services offered. Also, there are some basic services like finding and opening a file that are used by most programs.

It would be wasteful for OS/2 to have the code necessary to complete all possible services sitting in memory ready to roll at all times. A more efficient scheme is to have loaded and ready to operate only the code for services used at some point by the programs currently running. Also, it would be nice if all the programs that need a service could share the same copy of the code needed for the service rather than having a duplicate copy for each program.

In protected mode, OS/2 only loads those services
needed, and it allows multiple programs to share the same
copy of the code for the services used. To accomplish this,
OS/2 requires that program files contain a list of all the OS/2
services the program might use. In preparation for running a
program, this list of needed services is scanned. If a service
called for is already loaded to serve another program, the new
program is modified as it's loaded to refer to the proper location for the service code. If the code for a service used by a
program is not already in memory, OS/2 loads it and modifies
the new program to refer to the proper place for the code
needed.

The process of modifying a program to refer to other code
the program needs, but which is not part of the program file
itself, is called *linking*. It links the program with the external
code it needs. If this linking is done as the program is loaded,
it's called *dynamic linking*.

In DOS and OS/2's real mode, all the code for operating
system services is either permanently loaded into memory or
is made part of the program as it is stored. DOS programs are
linked when they're created. A programmer's tool, called a
linker, is run to link custom program code with standard code
from a file called a *library*.

After linking, this code becomes part of the program and
is saved in the program's file. DOS's linkage is not dynamic
because it is done when the program is built and does not re-
cur until the program is reconstructed by its programmer. This
is fine for DOS because most of the code needed for operating
system services can be kept in memory all the time without
being obtrusively large.

In order to perform dynamic linking, OS/2 needs the special program file format that specifies which services are used,
and it needs a file or files containing the library of standard
code that is the source for the dynamically linked services. To
get the right program file format, programmers use program-
building programs supplied by Microsoft to work with OS/2.

To tell OS/2 where to find linkage libraries when it loads
programs, you can specify to OS/2 a directory containing these

library files (using the LIBPATH command for CONFIG.SYS files).

There's a handy side advantage to dynamic linking. As new hardware becomes available, and as new services are added to OS/2, the dynamic link libraries can be changed to modify OS/2 without replacing it with an entirely new version. This represents a potential new product area for software companies. We will have to wait and see if any of them offer enhanced OS/2 linkage libraries.

Dynamic linkage is one of the most radical departures of OS/2 from previous practice in DOS. Operating system services are not only different from those offered in DOS, they are made available to programs in an entirely new way. This is yet another reason why the protected and real modes of OS/2 are so distinct from one another.

Chapter 4
The Command Interpreter

Chapter 4
The Command Interpreter

When you type a command, the command interpreter, which is part of OS/2, actually reads your entry and responds by executing the command. The command interpreter is a program. In general, it behaves like any other program. The only thing special about it is that it's the program used to load and execute other programs.

Internal Versus External Commands

All commands to the command interpreter program are of two types, internal commands and external commands.

Internal commands can be completed by the command interpreter without using any other program. External commands are actually commands to load and execute other programs.

The command interpreter pays special attention to the first word of any command given to it. If the first word matches the name for an internal command, the command interpreter performs the command. If the first word does not match any internal command, it is taken to be the name of a file containing a program or batch file. The external commands of OS/2 are separate programs just like any other programs, except that they were part of the package when you purchased OS/2.

It's important to remember that the name of an external command or other program is also the name of the file containing the program. OS/2 looks for no further meaning in the command name. For example, if you change the name of the file containing the XCOPY command, you also change the name of the command. OS/2 will not be able to find and run XCOPY unless it is in a file with XCOPY as its first name.

Finding External Commands and Programs

When the command interpreter is told to run a program, it must first find the file that contains the program. It starts by looking in the current default directory of the current default drive. If it doesn't find the program file, it looks in the directories listed in the environment variable named *path*.

The *path* variable is set with the PATH or SET commands. The character string value of the *path* variable is presumed to contain the names of directories with semicolons in between. The command interpreter continues to look for the program file in each directory listed in the *path* variable until it finds a match or until it has searched all of the directories specified in the *path* variable.

If it finds a matching program file, it runs the program contained in the file. If it fails to find a matching program file, it complains that your command was no good. While searching for a program file to match a command, OS/2 looks for any of three kinds of files:

• A .COM program file
• An .EXE program file
• A batch file

The structure of a program file can follow either of two sets of rules. If the program is constructed to one set of rules, it is a .COM program, if it follows the other set of rules, it is an .EXE program. Program files of the .COM and .EXE type have very different internal formats, and the programs are loaded and started differently. The only way OS/2 has to tell which way it should try to load a program is by its filename extension, which must be .COM or .EXE. (Do not rename a .COM to have a .EXE extension or vice versa. OS/2 will not be able to run such misnamed programs.)

While hunting for the file needed to execute a command, OS/2 looks not only for program files, but for batch files as well. In protected mode, batch files must have the extension .CMD. In real mode, the extension must be .BAT. Again, having the proper file extension is critical to the operation of commands that run batch files.

Here's an example of how OS/2 would look for a command or program in protected mode:

PATH=C: \ CMD;C: \ BIN;C: \ OS2;

Current Default Directory is C: \ USR \ YOU

Command is WP

Files OS/2 hunts for in trying to execute WP:

In the default directory:
C: \ USR \ YOU \ WP.COM
C: \ USR \ YOU \ WP.EXE
C: \ USR \ YOU \ WP.CMD

In the first PATH directory:
C: \ CMD \ WP.COM
C: \ CMD \ WP.EXE
C: \ CMD \ WP.CMD

In the second PATH directory:
C: \ BIN \ WP.COM
C: \ BIN \ WP.EXE
C: \ BIN \ WP.CMD

In the third and last PATH directory:
C: \ OS2 \ WP.COM
C: \ OS2 \ WP.EXE
C: \ OS2 \ WP.CMD

Remember that OS/2 stops looking as soon as it has a match for one of the files listed above. For that reason, the order of directories in your *path* environment variable is critical. If there were the files C: \ BIN \ WP.EXE and C: \ CMD \ WP.CMD, then the path shown above would cause C: \ CMD \ WP.CMD to be executed. With PATH=C: \ BIN;C: \ CMD;C: \ OS2, C: \ BIN \ WP.EXE would be executed. And, notice that if there were the two files C: \ BIN \ WP.EXE and C: \ BIN \ WP.CMD, the .CMD file would never be executed. (At least not without some fancy footwork.)

The search process in real mode is identical, except that .CMD files are ignored and .BAT files are sought instead.

Loading Programs

Once the command interpreter has found a file corresponding to a command, it must figure out how to use it. If the file has the extension .CMD in protected mode or .BAT in real mode, the contents of the file are input to the command interpreter's own stdin (standard input) and are treated as if typed at the keyboard. But in protected mode there's another trick OS/2 can perform. If the first line of a .CMD file contains the command EXTPROC, the command interpreter will run the program named in the EXTPROC command and reassign that program's standard input to be the batch file. The purpose here is to allow you to send commands to a program other than the command interpreter.

If the program file found is a .COM file, little special loading is performed. The file is copied into an area of memory and is executed. If the program file found is an .EXE file, the standard header information in the file is read, and the file is loaded into memory according to a complex set of options defined in the .EXE file.

In protected mode, as part of the loading process, the program is dynamically linked with any libraries required. Not only is the loading process for .EXE files fairly complex, but there are different kinds of .EXE files. Some .EXE files can run only in real mode, some only in protected mode, and some in both modes. Programs written for DOS will not run in protected mode, but programs written for OS/2 might run in either or both modes. The only way to be sure is to try.

If an .EXE file contains a program written exclusively for protected mode, you will receive an error message that the program is too big to fit in memory. (This isn't necessarily true, but it is the device OS/2 uses to keep protected mode programs from running in real mode.)

You will notice that these programs are loaded into memory. But where in memory? Since memory is shared by multiple concurrent programs, OS/2 has to do complex bookkeeping to track what's where and to make space when it's needed. If there is an unused gap in memory large enough for the program loading, it's placed in that gap. If there isn't a large enough gap, OS/2 tries to make one. It has two tools at its disposal:

- If there is enough total memory available, but it's split up into fragments too small to accommodate the program at hand, OS/2 can move other programs in memory to coalesce the unused gaps into one larger space adequate for the new program.
- If there isn't enough memory available, OS/2 can temporarily *swap* a program or two out to disk (save them to disk until they are called). When those programs run again, their contents will be swapped back into memory from disk.

You're not supposed to see swapping activity, but you might notice it because of the time required or because your disk runs when you don't expect it to.

OS/2 is able to move and swap programs because they are *relocatable*. This means that all memory location references in the programs are not simple addresses of memory locations. Instead, they are all stated in terms of offsets from a few key points. By changing the location of these key points in memory and passing them to the program, OS/2 can immediately shift all the memory references in a program to a new area of memory.

Starting and Ending Programs

When OS/2 has loaded a program into memory, it then prepares to run it. The program needs to be added to some internal tables where OS/2 keeps track of the active programs, their status, their turn at using the computer, their priority for computer time, and their location.

Once the bookkeeping is done, the program is ready to run and starts getting its share of computer time. During this process, the command interpreter has built a copy of the environment variables and command line for the program to use, and it has opened the standard files the program may use.

Once the program starts running, the command interpreter leaves it alone to run and waits for the program to terminate. Most often, programs do their tasks and then finish. However, you can interrupt the operation of a program by pressing the Ctrl-C or Ctrl–Scroll Lock key combinations. When you do this, you are telling the operating system to sidetrack the usual processing of input keys and immediately kill the process running in the currently visible session.

When building a program, a programmer can override OS/2's normal program-killing process and provide a special chunk of code to be executed whenever you signal the program to stop. This is because some programs need to put certain information away in files before quitting or the files might make no sense. As a result, you may see some programs that respond in a more complex way than just stopping when you press Ctrl–Scroll Lock.

When a program finishes, any files it opened are closed and the command interpreter makes ready for another command. Note that the standard files were not opened by the program that just ran. They were opened by the command interpreter. As a result, they can be used by other programs as input or output. It's one of the jobs of the command interpreter to make sure programs get the right standard files.

Where the Command Interpreter Is Found

In real mode, the command interpreter program is COMMAND.COM, just as it is in DOS. In protected mode, the command interpreter program is CMD.EXE.

In general, CMD.EXE is considerably smarter than COMMAND.COM and allows more complex command lines. Neither COMMAND.COM nor CMD.EXE is very flexible by modern standards, but each allows enough types of instructions to be useful. We will cover how to use command interpreter instructions in some depth in the commands section.

The Boot Process

One thing programmers know (and nonprogrammers usually don't know) is that getting a program set up and ready to run is more difficult to program than the actual running part of the program.

This is certainly true for operating systems. The computer's central processor can only execute instructions from memory, not directly from disk. But, when the power is turned off, memory loses its contents and turns to all zeros. In order to read a disk, the computer must execute instructions; to get instructions to execute into memory, the computer must read a disk.

This chicken-and-egg problem is solved by a special portion of memory that retains its contents when the power is turned off. This chunk of memory is permanently recorded and never changes its contents. It is called *ROM* (Read-Only Memory). Every modern computer contains some ROM and some special circuitry that causes the processor to receive its instructions from this ROM when power is first applied.

In PCs and compatibles, the contents of the ROM is the *BIOS* (Basic Input/Output System). The first part of the ROM BIOS contains instructions for testing the basic components of the computer. These are executed each time the computer is turned on.

After the tests comes the *bootstrap loader*. This is a generic term for a program fragment whose job it is to load some information from disk and then cause the processor to follow these newly loaded instructions.

The BIOS isn't as smart about disk files and directories as the full operating system is, so it has to limit its search to specific files in specific places on the disk. In the case of OS/2, the BIOS is expected to look first at the first file stored on a floppy disk in drive A:. If there is no floppy disk in A:, then the BIOS is supposed to look for the first file on the *currently active* hard disk partition. (You can break a disk into partitions and set which one is active with the FDISK command.) If BIOS can't find an operating system file that meets certain conditions, the operating system cannot be loaded and the computer will inform you of a boot failure, or you'll be prompted to insert a system disk.

If your system is properly installed, this won't happen, and the BIOS will load a file containing basic input/output code. (This file is called IBMIO.COM in the IBM release of OS/2.) Once these basic input/output services are loaded, they, in turn, are used to load the *kernel* or core programming of the operating system, which contains most of the code needed to access the file system. (In the IBM release, this is IBMDOS.COM.)

This loading business has just begun. OS/2 can run on computers with a variety of input/output hardware. To keep from having many versions of OS/2 itself, the portions of code that deal with input/output devices are separated into independent modules. As OS/2 is loading itself into memory, it selects those files containing *device drivers* appropriate to the hardware at hand and links them into OS/2 itself to handle I/O (Input/Output) in ways appropriate for the particular computer.

OS/2 automatically loads device drivers for the display, keyboard, printer, floppy disk drive(s), hard disk drive(s), and the system clock. But you can cause it to load other device drivers as well. After loading its standard device drivers, OS/2 looks for a file named CONFIG.SYS in the root directory of the drive from which OS/2 initially started loading.

In CONFIG.SYS, you can inform OS/2 of any device drivers you want loaded to support any special hardware you might have and to support ordinary hardware for special purposes. Generally, you should specify one or more device drivers in CONFIG.SYS; the defaults are usually not sufficient.

You should be aware that there are two flavors of device drivers. Some only support real mode operations. Others support both real and protected mode input and output requests. (The real and protected mode device drivers are difficult to write; it may take some vendors of special hardware some time to get them right.) In addition to specifying device drivers, you can use CONFIG.SYS to specify several options about how OS/2 works. Usually the default options are adequate, but you can fine-tune your system for your typical work pattern by altering CONFIG.SYS statements. You can also use it to start detached programs you want to run quietly in the background, like the SPOOL program that handles printer output.

After CONFIG.SYS is read and processed, OS/2 is still not finished loading itself into memory. It continues to put itself together, and, when it's done, it looks for another special file called STARTUP.CMD. This batch file must reside in the root directory of the boot disk. It's just like any other protected mode batch file. Its distinction is that it is automatically executed whenever OS/2 starts. STARTUP.CMD is a handy place to set things up. You can use it to *start* the sessions with which you normally work and to do housekeeping on backup files and the like.

By the time OS/2 progresses as far as executing STARTUP.CMD, it's complete with all of its faculties so you can do almost anything you want with STARTUP.CMD.

There are two other automatically invoked batch files that aren't run by the boot process, but which usually run shortly thereafter.

The first of these is the protected mode batch file OS2INIT.CMD. This batch file is invoked as the first step in any session you create and start with the program selector. It's a good place to put your standard PATH and PROMPT commands, along with any other commands you want as standard in all sessions.

In DOS, there has long been a provision to run the batch file AUTOEXEC.BAT automatically from the root directory of the boot disk when DOS starts. The same happens in OS/2's real mode, but AUTOEXEC.BAT doesn't run until the first time you select the real mode session screen. Like a combination of STARTUP.CMD and OS2INIT.CMD, AUTOEXEC.BAT is a good place for your PATH and PROMPT commands, along with any other setup commands of a general nature.

Chapter 5
Command Editing and Control

Chapter 5

Command Editing and Control

In both real and protected modes, OS/2 provides the computer user with some limited command-editing capabilities. At the most basic level, when you are typing a command, you can use the backspace or left-arrow key to delete characters to the left of the current cursor location. Your command is not read by the command interpreter until you press the Enter key. OS/2 also offers a few slightly more advanced command editing capabilities, but they don't work like those in most programs. The trick to using these capabilities is learning the meaning of the *command template*.

In the command interpreter, OS/2 keeps a copy of the last command line completed with an Enter Key or F5 key. You can't always see this copy, but it's generally there. (Rarely it goes blank.) When the OS/2 prompt appears, awaiting a command line, you can make use of the command stored in the template while making your new command. It's handy when you want to change an improperly typed command that failed, and it's handy for redundant sequences like

copy olddir newdir
del olddir
rd olddir

or

copy *.dbf a:
copy *.ndx a:
copy *.frm a:
copy *.prg a:

Think of the template as lying just above your command line. It's matched with your command line character for character. To actually see the template in this way, press F3 then

F5. (This is good way to get used to using the command template. The F3-F5 sequence doesn't send anything to the command interpreter, but it lets you see the template as you work.)

You can move characters from the template to the current command line one at a time or in groups. To copy the template character in the same position as the cursor, you press F1 or the right-arrow key. To copy several characters from the template to the cursor location, press the F2 key and then press the key for the character in the template after the last one you want to copy. For example, in the second sequence above, you would repeatedly press F2 and the first letter of the extension in the previous command. This would copy the "COPY *." part of the template to the command line.

To copy the entire template from the position corresponding to the cursor position in the command line to the end of the template, press F3. In our second sequence, your routine would be as follows.

You Type	You See
copy *.dbf a:	copy *.dbf a:
F2 d	copy *.
ndx	copy *.ndx
F3	copy *.ndx a:
Enter key	5 files copied
F2 n	copy *.
frm	copy *.frm
F3	copy *.frm a:
Enter key	7 files copied
F2 f	copy *.
prg	copy *.prg
F3	copy *.prg a:
Enter key	4 files copied

To skip one character in the template and prepare to copy from the location past the skipped character, press the Del key. To skip up to a particular character, press the F4 key and the character. For example, you could enter our first example sequence as follows.

You Type	You See
copy olddir newdir	copy olddir newdir
Enter key	14 files copied
del Space bar	del
F4 o	del
F2 Space bar	del olddir
Enter key	Are you sure?
Y	
rd	rd
Del key	rd
F3	rd olddir

It takes some time to get used to these procedures, but they're worth it. They not only save keystrokes, they also reduce your chances of entering an incorrect filename and inadvertently doing damage.

When practicing, use the F5 key. It makes the current command line become the template and gives you a fresh command line to work with, but it doesn't send anything to the command interpreter for processing. If you run out of space on the screen but have more command to type, press Ctrl-J. This is a linefeed character that gives you a new line but doesn't send it to the command interpreter. If you want to start a command line over with the same template, press the Esc key. It gives you a new command line and leaves the template unchanged.

Special Keys

While we're on the subject of keystrokes, there are a few other special keys and key combinations you should learn. Ctrl-S will normally stop output to the screen so you have time to read it before it escapes off the top of the monitor screen. Pressing any other key will resume output.

Sometimes Ctrl-S will not stop a process. In that case, press Ctrl-NumLock. This doesn't just stop output scrolling, it stops the whole computer until you press another key. If you want to unceremoniously terminate a program, make sure its screen is displayed and then press Ctrl-C. If you have typed anything since you ran the program you're trying to stop, Ctrl-C may not work. In such cases, press Ctrl–Scroll Lock. (The program won't respond immediately.) If you have troubles with this in real mode, put the command BREAK=ON in your AUTOEXEC.BAT file. It makes the system check for Ctrl–Scroll Lock more often in real mode.

When the keyboard is being used as if it were an input file (for instance, after issuing the command COPY CON *newfile*), you must be able to tell OS/2 you're through providing input. To do this, press either Ctrl-Z or F6 (they do the same thing) to enter an end-of-file special character. But remember that your line is only read after you press Enter, so press F6 and Enter to get the job done.

You can reboot the computer with the key combination Ctrl-Alt-Del. But use Ctrl-Alt-Del sparingly and as a last resort. Programs running at the time of the reboot may leave files incomplete or with missing data.

When the OS/2 print spooler program is active (as it nearly always should be), some DOS programs in real mode may not start printing when you want them to. They can save material to be printed until the program ends. To force immediate printing from such programs, press Ctrl-Alt-PrtSc.

I/O Redirection

Normally, real mode command lines start with a command or program name often followed by options or files for that command or program. That's all you need for many commands, but you can do a good deal more. Most command line tricks involve using I/O redirection.

Input/Output redirection. With redirection, you can connect programs to files and to each other. To send the output of a program named PROG to the FOO, use the command PROG /P FII >FOO. In this example, /P and FII are options interpreted by the program PROG. The > is the symbol that sends PROG's output to FOO. Generally, the program PROG doesn't "know" that it isn't outputting to the screen. The command interpreter doesn't inform PROG about the redirection. PROG is only given the PROG /P FII part of the command.

Similarly, you can redirect input to a program from a file:

prog /p fii >foo <fee

In this case, PROG still only sees the PROG /P FII part of the command, but when PROG looks for keyboard input, that input is from the file FEE instead of the keyboard. There adds another wrinkle to redirecting output to a file. Sometimes, you'll want to collect output from several sources into one file. When you use the > symbol, any prior contents of the recipient file will be destroyed. But, if you use >> instead, the redirected output will be added to the end of the file if it contains anything. If the file is empty or doesn't exist, >> acts just like >. Here's an example:

echo Directory of three directories > dirs3
dir \letters >> dirs3
dir \notes >> dirs3
dir \lovenots >> dirs3
echo That's all folks >> dirs3

When these commands are done, DIRS3 will contain the first echoed message followed by the three directory listings and will end with the *That's all folks* line.

Sometimes you'll want to use redirection in order to throw output away. This is most often done in batch files to keep output neat. For example, the COPY command provides a great deal of information about what it's doing. If you don't want to see it, redirect its output to the special file NUL, which is a "black hole" for characters:

COPY . A: > NUL

This line will cause the COPY operation not to list all the files in the current directory.

Unfortunately, I/O redirection is a sometime thing. Programs can receive keyboard input in several ways. If they use the simplest, slowest, and most standard way, they will get what looks like keystrokes redirected from a file. If they use a more fancy way of getting keys, they will still see the real keyboard and ignore the redirection. Some programs even use both methods at different times. The same goes for output. Not all programs send their output to the stdout standard output, which is redirectable. Some send their output directly to the screen, thus bypassing redirectability.

The only way to know for sure how a program behaves with redirection is to try it. Besides redirecting output and input to and from files, you can *pipe* them between programs. Here's a common example:

dir ¦ sort

In this case, the ¦ (vertical bar) causes the first command's output to become the input for the second program. If redirection to and from files works for a program, this style of redirection between programs will also work.

The FOR Command

One of the most often overlooked commands in DOS and the real mode of OS/2 is the FOR command. Some examples of the FOR command follow.

for %%f in (*.doc *.nts) do find "needle" %%f

In this example, the FIND command would be applied to all files matching *.DOC and *.NTS in a search for *needle*.

for %%f in (1 2 3 4 5 6 7 8 9) do find "%%f" plan

In this example, all lines of the file PLAN containing any numeral would be output.

```
echo echo Here is %%1 > quickee.bat
echo type %%1 >> quickee.bat
echo echo That's all for %%1 >> quickee.bat
for %%g in ( *.* ) do command /c quickee %%g > listing
del quickee.bat
```

In the final example, another trick is added. It's easy to create a simple batch file using redirection of ECHO commands. The first and last redirected ECHO commands actually create ECHO commands in the batch file (that's why you see ECHO ECHO).

QUICKEE.BAT would look like this:

```
echo Here's %1
type %1
echo That's all for %1
```

The FOR command is used to apply QUICKEE.BAT to every file in the current directory. The COMMAND /C command causes control to return to the FOR command after QUICKEE.BAT is done each time. Without it, QUICKEE.BAT would return to the command interpreter and the FOR command would be over prematurely. COMMAND /C acts to encapsulate QUICKEE.BAT into a single command rather than a series of commands in a batch file. The %1 parameters in the batch file are replaced by the first word after QUICKEE on the command line each time it is called. When all is done, a *Here's . . .* line, the full text of a file, and a *That's all . . .* line for each file in the current directory will be printed—pretty neat for five commands, especially if there are 100 files in the current directory.

Batch Files

Batch files, sometimes called *command files*, are merely sequences of OS/2 commands stored in a file. When you tell OS/2 to execute a batch file (by typing the name of the file as a command), OS/2 takes its subsequent commands from the file. When all of the commands in a batch file are exhausted, OS/2 returns with a prompt and expects its commands to come from the console (keyboard).

There are a few special things about the commands in batch files that don't apply to console command-line commands. First, a batch file containing real mode commands must have the extension .BAT, and it will only be recognized as a command in real mode. A protected mode batch file must have the extension .CMD.

Within a batch file, the special variable names %0–%9 are replaced at the time the batch file is run by words on the command line used to invoke the batch file. The variable %0 is replaced by the first word of the command which will have been the name of the batch file itself. The variable %1 is replaced by the next word from the command line, and so on through %9. The variable %10 is not understood in batch files; it's treated as a %1 followed by 0.

If you need more than ten varaibles (%0–%9), you can use the SHIFT command to cause %0 to take the value of %1, %1 to take the value of %2, and so on until %9 takes on what would have been the value for %10 if it were understood. On the protected mode command line, a variable word of the form *%variable%* is replaced by the value of the environment variable named *variable*. If no such variable is in the current environment, then *%variable%* would be replaced by nothing. It would be treated as if it were not there.

You can't use this facility on the real mode command line, but it works within real mode batch files. Of course, it also works within protected mode batch files. To set the value of a variable within a batch file, you use the SET command just as you would on the command line.

Normally, the variables set within a batch file persist after the batch file is complete. This is often desirable because it is a way for a batch file to leave a value behind which the system or a later batch file may use.

Sometimes, however, you may want the values set within a batch file to disappear after the batch file is complete. This is usually simply to keep temporary variables only useful within the batch file from hanging around and cluttering the environment. To do this in protected mode, use the commands SETLOCAL and ENDLOCAL. All environment variable and current directory changes made between these two commands will be forgotten as the batch file ends. If you use only the SETLOCAL command, OS/2 treats the end of the batch file as if were an ENDLOCAL command.

In real mode, you can accomplish something similar by invoking the batch file with the command COMMAND /C *batch*, where *batch* stands for the name of the batch file. This causes a secondary copy of the command interpreter program COMMAND.COM to run the batch file. The /C option causes that copy of COMMAND.COM to exit when the batch file is completed. Since environment variables are inherited by child programs from parent programs, your batch file will have all currently set environment variables available to it. However, when a child program changes an environment variable, the change isn't passed back to the parent. Therefore, any changes, additions or deletions of variables made in the batch file will not alter those in the original COMMAND.COM.

This technique is not quite as good as the protected mode SETLOCAL command, as changes to the current directory will persist and the need to invoke the batch file with COMMAND /C is cumbersome.

Within a batch file, you can cause the sequence in which instructions are executed to change using the GOTO command and labels. *Labels* are command lines within a batch file which begin with a colon. The colon is immediately followed by a string of normal characters (usually just letters or numerals). You may not include spaces or any of the special characters used for I/O redirection or command grouping within a label.

When OS/2 encounters a label, it skips it. When the command GOTO *label* is executed, OS/2 searches the batch file for a label matching the *label* given in the command.

The colon is not included in the label name, as stated in the GOTO command. When OS/2 finds the label, it continues executing commands with the statement immediately following the line containing the label. GOTO commands are usually combined with IF commands to cause different sections of the batch file to be executed under different conditions. Since OS/2 ignores all labels until they are referenced in a GOTO command (if they are ever referenced at all), you can insert comments into a batch file by preceeding them with a colon. OS/2 will ignore the rest of the line after the colon. (These comments look neater than comments that use REM.)

Batch files in both real and protected modes are one of the most powerful facilities of OS/2, especially for the nonprogrammer. Get used to making and using them.

Protected Mode Commands

In general, protected mode commands work like real mode commands. The differences between the two result from the expanded capabilities of the protected mode command processor CMD.EXE. You can still perform I/O redirection in protected mode, but you can redirect more than just standard input and standard output. Also, there are a variety of ways of

combining commands into complex command lines in protected mode.

The simplest way to combine two commands in protected
mode is to use the ampersand (&) operator. Placing this character between two commands simply means to perform them
both. For example:

dir myfile & dir yourfile

means simply to perform a directory search for MYFILE and
then to perform a directory search for YOURFILE.

You can make this a little fancier by using && instead of
&. When you use two ampersands (with no spaces between
them), the meaning changes. Now you're telling OS/2 to perform the command on the left and then, if that command is
successful, to perform the command on the right. If the first
command fails, the command on the right will not be executed. For example:

dir myfile && dir yourfile

will do a directory search for MYFILE. If MYFILE is found, a
search for YOURFILE will be performed. If MYFILE is not
found, the DIR YOUFILE will not be executed.

But, you might want to look for YOURFILE only if
MYFILE is NOT found. Then you use the ASCII bar character
(¦) twice in succession (again, no spaces between the bars). For
example:

dir myfile ¦¦ dir yourfile

will perform a directory search for MYFILE. If MYFILE is
found, the DIR YOURFILE will be skipped. If MYFILE isn't
found, then a directory search for YOURFILE will be
performed.

In OS/2 terminology, && is the AND operator and ¦¦ is
the OR operator.

Combining these operators can get a bit complicated. To
make sure that the combinations are taken by OS/2 the way
you mean them, you may use parentheses to clarify your
meaning. For example:

(dir myfile ¦¦ dir yourfile) && dir herfile

means that if MYFILE isn't found, YOURFILE is sought. If YOURFILE is found, then HERFILE is sought. If MYFILE is found, then YOURFILE is not sought, but HERFILE is. In other words, if either MYFILE or YOURFILE is found, then HERFILE will be sought. If neither MYFILE nor YOURFILE are found, HERFILE will not be sought. Now, maybe the reason for calling ¦¦ OR and && AND will be clear.

&& Both commands must succeed for the combination to succeed.

¦¦ Either command must succeed for the combination to succeed.

On the other hand,

dir myfile ¦¦ (dir yourfile && dir herfile)

means if MYFILE is found, then YOURFILE and HERFILE will not be sought. Or, if MYFILE does not exist, HERFILE will only be sought if YOURFILE exists. The parentheses make a difference. In the first example, you're dealing with an ANDing of a combination command on the left and a single command on the right. In the second example, we are dealing with an ORing of a simple command on the left and a combination command on the right. Whenever you use combinations of combinations, use parentheses. Otherwise, you quickly will become lost.

In real mode, you could redirect standard output and standard input using the >, <, and ¦ characters. In protected mode, you have more I/O streams than just standard input and standard output to deal with. Many programs use a third stream called *standard error*.

You may have noticed that redirecting the output of some commands does not cause error messages to be redirected. They still appear on the screen. That's because well-written programs send errors to the standard error stream instead of to standard output. In real mode, you can't do anything about where the standard error output stream goes. In protected mode, however, you can redirect it just as you redirect standard output. (These streams are named *stdin, stdout,* and *stderr.*)

Not only does OS/2 allow you to redirect stdin, stdout,

and stderr, but it has additional streams named simply 3–9. But, since there is no standard usage of these I/O steams, they're not generally used.

Here's how to redirect stderr:

dir myfile 2>errfile

The 2>ERRFILE causes stream number 2 (that's stderr) to go into the file ERRFILE. But, you can also combine streams:

dir myfile >outfile 2>&1

In this command, stdout is redirected in the usual way to OUTFILE. In addition, the 2>&1 means to send the output of stream 2 (stderr) to the same destination as stream 1 (stdout). The result is that all data written to either stdout or stderr will go into the file OUTFILE. And they may be mixed. If the command were to send some output to stdout, then some to stderr, then some more to stdout again, that's the order in which the material would appear in the combined output stream.

Note that some programs perform internal buffering which may cause output from combined streams to not appear in strict chronological order, but even if so, it will all get to the same place eventually. The sequence >file 2>&1 is very handy for keeping a command entirely quiet. Since most programs only write to stdout or stderr and no other streams, this sequence will cause all output from the program to go into a file. This is particularly useful for detached processes (see the DETACH command).

Also, combined commands within parentheses can be redirected. The redirection applies to the entire combination within the parentheses.

The only way to get to know all the things you can do with the protected mode command combinations and redirection is to experiment. You will get a good deal more out of your computer if you do.

Chapter 6
Command Details

Chapter 6
Command Details

What follows is an alphabetized, comprehensive list of the commands available under OS/2. You will see the mode under which the command operates, depending on whether it is network-compatible, whether the program is internal or external, and how frequently it is used.

Following that brief analysis, you will be given a complete explanation of the command along with examples, warnings, and related commands.

ANSI

• Protected mode only.
• Network-compatible.
• External program.
• Frequently used.

Purpose

Adds to the display system's capabilities. Specifically, allows the display system to respond to commands in the form of escape sequences. Escape sequences can alter display colors and renditions, change the display cursor location, and reassign keys.

Use if you have programs which make use of ANSI support or if you want a fancy prompt which uses ANSI escape sequences.

Formats of Command

ANSI ON   Turns ANSI support on.
ANSI OFF Turns it off.
ANSI   Outputs whether ANSI support is on or off.

Description

ANSI stands for American National Standards Institute, which developed a standard for the meaning of escape sequences sent to terminals. The standard was originally for stand-alone terminals generally connected to minicomputers. (The standard is based largely upon Digital Equipment's VT52 and VT100 terminals.)

Escape sequences are strings of characters that begin with an escape character. The sequences are not displayed by an ANSI-standard device. Instead, they are taken as commands to change the operation of the device in some way. OS/2 only implements a small subset of the full ANSI standard escape sequences.

ANSI support is only useful if you want a more colorful prompt or are running programs that output ANSI escape codes. Today, such programs are rare, but not unheard of, in the PC world.

APPEND
• Real (DOS) mode only.
• Network-compatible.
• External program which loads and becomes resident with OS/2.
• Rarely used.

Purpose

Makes the files in specified directories appear as if they are in the current directory. This allows programs to look for files in more than one directory at a time. APPEND does not influence where new files are written, only where existing files are found.

Formats of Command

APPEND /E Only effective as the first APPEND command since the last system start. Causes APPEND to keep its list of directories in a conventional environment variable rather than in a hidden data area within the APPEND command code.

APPEND Outputs the current list of appended directories regardless of whether the list is stored in an environment variable or hidden within the APPEND code.

APPEND *pathname;pathname...;* Causes the files in the specified directories to appear to programs as if they are in the current directory (regardless of what is the current directory). *Pathname* must designate a directory and may include a drive prefix. APPEND places no limit on the number of directories. Their number is limited only by the length of the command line. Any previous list of appended directories in the current instance of COMMAND.COM is overridden by this command.

APPEND ; Causes no directories to appear within the current directory. Inactivates the APPEND command (but does not remove the memory-resident code added to OS/2 with the first APPEND command).

Warnings

APPEND does not influence where files are written. Thus, a new version of a file may be placed in the current directory while the old version is in another directory (unknown to the program creating the file). The program's behavior depends upon how it updates files. Programs that update a file by directly altering the original will leave it in its original place. Programs that make a new version of a file, delete or rename the original and then rename the new version to the old name will generally cause the new file to appear in the current directory even though the original was in a different (appended) directory. By its very nature, APPEND allows a program to reach out and alter files beyond its usual limits. This can lead to surprises even with old, reliable programs.

Examples and Description

```
append /e
append c: \ data;d: \ docs
c:
cd  \ lib \ bees
command
drone
append ;
worker
exit
queen
```

In this sequence, the program DRONE would see all files in C: \ LIB \ BEES followed by those in C: \ DATA and D: \ DOCS as if they were in the default directory C: \ LIB \ BEES. The program WORKER would see only the actual contents of C: \ LIB \ BEES. But since the changes to environment variables made in the instance of COMMAND.COM running DRONE and WORKER will be cleared by the EXIT command, the program QUEEN would again see the files in C: \ DATA and D: \ DOCS.

Note in the above example, if APPEND /E had never been entered, QUEEN would see the same files as WORKER. The difference is in how APPEND saves its list of added directories. If the list is saved as an environment variable (because of the APPEND /E command), it follows the rules for environment variables. One of these rules is that the environment variables of one instance of COMMAND.COM are passed to any child program (a program called by another program) run within that parent (the program that calls the child program), but environment variable values of a child are not passed back to the parent when the child expires. The result above is that the APPEND ; command only influences the appended directories list for the child COMMAND.COM and when that child is ended with the EXIT command, the parent reverts to its previous environment variables and the changes made in the child are lost.

When APPEND uses an internal data area to save the list of appended directories, that list does not change as COMMAND.COM comes and goes. Remember, APPEND uses an internal data area unless you tell it otherwise with the APPEND /E command given before any other APPEND command.

It is generally best not to use APPEND. There are two occasions when you may need to use it:

• When your file system directory structure does not make good sense.
• When you are using a program that doesn't make good use of the file system.

If your file system is poorly structured and you find related files are not stored together, rather than use APPEND, your best course is to move the files around until they are better grouped. In practical situations, you may want to use the APPEND command as an expedient, especially to meet a deadline or if you won't be using these files for long. In most cases, if you have a problem with related files in unrelated directories, the APPEND command is usually not a good answer because other problems will arise that are not solved by appending.

Sometimes you need to append because you are using a program which makes poor use of the file system. Some programs require certain files to be in their current directory when they start. Better written, newer programs usually do not. They can find the required files in the command path, or as directed by an environment variable, or by reading a configuration file that says where other needed files reside.

Some accounting systems, word processors, and programs that use nonstandard display interfaces make specific demands with regard to directory placement of files and support programs. Before you convict a program of this offense, check the manual (usually under "Installation" or in an appendix) for an explanation of how the program finds the files it needs when it starts. Appending slows file searches and often is improperly left active when it is no longer needed.

If you don't find a clue in the manual, you're better off to append a directory with needed startup files than to force yourself to always start in a directory specially suited to the program. After all, your file system should generally be built around the contents of files, not the demands of the tools used to manipulate them. See the common command sequence that follows for an example of this technique.

In the following example, PIG is a mythical program that requires up to 37 particular files (mostly drivers and configuration files) to be in the current directory when PIG starts. The PIG manual assumes you will always start PIG in the same directory and that all the files PIG works on will be there as well.

append c: \ lib \ sty;
pig slop
append;

To fool PIG, append its home directory STY so PIG sees all needed files as part of the current directory, wherever that directory may be. If your data file, SLOP, is not in PIG's home directory, it won't matter: PIG thinks SLOP is in the STY because it finds its startup files as a result of the APPEND. So you can feed SLOP to the PIG when you and SLOP are not in the STY. Note that the APPEND is undone as soon as the PIG leaves. This is good practice, but means that you can't count on APPEND lasting through multiple commands from the operator, any one of them might be a batch file that clears the APPEND path. Usually a sequence like the above is saved in a batch file and looks something like batch file SWINE.BAT:

```
append c: \ lib \ sty;
pig %1 %2 %3 %4 %5 %6 %7 %8 %9
append;
```

The items %1, %2, and so on, are parameters. They allow you to specify some parameters and files for PIG on the command line. When you run the batch file, the parameters %1, %2, and so on, are replaced by the corresponding words on the command line after SWINE. If there is no corresponding parameter, the parameter (%9, for instance, will rarely be used) will be ignored and will do no harm. Now you would type

swine slop

to start the PIG program to work on the file SLOP in the current directory. If you require that SWINE doesn't wipe out appends used by other programs, make sure that the command APPEND /E appears in your AUTOEXEC.BAT file and modify SWINE.BAT to batch file SOW:

```
set oldappnd = %append%
append c: \ lib \ sty
pig %1 %2 %3 %4 %5 %6 %7 %8 %9
append %oldappnd%
```

When you run SOW.BAT, the environment variable *oldappnd* will be set to the APPEND path at the time SOW starts, and the final APPEND will restore the same APPEND path just before SOW finishes because *%oldappnd%* will be replaced by the value you set in the first line. SOW is much better behaved than PIG alone, and it's about as elegant as a PIG can get.

Related Commands

DPATH   Performs a similar function in protected mode.

JOIN   More appropriate when you want an entire drive to appear attached to a specific directory.

SUBST   If you are thinking about using APPEND in order to get around a program's inability to access subdirectories properly, the SUBST command is often a better choice. It makes a particular directory appear as a separate drive.

ASSIGN
- Real (DOS) mode only.
- Network-compatible (usually).
- External program.
- Rarely used.

Purpose

Causes a disk drive to appear as a different drive. For example, if you want operations designated as dealing with drive A: to actually use drive D:, you might use the ASSIGN command. Normally used to fool programs that require certain files to be on certain drives.

Formats of Command

ASSIGN *drive1=drive2* Causes references to drive A: to actually use drive B:. Note that there are no colons in the command.

ASSIGN *drive1 drive2* Same as prior command. A space between drive letters is required.

ASSIGN Undoes all previous assigns.

ASSIGN *drive1=drive2 drive3 drive4 drive5=drive6* Multiple assignments with one command are allowed.

Warnings

Don't leave in effect assignments you may forget. You can easily unintentionally alter a disk when you think you're working with another disk. For example, if you issue the command DEL A: while A: is assigned to C:, you might get a big surprise when you find an empty directory on your hard disk. Commands that need to know the details of the type and format of a disk will not work with assigned drives. For example, the FORMAT and DISKCOPY commands ignore assignments. Many disk utility programs will either ignore or gag on assignments. Using the PRINT or BACKUP commands with assigned drives is not recommended.

Example and Description

ASSIGN A=C B=C Be careful with this one. After this command, commands issued to drives A: and B: will actually alter drive C:. You might later think you are working with a floppy when in fact you are using the fixed hard disk C:.

```
assign c=d
dummy
c:myfile
assign
```

The above batch file might be used with a program named *dummy*. Dummy is a hypothetical, poorly designed program that can't deal with any drive that has a letter later in the alphabet than C, but you want to use it on drive D:. These three commands make D: look like C: to dummy.

The last line of the batch file removes the assignment as soon as it is no longer needed. However, if you break out of dummy with a Ctrl-Break keystroke, the last ASSIGN (that undoes the assignment of C: to D:) may not be executed. You could then become very confused. Your computer will think drive D: is a clone of drive C:. Whenever in doubt, issue the command ASSIGN with no following drive letters to make sure all the drives are named as you expect. Better than using ASSIGN, buy a new version of dummy or another, smarter program that does the same job. And put dummy out to pasture.

The ASSIGN command is intended to rename disk drives to letters other than their normally assigned names. The only reason for the existence of ASSIGN is to accommodate old programs built before the full variety of DOS drives was available. These days, such programs are out of date and are likely to have other problems as well.

The best solution is to avoid the ASSIGN command and programs that require its use. In addition to renaming a drive, the ASSIGN command hides the physical characteristics of the drive from programs. DOS and OS/2 real mode provide programs with information about how a disk is organized when asked by the program. If the drive is assigned, that information is not accurate.

Most programs don't use such information, but those that do can become very confused by assigned drives. Programs that ask for this information should also check to see if the drive is assigned (as FORMAT and DISKCOPY do), but some don't.

Avoid the ASSIGN command. Use it only when you have no choice. When you use it, cancel the assignment as soon as possible. Usually, you can use the preferable SUBST command to solve problems where you might think you need to use the ASSIGN command.

Related Commands

SUBST   SUBST allows you to treat a particular subdirectory as if it were a disk with its own letter designation. Where possible, use this command rather than the ASSIGN command.

APPEND   When a program expects to find a file in the current directory of a drive, you can use this command to make it appear that a file from another directory is in the current directory. You can sometimes use this instead of an AS-SIGN command.

JOIN   JOIN makes a drive appear to be a subdirectory.

ATTRIB
- Real (DOS) mode or protected mode.
- Network-compatible.
- External program in file ATTRIB.EXE.
- Can operate on entire directories and on all descendants of a directory.
- Used occasionally.

Purpose

Outputs, sets, or resets archive file attribute or read-only file attribute. Shows if a file (or files) is currently marked for read-only operation or if it has changed since last archive of the file. Marks or unmarks file(s) as read-only, prohibiting changes to the file(s). Marks or unmarks file(s) as changed since last archived with BACKUP or XCOPY commands.

Formats of Command

ATTRIB *ambiguous_filename* **[/S]** Displays current status of read-only and archive attributes.

ATTRIB +R *ambiguous_filename* **[/S]** Marks file(s) as read-only, thus protecting against changes and deletion, but not against renaming.

ATTRIB −R *ambiguous_filename* **[/S]** Marks file(s) as not read-only, thus allowing changes and deletion.

ATTRIB +A *ambiguous_filename* **[/S]** Marks file(s) as in need of archiving with BACKUP or XCOPY commands.

ATTRIB −A *ambiguous_filename* **[/S]** Marks file(s) as not in need of archiving with BACKUP or XCOPY commands.

Warnings

This command format is unusual. ATTRIB.EXE interprets the filename supplied to it in an unusual way. It views the filename as two parts: a path and an ambiguous file pattern. If the name you supply contains a backslash or a colon, the characters after the last backslash or colon in the name are taken to be the pattern and all characters preceding are taken to be the path. If the name you supply does not contain a backslash or a colon, the entire name is taken to be the pattern, and the working directory is used as the path.

If you don't supply a valid pattern, ATTRIB won't find any files on which to work. ATTRIB starts in the directory specified by the path. It then compares all files against the pattern. Matching files are processed as specified by the R and A switches or output with attribute marks shown. If the /S switch is specified, ATTRIB goes on to do the same matching and processing for all descendants of the path.

If no files match the pattern, or if the pattern is not specified, ATTRIB will issue an error message. This implies the results shown in Table 6-1.

Table 6-1. ATTRIB and Operative Patterns

Will Not Work	Will Work	Comment
ATTRIB	ATTRIB *.*	These results are regardless of the R, A, and /S settings.
ATTRIB .	ATTRIB . \ *.*	
ATTRIB ..	ATTRIB .. \ *.*	
ATTRIB C: \	ATTRIB C: \ *.*	
ATTRIB C: \ TEMP	ATTRIB C: \ TEMP \ *.*	

Once a read-only file is reset to normal with ATTRIB −R, it doesn't again have read-only protection until explicitly made read-only again with ATTRIB +R. Renaming a file does not turn on its archive attribute. It may not be backed up as appropriate. A read-only file may be renamed and thereby lost.

You can't delete a file marked read-only by accident, but you can lose it by renaming it and forgetting the new name. Haphazard use of the −A option may keep critical files from being included in your regular backup routine even if a backup program other than OS/2's BACKUP or XCOPY is used. This may result in loss of important data in the event of an error or failure. When in doubt, mark a file with +A to make sure it will be included in the next backup operation.

You must use the −R option to prepare a read-only file to be changed. After the change, you will probably want to use ATTRIB +R to again protect the file with the read-only attribute. If you don't, the file will no longer be protected. If you rename a file that hasn't been changed and that has its archive attribute off, the renamed version will also have its archive attribute off. You won't lose any data from this, but the file under its new name may not be included in the next incremental backup and should be. Use ATTRIB +A either before or after the rename to make sure the file, under its new name, will be included in your next incremental backup.

Some files used by programs are routinely changed by the program. These must not be set to read-only. If this attribute is set on, OS/2 will experience subtle failures. For example, you might have a project management program that uses a file (entered when you installed the program) to store information about your system. If you set it to read-only to make sure it is not inadvertently deleted, the program may work fine for months. Then, when you buy a new monitor, your project management program may quit when you try to tell it about your new display. The cause of the failure is OS/2, which is preventing the program from writing to its configuration file.

Many programs will give misleading error messages, or no error message at all, in such a situation. When a program quits for no apparent reason, or when it gives a message about not finding or being unable to open a file you know is present, the problem may be a file with its read-only attribute set.

An additional hazard associated with ATTRIB is that some programs will remove the read-only protection and change the read-only file without telling you. Don't rely heavily on read-only protection unless you check that it's still in force.

Examples and Description

ATTRIB *.* Outputs the read-only and archive attribute settings for all files in the current directory.

ATTRIB +R *.* Protects all files in the root directory from inadvertent alteration or deletion (a good idea).

ATTRIB +A *.* Prepares all files in your root directory for back up the next time you use the BACKUP command with the /M option or the XCOPY command with the /A or /M option.

ATTRIB +A *.* /S Marks all files on the default drive as changed and ready to be copied by the next BACKUP command using option /M or to be copied by the XCOPY command using options /M or /A.

All directory entries for files contain markers called *file attributes*. Two of these are the archive attribute and the read-only attribute. The archive attribute is set on whenever a file is created, changed, or the subject of an ATTRIB +A command. The BACKUP command with the /M option and the XCOPY command with the /M or /A options copy only those files with their archive attribute on. Once copied by BACKUP or XCOPY /M (but not XCOPY /A), the file's archive attribute is again set to off. This makes it easy to make incremental backups that only include changed files. Use the ATTRIB +A command to make sure a file will be seen as changed and copied. Use the ATTRIB −A command to exclude a file from an incremental backup.

A file with its read-only attribute set on will not be changed or deleted by OS/2. Mark critical files with ATTRIB +R to set their read-only attribute on and prevent accidental damage. Unmark them with ATTRIB −R to remove this protection. See Chapter 2, "OS/2 Concepts," for more information about these and other file attributes.

The following is a common sequence to edit a critical document stored with read-only protection:

attrib −r critical.doc   Make critical.doc free to be modified.
wp critical.doc   Run the word processor with this file.
attrib +r critical.doc   Again protect the file as read-only.

A better way for really critical data:

copy critical.doc newcrit.doc	Work on a copy because the copy will not have read-only protection.
wp newcrit.doc	Run the word processor on the copy.
attrib +r newcrit.doc	Protect the new version.
attrib −r critical.doc	Unprotect the original.
del critical.doc	Delete the original.
rename newcrit.doc critical.doc	Make the new file have the original name; it's still read-only.

Using the first method, the critical file was not protected during the word processing session. Also, you had to remember during the entire session to again make the file read-only after your editing was complete. If your word processing session were to be interrupted by a phone call, it would be easy to forget and leave the file unprotected. In the second method, there's always a read-only copy of either the old or new version. Note that renaming a read-only file does not change its read-only attribute. The following is a sequence for conducting a complex copy operation from the current directory:

ATTRIB −A *.*	Turn off all archive attributes.
ATTRIB +A A*.*	Turn on archive attribute for files beginning with *A*.
ATTRIB −A AB*.*	Turn off archive attribute for files beginning with *AB*.
XCOPY *.DOC B: /A	Copy files with the extension .DOC, but only if their archive attribute is turned on.
ATTRIB +A *.*	Reset all archive attributes to on in case they need backing up.

Only those files beginning with *A*—but not beginning with *AB*—and having the extension .DOC will be copied to the disk. This technique allows you to add and subtract files matching various patterns to or from the group that will be copied. You might have many ATTRIB commands before the XCOPY command.

To check which files are marked for archive and will be copied, use ATTRIB *.*.

Note the last ATTRIB command to make sure you haven't inadvertently excluded any files from your next regular backup operation. The following is a sequence to find all read-only files on the volume in the current default drive:

ATTRIB *.* /S I FIND " R "

This command pipes ATTRIB output to find and look for *R*'s with spaces.

Note that you can use ATTRIB for many of the jobs normally done with the DIR command. ATTRIB presents a compact list of files and can access multiple subdirectories. DIR does neither.

Related Commands

There is no clear alternative to ATTRIB within OS/2. However, there are public-domain and commercially available programs (some also named ATTRIB) which can perform the same functions. Other ATTRIB programs usually allow you to also set and reset the hidden and system file attributes. Another traditional name for programs like ATTRIB is CHMOD for *change mode*. Some alternative programs have this name. BACKUP (especially the /M option), XCOPY (especially the /M and /A options), and RESTORE are related commands.

BACKUP

- Real (DOS) or protected mode.
- Not network-compatible.
- External program.
- Can operate on entire directories and trees of directories.
- Better if used often.

Purpose

To make copies of your file system for restoration (with the RESTORE command) later in the event of an inadvertent loss of data.

Format of Command

BACKUP *pathname drive options* Copies files in a BACKUP format from *pathname* to *drive*. *Pathname* may be a directory, a file, or a file pattern. *Drive* must include a colon, as in A:.

/S This option copies the files in *pathname's* subdirectories and their subdirectories and so on.

/F If BACKUP is followed by an /F option, BACKUP will format the disk on which the backup copy is to be made. It will not do this if *drive* is a fixed hard disk. It will attempt to format floppy disks to the highest capacity the drive allows. Make sure you are using a high-density disk if you are using this option with a 1.2MB floppy drive.

/A Adds the backup copies to the files already on the target drive. Otherwise, files on the disk in that drive will be quietly erased.

/D:MM-DD-YY Causes only those files with last modification dates of the specified date (in the form MM-DD-YY) or later to be included in the backup. If your system clock is not always correct, this option may surprise you.

/T:HH:MM:SS Causes only those files with specified last modification times (in the form HH:MM:SS) or later to be included in the backup. (Again, be careful about trusting the accuracy of these times.)

/M Causes only modified files to be included in the backup. *Modified* means the file has its archive attribute turned on. Any change to a file turns on the archive attribute, but the archive attribute may be turned off by the ATTRIB, XCOPY, and BACKUP commands. (See the ATTRIB command and the File System text for more on file attributes.)

/L Makes a file named BACKUP.LOG in the root directory of the source drive describing the files included in this backup and when the backup occurred. If this log file already exists, the new information is added to the end of the existing log file.

/L:*file* Like /L, /L:*file* only uses a specified *file* rather than BACKUP.LOG for the log information.

Warnings

If you don't use the /A option, files on the target drive will be erased as necessary to make room for the backup copies.

Heavy reliance on file dates, times, and archive attributes for determining which files to back up tends to reduce the insurance value of backups. Perform comprehensive backups from time to time, just in case some files are marked incorrectly.

Don't rely on backup copies being intelligible to someone else's compatible computer. They can only restore these files if they have DOS 3.3 or higher, or OS/2, and their file system must have directories of the same names as those included in the backup. BACKUP is intended for backup and restoration on the same computer. It will not handle hidden and system files like IBMIO.COM, IBMDOS.COM and some created by copy-protection schemes. BACKUP will not handle COMMAND.COM or CMD.EXE properly, so use COPY or XCOPY.

Be careful about relying on the /M, /D or /T options. Be careful about where you store backups. Keep your operating system files in a non-BACKUP form because BACKUP won't work with them all.

The XCOPY command can do much the same job as BACKUP, but it can't split large files across more than one target disk. Repeated use of the COPY command can do much of the backup job, but again there's a problem with large files, and it's easy to miss copying an essential file. There are many commercial backup programs that work more rapidly. Combining backups with an archive utility that compacts multiple files and then stores their compacted forms together in one archive file often saves time and disk space and provides better error detection. (Get the excellent shareware program PKARC for this purpose and others.)

Tape drives (including some using VCR technology) are probably the best solution for the long run, if you can afford them.

Examples and Description

BACKUP C: \ *.* A: /S Copies all the files on drive C: (except as noted in the warnings).

BACKUP C: \ *.* A: /S /M Copies all the files on drive C: that have changed since the last backup, (except those altered with the ATTRIB or XCOPY commands and those mentioned in the warnings above).

BACKUP C: \ USR \ ACCOUNTS \ *.DAT A: /S Copies all of the .DAT files in your accounting system (a very good practice).

BACKUP is your insurance policy. Taking the time to do it is the premium you pay. You use the RESTORE command to recover from your losses. BACKUP's greatest virtues are

- Its systematic, file-by-file action, which can insure you don't miss any essential files.
- Its ability to break up huge files into pieces that fit on floppy disks.

Its weaknesses are

- Its many options—there are so many that it's easy to think you have everything when you haven't.
- Your backup is only as good as the disks that hold it.

The best way to use BACKUP is in a regular routine carefully implemented with tested batch files that don't let you inadvertently skip any files that should be copied.

If you frequently make incremental backups of only

changed files (using the /M option), make sure you have a fil-
ing system that keeps a complete backup (made without the
/M, /D, or /T options) and all incremental backups since the
complete backup. Also, be sure you don't turn off any archive
attributes (which mark the file as having been changed) with
the ATTRIB or XCOPY commands. If you don't do backups
often because of the time required, your best system invest-
ment would be additional hardware to speed the process. You
can choose tape or some kind of removable or detachable hard
disk. Remember—backup copies fade, burn, get lost, and get
overwritten by desperate disk hunters. Nothing is forever.
Make complete backups frequently.

Related Commands

See the RESTORE command, which performs the comple-
mentary function to BACKUP. Also see the COPY and XCOPY
commands for a less reliable, more manual approach to data
safety.

BREAK

- Real (DOS) mode only.
- Network-compatible.
- Internal subprogram in COMMAND.COM.
- Normally used at the beginning of each real mode session.

Purpose

Makes OS/2 check for Ctrl-C and Ctrl-Break keystrokes while programs are running.

Formats of Command

BREAK ON Causes OS/2 to check for Ctrl-C and Ctrl-Break whenever the keyboard, display or disk services of the operating system are used by the program running.

BREAK OFF Causes OS/2 to check for Ctrl-C and Ctrl-Break only when its keyboard or display services are used by the program running. BREAK is off in real mode unless you tell OS/2 otherwise.

BREAK Tells you whether BREAK is on or off.

Warnings

If BREAK is off, some programs can be very difficult to stop without rebooting the system.

Placing the line

break = on

in the CONFIG.SYS file used at the time the system boots has the same effect as the command BREAK ON. As a rule, either put BREAK=ON in CONFIG.SYS, or put BREAK ON in your AUTOEXEC.BAT, the batch file that runs when real mode is first started.

Description

Generally, it's best to have BREAK on. It gives you more control over the computer's operation. It makes the computer work slightly harder, but the lost time is imperceptible. Pressing the Ctrl-C or the Ctrl-Break key combination is supposed to abort the program currently running, but this only happens if OS/2 checks to see if these keys have been pressed.

With BREAK on, nearly all programs not malfunctioning will respond to Ctrl-Break. Ctrl-C and Ctrl-Break are handled somewhat differently. If you type ahead of the system (that is, if you type characters before the system stops to accept them), the characters are stored in the order typed until they're requested by a program. There's a limit to the number of keystrokes that can be buffered in this way. When that limit is reached, the speaker beeps and further keystrokes will not be stored. The number of keystrokes that can be saved is generally 15, but it may be much more if software modifications or additions have been made. When you press Ctrl-Break, this key combination is processed immediately. It is not placed in type-ahead storage to wait until a program requests keyboard input.

Ctrl-C, on the other hand, is only recognized as a special combination when it is the next keystroke that would be read by a program requesting keyboard input. That's why Ctrl-Break sometimes works when Ctrl-C doesn't. How programs respond to Ctrl-Break and Ctrl-C varies. Programmers have the option to let OS/2 handle breaks by aborting the program, or programmers may replace the OS/2 method with one of their own. Still, reasonable programmers let Ctrl-Break stop the program, but they may ask for confirmation from the user, and they often have the program do some essential file housekeeping before stopping. BREAK is always on in protected mode.

CALL
• Real (DOS) or protected mode.
• Network-compatible.
• Internal subprogram in COMMAND.COM and CMD.EXE.
• Frequently used in batch files.

Purpose
If you use a command in a batch file that is carried out by a second batch file, the original batch file will not continue when the second is completed. It will be forgotten. If you precede the name of the second batch file with the CALL command, the original batch file will resume operation immediately upon the completion of the second.

CALL allows you to call other batch files inside a parent batch file without killing the parent batch file. CALL makes batch commands behave like program or internal commands within a batch file.

Format of Command
CALL *batch_file_command* The *batch_file_command* is called just as you would normally call it from the keyboard. It may contain parameters or arguments after the name of the batch file. The CALL command only changes what happens after the command is completed.

Example and Description
In a batch file:

dir
call mybatch c: \ valuable \ data \ file
copy thisfile thatfile

After the DIR command is executed, the command MYBATCH C: \ VALUABLE \ DATA \ FILE is executed. When the batch file is finished with its work, the COPY command is executed. Without the CALL command, the batch file would not resume and the copy command would never be executed.

CALL makes batch commands within batch files behave as they should have all along. Preceded by CALL, batch commands work like any other commands in a batch file. The rea-

son for the CALL command is simply that earlier versions of
DOS handled batch files in a very simplistic way that could
not cope with a batch file command within a batch file. CALL
is a patch to solve this problem. In general, you should use
CALL before any batch command within a batch file. It's good
programming form to always return to where a command
came from before exiting. Otherwise, you can get into a tangle
of batch files calling other batch files that call other batch files,
and so on, without ever returning to the first batch file. Such
chains of commands can be difficult to debug.

Related Commands

COMMAND /C In DOS, programmers used the trick of using
COMMAND /C in just the same way CALL is
now used. This is no longer needed: CALL is
better.

CD (CHDIR)

- Real (DOS) or protected mode.
- Network-compatible.
- Internal subprogram in COMMAND.COM and CMD.EXE.
- Very frequently used.

Purpose

Changes the default working directory associated with a disk drive (usually the current default drive).

Formats of Command

CD This command outputs the current default directory for the current default drive. (That is, the directory you're in on the drive you are in.) You shouldn't need to do this. Your command prompt should tell you (see the PROMPT command).

CD C: Outputs the current default directory for drive C:.

CD C:\ *directory1* \ *directory2* Makes \ *directory1* \ *directory2* the current default directory for drive C:. When you refer to a file (or files) on drive C: without specifying a directory, it's presumed you are referring to C:\ *directory1* \ *directory2*.

CD \ *directory1* \ *directory2* This is the same as last example, but it selects the default directory on your current default drive. If the drive is C:, the effect would be identical to that described above.

CD .. Changes your default directory to the next higher directory. (Remember, .. is a short name for the directory which is the parent of the current default directory.)

CD ..\ *directory* Causes your default directory to change to the directory named *directory* which has the same parent directory as your starting default directory.

CD *directory* Changes your default directory to a directory named *directory* which is a subdirectory of your current default directory.

Examples and Description

For each drive of your system, OS/2 keeps track of one current default directory. OS/2 assumes that you are operating in this directory unless you specify otherwise. OS/2 also keeps track of a single default drive. So, if you refer to a file without mentioning either drive or directory, OS/2 assumes that you're referring to a file in the default directory of the default drive. If you refer to a drive, but you don't mention the directory, OS/2 assumes you mean the current directory for that drive.

All references to files or directories must ultimately be decoded by OS/2 into a drive, a directory (including the full path or parentage of that directory) and usually a particular file or set of files matching a pattern. OS/2 needs to know all of these things before it can access a file or directory, but your hands would fall off if you had to type each of these paths each time you wanted to access a file. The business of having a default drive and default directory is a convenience that saves typing yet provides OS/2 with all the information it needs.

If this shorthand is to work, you must be able to change the defaults OS/2 uses for unentered pieces of a full file specification. The CD command sets the default for the directory part of file specifications. That's all it does. But it's very handy, and it should be one of your most frequently used commands. Of course, if OS/2 is going to use a default for the directory part of filenames, the default directory must exist or some useless file specifications will result. If you specify a directory that doesn't exist for the CD command, OS/2 will squawk and ignore the command.

Note that most of the time you will not type the full name of the directory you want to become the default, you will refer to it in terms of the default at the time the CD command is typed. Thus, if you mention a directory name in the CD command that doesn't start with \, that directory is presumed to be the default at the time the CD command is entered. It sounds complicated, but it isn't. After a few minutes of experimentation, you'll be a master of directory navigation.

cd c: \ tmp
cd a: \ source
c:
copy a:*.doc
copy a:*.bay
copy a:*.pir

This sequence is typical. You set the default directory of C: to \ TMP. Presumably, you want to copy some files into this directory from a disk in drive A:. Then you make the directory on A: containing the files you want become the default directory for A:. Finally, you can do some quick copy commands without having to type the directory names repeatedly. (Note: You don't even need to mention the destination of the files in the copy commands as it is the default directory of the default drive.)

cd \ state	\ state (default directory)
dir	
cd county	\ state \ county
dir town	
dir city	
cd town	\ state \ county \ town
dir smalvile	
cd smalvile	\ state \ county \ town \ smalvile
dir farms	
cd farms \ super	\ state \ county \ town \ smalvile \ farms \ super
dir	
copy . a:	
cd .. \ ..	\ state \ county \ town \ smalvile
cd .. \ ..	\ state \ county
cd .. \ metropol	\ state \ metropol
copy . a:	

This is a typical hunt through a directory tree. In this process, you may have sifted quickly through hundreds or even thousands of files to find a few particular files to copy to drive A:. (Remember . is a shorthand name for the current default directory. So, COPY . A: copies all of the files in the default directory of the default drive to the default directory of drive A:.)

Related Commands

RD   Removes an empty directory.
MD   Creates a new directory.

CHCP

- Real (DOS) or protected mode.
- Network-compatible.
- Internal subprogram in COMMAND.COM and CMD.EXE.
- For international compatibility only.
- Rarely used.

Purpose

OS/2 can, to a limited extent, use character sets that conform
to foreign languages. This is accomplished with special code
pages. Each code page represents a correspondence between
character codes and the characters displayed or printed. This
facility is rarely needed, and most real mode programs and
most popular printers will ignore code pages. In general, code
pages will only work if you are careful to buy hardware and
programs specifically designed to support them.

Format of Command

CHCP *nnn* Where *nnn* is an IBM-assigned code page number
    representing a particular set of character-to-code assign-
    ments, this command will cause code page number *nnn* to
    be used until OS/2 is told otherwise, or until a program
    that ignores the code page setting is run.

Warnings

You can't use more than two code page numbers in any one
session. OS/2 can handle only two code pages. You may use
CHCP to switch between these two and no others.

Description

To tell OS/2 which two code pages to use, you must use the
CODEPAGE command in your CONFIG.SYS file. And only
certain code pages are allowed for a particular setting of the
system's COUNTRY information specified in a file named in
the COUNTRY command in your CONFIG.SYS file. In addition, for each device (keyboard, display, or printer) to use
code-page switching, you must include a DEVINFO command
in your CONFIG.SYS file and the hardware device must be

capable of supporting code pages (it probably isn't, unless it is an IBM). All in all, code pages are a good idea and are almost never used and rarely work very well. If at all possible, forget all about them. If you need to share documents with larger IBM computers, get technical help to implement the sharing. Getting code pages to match is one of the less difficult parts of such sharing arrangements. If you want characters other than those used in American English, get your dealer to set up code pages for you.

Related Commands

CODEPAGE
COUNTRY   Selects the date, time, and currency format for a given country.

CHKDSK

- Real (DOS) or protected mode.
- Not network-compatible.
- External program.
- Normally operates on entire disks.
- Frequently used. (The more frequently used, the better.)

Purpose

CHKDSK checks disks, partially fixes some disk errors, lists filenames, shows memory available (in real, DOS mode only), and can show how a file is stored on a disk. Most often, CHKDSK is used to check that a disk is in good condition. In real (DOS) mode, it's often used to report how much memory is assigned to DOS and is available. Sophisticated users use CHKDSK to see if files are stored in one or several physical regions of a disk, as this can make a big difference in disk performance.

Formats of Command

CHKDSK In protected mode this command will report:
Total disk space for the current drive.
How much space is used by hidden files like the operating system boot files.
How much space is used for special directory files listing regular files.
How much space is used by ordinary user files.
How much space has been marked as unusable in bad sectors.
How much space if left available.

CHKDSK In real (DOS) mode, it will report all of the above information, plus:
How much total RAM is available to DOS.
How much is available to programs to use.

CHKDSK *drive:* Same as the previous command, but information is for the specified drive.

CHKDSK /V

CHKDSK *drive:* **/V** Same as the first command and the previous command, but also lists the path name of every file on the specified (or default) disk.

115

CHKDSK /F

CHKDSK *drive:* **/F** Same as previous command, but if CHKDSK finds errors in the file organization on the disk, it will destroy, truncate, or create files as necessary to get the disk properly organized again. There are special restrictions on when the /F parameter may be used. See the sections "Warnings" and "Examples and Description," below.

CHKDSK *filename* The filename may be a full path name with drive and/or directory, and it may be a file pattern using ? and *. This command will do the same as CHKDSK without a filename, but it will also report any files matching the filename pattern which are stored in noncontiguous blocks (see "Examples and Description").

CHKDSK *filename* **/V /F** Performs all the above functions.

Warnings

With the /F option, CHKDSK can destroy files by the thousands. Some of these might be damaged but still may be recoverable before using CHKDSK. They won't be available after CHKDSK. CHKDSK /F works hard to straighten out your disk. It cares little about saving damaged data. Always run CHKDSK without the /F parameter first. If it only finds lost clusters, running CHKDSK /F will do no harm. But, if CHKDSK (without the /F) finds other errors in disk organization, make sure any recovery efforts you plan to make are done before running CHKDSK /F.

Don't use CHKDSK /F before reading "Examples and Description," below.

When running CHKDSK with the /F option, make sure that no other processes in protected mode are using the disk under repair. Also, make sure that the CHKDSK program is not on the disk to be fixed. If necessary, copy the CHKDSK program to another disk and be sure to invoke that copy of CHKDSK rather than the original.

Since you can't fix a disk while any other activity involves that disk, you can't fix your boot disk: The operating system itself uses the boot disk frequently without asking your permission. You must create a system disk (see the FORMAT and

SYS commands), copy the CHKDSK program to it, and boot with that disk in drive A:. Then you can use CHKDSK to fix your usual boot disk (most often hard disk drive C:).

If you have placed a SWAPPATH command in your CONFIG.SYS file that specifies the disk to be fixed, you should reboot with a different CONFIG.SYS that doesn't direct swapping activity to the disk to be fixed. Usually, your regular boot disk and the disk used for memory-segment swapping are the same. If so, the approach of creating a system disk and removing the CONFIG.SYS file from that disk will solve any conflict between CHKDSK and the boot disk or swap disk. (If you boot from a floppy with no CONFIG.SYS file, memory-swapping is disabled, so it won't be a problem.)

Examples and Description

CHKDSK C: \ DATABASE If C: \ DATABASE is where you keep a set of database files, this command is a good one to see if your files are contiguous and in the best form for fast operation. (See description below.)

CHKDSK C: /V > C:*filelist* This is a good way to gather a complete, compact list of all files on drive C: into a file named FILELIST for reference or printing.

CHKDSK A: /F May be able to rejuvenate a sick floppy without having to wait for a FORMAT command to finish. Don't count on all files on the floppy being complete after the fix.

CHKDSK

CHKDSK D: Do this check-only version of the command frequently on your hard disks to make sure everything is all right. If it isn't, less damage and more successful recovery are likely if the problems are found earlier rather than later.

OS/2 disks are organized according to a rigid and specific plan. Because of this, CHKDSK can analyze the organization of a disk to be sure it all makes sense. Fundamentally, every disk is broken into equally sized physical blocks called *clusters*. These clusters are then assigned to files and are linked together to make long files.

When OS/2 deletes a file, it simply removes the links between the filename and every physical cluster used by the file. The clusters are then marked as being unlinked and therefore available for use. If clusters are linked to one another, but not to a filename, something has gone wrong. This group of linked clusters is called a *chain of lost clusters.* CHKDSK will find any chains of lost clusters which presumably were part of a file which has been damaged.

When CHKDSK is used with the /F option, chains of lost clusters are made into files by giving them an arbitrary filename. One filename is created for each chain of clusters, and the chain is linked to that filename. (The names given are \FILE0000.CHK, \FILE0001.CHK, and so on.) You can then look at the contents of these new files containing the lost chains and see if they contain data which should be in some other file.

Usually, lost chains are from temporary files which were deleted incompletely because a program was interrupted by a power failure or some similar catastrophe. CHKDSK's fixing action of giving lost chains a name does not alter or damage any other files, as it only deals with chains of clusters that are not part of any file. It's not good to find chains of lost clusters, but it's usually not disastrous, either.

There are worse errors. Some file system errors involve extra links rather than broken links. If a cluster is linked into two or more chains, the files represented by those chains are said to be *cross-linked.* CHKDSK will find and report any cross-linked files. Usually you can recover the information in cross-linked files, but you may find extraneous junk from another file or even empty disk space amidst the valuable information in the file.

The first thing to do is to copy a cross-linked file to a new filename, and then, if it is a text file, edit it to remove any junk. If the original was a binary file (like a program), you probably cannot do the editing without laborious technical assistance, and you should restore the file with your most recent backup.

When the CHKDSK /F option attempts to fix cross-linked

files, it almost always damages some of the files involved because it has no way of knowing which part of the crossed path belongs to which file. It can make a real mess out of something you might be able to save otherwise. If the simple copy operation doesn't work, there are various utility programs available at reasonable cost that can help you, but most require some degree of technical background. The best known of these are the *Norton* and *Mace* utilities.

CHKDSK /F will always force cross-linked files into a proper single-chain organization, but CHKDSK by itself only aims to get the disk back into proper form—it doesn't pay any attention to content.

Filenames are attached to chains of clusters by directory entries. Directories also contain a number representing the number of bytes in the file. Using this number, CHKDSK can easily calculate the number of clusters that should be attached to the file's cluster chain (it's the number of bytes in the file divided by the number of bytes in a cluster rounded up to the next whole cluster). If the number of clusters in the file and the number of bytes in the directory entry don't correspond, CHKDSK with the /F option can be used to trim the chain to match the number of bytes in the directory entry. Once this has been done, it can be hard to find the detached clusters and reattach them if the chain was right and the directory entry was wrong. Again, files with *goofed-up allocations*, as these are called, should be recovered with utilities before CHKDSK /F is used to reorganize them.

Information about the characteristics of a disk, like the cluster size and total number of clusters, is stored in a *disk parameter block* at the beginning of the disk. Immediately after this is a table where all the links between clusters are stored. This is the FAT (File Allocation Table). If either of these is damaged or contains invalid values, the entire contents of the disk are unavailable to OS/2.

In some cases, such damage can be repaired with utilities not available in OS/2 itself, but only if the damage is limited. If CHKDSK or any other operating system command reports a bad FAT, you must either find very skilled and patient assistance or write off the disk as a total loss and simply reformat it.

There is one class of disk errors that CHKDSK does not deal with: When a program is reading or writing a file, the system may report a failure in the reading or writing process. This is generally because of a flaw on the surface of the disk that has caused one or more bytes to be read differently from the way they were written. Bad spots on disk surfaces are common. Remember the bad sectors part of the normal CHKDSK report. They usually don't cause problems because the format process finds them and marks as bad the clusters that contain them. Thereafter, OS/2 will not use these clusters for any purpose. Problems occur when a good cluster turns bad. Then OS/2 will use it until the disk is reformatted or the RECOVER command is used to mark the cluster as bad. The techniques for working around such problems don't involve CHKDSK. See the RECOVER command for handling damage within clusters.

A note on terminology: *Disk sectors* are a set size for a particular disk format. *Clusters* are made up of one or more sectors. The cluster is the smallest unit of disk space that OS/2 can mark as part of a file or as bad. Though documentation often refers to *bad sectors*, a cluster is actually the unit marked as bad in the FAT if any of the sectors within the cluster are bad.

When using CHKDSK with the /F option, the subject drive must not have any activity on it other than that of CHKDSK while CHKDSK is making changes. Multiple processes may be running that access disk without letting you know, and since the operating system automatically swaps some processes or parts of processes to disk from memory and back again, it can be difficult to make sure CHKDSK will be the only process dealing with the subject disk.

See the warnings section above to see how to deal with this problem.

Related Commands

RECOVER   Deals with errors within a file while CHKDSK deals with errors in the organization of the clusters that compose a file.

CLS

- Real (DOS) or protected mode.
- Network-compatible.
- Internal subprogram in COMMAND.COM and CMD.EXE.
- Frequently used.

Purpose

The command CLS simply clears the screen. It has no options or arguments.

Format of Command

CLS

Example

CLS Clears the screen of text.

CMD

- Protected mode only.
- Network-compatible.
- The command processor program for protected mode.
- Rarely used.

Purpose

All commands in protected mode are processed by the program CMD.EXE. When CMD.EXE receives the CMD command from you or a batch file, it starts another copy of itself. This copy is called a *child process* or a *child instance* of the original *(parent instance)* CMD.EXE.

When the child of CMD exits, the parent again regains control and proceeds to process the next command.

When the child of CMD begins, it receives a copy of all environment variables known to the parent CMD. If the child changes any of these variables or adds new ones, these changes and additions will be forgotten when the child exits, and the parent will continue with its original copy of the variables. Thus, you can use the CMD command to obtain a temporary environment which will disappear when you EXIT the child CMD.EXE.

In batch files this is not necessary because the SETLOCAL and ENDLOCAL commands are available.

Formats of Command

CMD Starts a child of CMD.EXE.

CMD /C *"command"* Starts a child of CMD.EXE that will execute the specified command and then immediately exit to the parent instance of CMD.EXE. If the command contains any of the characters <, >, &, (,), or |, it should be enclosed in quotation marks as shown. Otherwise, the quotation marks are optional.

CMD /K *"command"* Starts a child of CMD.EXE that will execute the specified command and then look to the console for the next command. It will not automatically exit until you use the EXIT command. If the command contains any of the characters <, >, &, (,), or |, it should be enclosed in quotation marks as shown. Otherwise, the quotation marks are optional.

Warnings
If you use CMD multiple times without causing the children to exit and remove themselves from memory, you will waste system resources.

Examples and Description
CMD /C DIR *.DOC & SET DOCS=FOUND This command will run CMD with the command DIR *.DOC. The child of CMD will then exit, and the command SET DOCS=FOUND will run in the parent of CMD.EXE. When all is said and done, the environment variable DOCS will equal FOUND in the parent instance of CMD.EXE.

CMD /C "DIR *.DOC & SET DOCS=FOUND" This command will run a child CMD.EXE with the command DIR *.DOC & SET DOCS=FOUND, which it will execute and then exit. When all is done, there will be no change to the environment variable DOCS in the running parent instance of CMD.EXE because it was only changed in the child's environment. The child's environment disappeared when the child exited.

CMD.EXE is special in that it's the command processor program for protected mode. But it's still a program and can be run like any other program. That's all CMD command does: It runs the CMD program. When the program finishes, control returns to the parent CMD.EXE that started the child CMD.EXE, just as it does after any other program.

The only thing special about this is that the current copy of the environment is passed to any program that starts, but the environment of the parent is never changed. Therefore, the child CMD.EXE has a cloned copy of the environment which may be changed without changing the parent's copy.

It's often important to have a temporary copy of environment variables in a batch file, but this is better accomplished by using the commands SETLOCAL and ENDLOCAL. As a result, you'll rarely have occasion to use the CMD command. Note that to create a sibling (concurrent) CMD.EXE to run alongside the one in use, you must use the START command or the program selector. The CMD command will not start a sibling. CMD causes the parent CMD.EXE to lie dormant until the child exits.

Related Commands

START   START and the program selector create new copies of CMD.EXE that are not child processes, but are concurrently running siblings of any running CMD.EXE.

COMMAND COMMAND in real (DOS) mode is similar to the CMD command in protected mode.

COMMAND

- Real (DOS) mode only.
- Network-compatible.
- COMMAND.COM is the command processor program for real (DOS) mode.
- Rarely used.

Purpose

In older versions of DOS, before the CALL command was available, the idiom COMMAND /C *batchcommand* was used to call a batch file from a batch file and cause control to return to the calling batch file after completion of the called batch file. Since the advent of the CALL command, this is no longer necessary. CALL does the job more neatly. One remaining use for COMMAND is to run a child instance of COMMAND.COM which inherits the parent's environment variables but which will not pass back to the parent any changes to these environment variables. It allows a temporary copy of the environment variables which will not have lasting effects. Since the SETLOCAL and ENDLOCAL commands are not available in real mode, it may be useful to invoke batch files that change environment variables by prefixing them with COMMAND /C so the changes have no lasting effect. If you are familiar with output redirection in real mode, you can use COMMAND to redirect the output of a batch file. If you get errors that say *Out of Environment Space*, you can use COMMAND with the /E option to expand your available space for environment variables. The better solution is to alter the SHELL statement in your CONFIG.SYS file to use the /E option with a large enough environment to suit your needs.

Formats of Command

COMMAND Invokes a child instance of COMMAND.COM that inherits the environment variables of the parent instance of COMMAND.COM, but will not alter those values for the parent, only for itself. The child instance of COMMAND.COM started with this command is exited when it processes an EXIT command.

COMMAND /C *dos_command* Similar to the previous form, except that the command *dos_command* will be executed by the child instance of COMMAND.COM, the child COMMAND.COM will immediately exit after the command is finished, and control will return to the parent COMMAND.COM. The command *dos_command* may not contain the characters <, >, or |. If these redirection characters are used, they will redirect the input or output of the child COMMAND.COM, not *dos_command*, usually with undesirable results. (You can experiment with this, but if you use <, make sure the input file ends with an exit command, or your real mode session will be frozen. If you use >, you can effectively redirect the output of a batch file—a trick not usually allowed in real mode.)

COMMAND /P This form prevents the child of COMMAND.COM from exiting. It leaves the original instance dormant in memory until you boot again. Don't use it. It only wastes resources and can do you no good. (It might do you some good, if you also use the /E option to expand a deficient environment size, but you should do this in your CONFIG.SYS file's SHELL command where the /P and /E options were designed to be used.)

COMMAND /E:*nnnn* Where *nnnn* is a number from 160 through 32768, this command will invoke a child instance of COMMAND.COM that has an environment variable space equal to the number of bytes specified with *nnnn*. If you find you are running out of environment space, this can be useful.

Warnings

If you use COMMAND multiple times without the /C option and without exiting from any of the child instances with the EXIT command, you will waste real mode memory, which is often in short supply. All of the old instances of COMMAND.COM that processed your COMMAND commands will still be in memory doing nothing.

Examples and Description

Batch file D.BAT contains:

dir | sort
command /c d > filelist

This command with the batch file D.BAT will cause a sorted directory output to appear in the file named FILELIST. The command D > FILELIST won't do this: The output from the sort will go to the console instead of to the file FILELIST.

command /c d | sort /r >filelist

This line works just like the last command, except this time the sorted output of D.BAT will be sorted again, only in reverse order this time. This is just to show that OS/2 looks at COMMAND /C D as one command and redirects its output to SORT after the child COMMAND.COM has exited.

command /e:32000

This command gives you nearly the maximum environment variable space COMMAND.COM can manage. (This is nearly always an excessive and wasteful size.) Upon using the EXIT command, the environment variable space and all environment variable values return to their values before this command was issued.

Batch file ECHOER.BAT contains:

set prompt=command from batch file:
call %1
command /c echoer mybat.bat

This command, with the described batch file ECHOER.BAT, causes a child instance of COMMAND.COM to be run. It in turn will execute the prompt-setting command in ECHOER.BAT and then the batch command MYBAT.BAT, which will be substituted for the parameter %1 in ECHOER.BAT. While MYBAT.BAT runs, if it has no ECHO OFF command, each command of MYBAT.BAT will be echoed to the console prefixed with the prompt *COMMAND FROM BATCH FILE:*. When MYBAT.BAT finishes, control will return to ECHOER.BAT, which has no more to do. As a result, ECHOER.BAT will finish. Since COM-MAND was invoked with /C and its one command was completed, it in turn will exit back to the original COMMAND.COM where this all started. In that parent instance of COMMAND.COM, the change in the prompt is unknown, and the prompt appears as it did when this example command was first issued.

COMMAND.COM is special in that it is the command processor program for real mode. However, it's still a program and can be invoked like any ordinary DOS program. The differences are that COMMAND.COM keeps the current environment variables so a child instance of COMMAND.COM can be used to obtain a larger environment or a temporary environment which will not alter the environment maintained by the parent instance of COMMAND.COM. Otherwise COMMAND.COM behaves like any other program. All of the redirection tricks shown in the examples are of the same logical form as for any program, they just tend to be more handy with COMMAND.COM.

The /P option for COMMAND.COM is intended for use in the SHELL command of your CONFIG.SYS file. All it does is tell COMMAND.COM to not allow an exit; in other words, it never returns to its calling program. This can be done by any ordinary program as well, but programmers usually have no reason to build ordinary programs this way.

Related Commands

CMD Executing the protected mode command processing program CMD.EXE is very similar in concept to COMMAND.

COMP

• Real (DOS) or protected mode.
• Network-compatible.
• External program.
• Can operate on entire directories.
• Occasionally used.

Purpose

The COMP command calls a program that compares files or groups of files. It's useful when checking that copies are accurate. It will find errors in copies, changes to copies, and files missing from a copied set of files.

Formats of Command

COMP In this form, COMP prompts you to enter the names of the files to be compared.

COMP *drive_path_or_filename drive_path_or_filename*
The files specified in the first argument are compared to the files specified in the second argument. The arguments may contain a drive designation, directory path, and/or filename or file pattern using * or ?. COMP attempts to find all files matching the first argument. For each of these, it attempts to form a filename using the second argument. If the second argument does not specify a filename or file pattern, but a drive or directory path only, COMP presumes the filename will be the same as that for the first argument, but in the drive or directory specified in the second argument. If the second argument contains a file pattern using * or ?, COMP fills in the variable parts of the second filename using the corresponding characters of the filename developed from the first argument. If the second argument designates a specific filename, COMP compares the file found with the first argument against that specific file.

Warnings

It's possible to compare a file to itself. But the results don't tell you much and may mislead you.

Examples and Description

COMP C: \ OLDDIR A: \ NEWDIR All files in the directory
C: \ OLDDIR are compared against files of the same name
in A: \ NEWDIR. If no file in C: \ OLDDIR has a corresponding file (of the same name) in A: \ NEWDIR,
OS/2 will inform you. If any of the files compared differ,
you'll be told where in the file the differences begin.

COMP C: \ OLDDIR \ *.DOC A: \ NEWDIR \ *.LTR Each
file matching C: \ OLDDIR \ *.DOC is compared against
the file in A: \ NEWDIR having the same name but having the extension .LTR. If a file in C: \ OLDDIR has no
corresponding entry in A: \ NEWDIR, you will be informed. If any of the corresponding files differ, you'll also
be informed.

COMP C: \ OLDDIR \ *.DOC A: Each file matching
C: \ OLDDIR \ *.DOC is compared against a file having
the same name in the current directory for drive A:. If no
corresponding file is found, you will be told. If corresponding files differ, you'll be told.

When COMP compares files, it first attempts to find corresponding files matching the first and second arguments as
described above. If any file matching the first argument has no
corresponding file matching the second argument, COMP will
inform you of this. When corresponding files are found,
COMP reads and compares both files. If they have different
lengths, COMP tells you so and asks if you want to continue
the comparison. If you respond *yes*, COMP compares the files'
contents byte by byte.

At the first differing byte, COMP outputs the number of
the byte in the file (that is, the *offset*—the first byte is byte 0)
and the value of the byte as found in each corresponding file.
It continues reporting such differences until it has reported
ten. Then it gives up the comparison of the specified pair of
corresponding files.

Unfortunately for nonprogrammers, the offset and the
byte values are given in the base 16 (or *hexadecimal*) number-
ing system. In this system, 16 is used rather than 10 as the basis for digit values, and the numerals run from 0–9, and then

letters *A–F* are used for the values 10 through 15. (The hexa-decimal number AB represents the value 171—or ten 16s and eleven 1s).

Generally, COMP tells you if a file is missing or if two corresponding files are not exactly the same. If you have been having disk problems, a COPY command followed by a COMP command with the same file arguments is a good idea, if only for your peace of mind.

COPY

- Real (DOS) mode or protected mode.
- Network-compatible.
- Internal command.
- Can operate on entire directories.
- Can accept * and ? in filenames.
- Used very frequently.

Purpose

COPY's purpose is to copy files. COPY copies single or multiple files from a single directory to a single directory, copies multiple files into a single file, updates the modification date and time, and sets the archive attribute of files.

Warnings

If any existing file has the same main name, extension, and parent directory as a file that will receive a copy, the existing file will be overwritten. You must check that you will not overwrite desired data. This problem is most critical if the existing file has the hidden or system attributes set, as you will not see the file to be replaced until after it is gone. To avoid overwriting hidden or system files, mark them read-only as well. (See the ATTRIB command.)

In COPY F1 + F2 + F3, files F2 and F3 should be appended to F1. However, if file F1 doesn't exist, COPY appends F3 to F2 without warning or error message. Also, if F2 is a non-ASCII file, some data in F2 may be irretrievably lost (see "Known Bugs" section).

By default, in any copy operation that copies multiple files into one file, the source files are truncated at the first end-of-file character (the character generated by pressing Ctrl-Z—holding down the Ctrl key and pressing Z). The remainder of the file will not be copied. For non-ASCII files, data loss may result. This applies to commands of the forms COPY *directory file* and COPY B*.* *file* as well as those that use +. Avoid this by using the /B switch before the destination file. COPY will not alter a file marked read-only. This may defeat some copy operations.

Formats of Command

COPY *source* **[/A] [/B] [/V]** *destination* **[/A] [/B] [/V]**
Copies the source to the destination. The source may be a simple filename, an ambiguous filename using * or ?, a directory, or a series of filenames or ambiguous filenames separated with +. The destination may be blank (meaning the default directory), a simple filename, an ambiguous filename, or a directory. Except in the *touch* operation, it's an error to copy a file to itself, regardless of whatever different names may be used for the file.

COPY *filename* **[/A] [/B] [/V]** Copies the file from another directory to the default directory. There the copy will have the same main name and extension as the original.

COPY *ambig_name* **[/A] [/B] [/V]** Copies the matching file(s) to the default directory. The copies will have the same main names and extensions as the originals.

COPY *directory* **[/A] [/B] [/V]** Copies all files in the specified directory to the default directory. The source directory itself will not be copied, only the files within it. The copies will have the same main names and extensions as the originals.

COPY *filename* **[/A] [/B] [/V]** *directory* **[/A] [/B] [/V]**
Copies the specified file to the specified directory. In the destination directory, the copy will have the same main name and extension as the original.

COPY *ambig_name* **[/A] [/B] [/V]** *directory* **[/A] [/B] [/V]**
All matching files are copied to the specified directory. The copies will have the same main names and extensions as the originals.

COPY *directory* **[/A] [/B] [/V]** *directory* **[/A] [/B] [/V]**
Copies all files in the first directory to the second. The source directory itself is not copied, only the files within it are. The copies will have the same main names and extensions as the originals.

COPY *filename* **[/A] [/B] [/V]** *filename* **[/A] [/B] [/V]**
Copies the first file to the second. The two filenames must not refer to the same file.

COPY *ambig_name* **[/A] [/B] [/V]** *filename* **[/A] [/B] [/V]**
Copies the first matching file to the destination file, then appends the next matching file, then the next, and so on. All files are treated as ASCII unless the /B switch is used. If the destination filename also matches the source *ambig_name*, the old contents of the destination file are lost and a warning is issued indicating it is not included in the copy.

COPY *ambig_name1* **[/A] [/B] [/V]** + *ambig_name2* **[/A] [/B] [/V]** + *ambig_name3* **[/A] [/B] [/V]...** *file* Copies files matching *ambig_name1* to the destination file as in last format, then files matching *ambig_name2* will be appended, then those matching *ambig_name3*, and so on. All files are treated as ASCII unless the /B switch is used. If the destination filename also matches the source *ambig_name*, the old contents of the destination file are lost and a warning is issued indicating it is not included in the copy.

COPY *directory* **[/A] [/B] [/V]** *filename* **[/A] [/B] [/V]**
Copies the first file in the directory to the destination file, then appends the next, then the next, and so on. All files are treated as ASCII unless the /B switch is used. If the destination filename is in the source directory, the old contents of the destination file are lost and a warning is issued indicating it is not included in the copy.

COPY *ambig_name* **[/A] [/B] [/V]** *ambig_name* **[/A] [/B] [/V]** Copies the files matching the first *ambig_name* to files with names formed from the name of the individual source file and the destination *ambig_name* by overlaying the source filename on the ambiguous destination name and replacing any variable portions of the ambiguous name with characters from the source file's name. (See description below for more explanation of these names.) Please note that if two or more newly formed destination filenames are the same, the more recent copy will overwrite the older one leaving only the last copy.

COPY [/A] [/B]) [/V] *filename1* **[/A] [/B] [/V]** + *filename2*
[/A] [/B] [/V] + *filename3* ... Copies the contents of
filename2, filename3, and so on to the end of *filename1.*
Spaces before and after + are optional. Please note that if
filename1 is not an existing file, it will be ignored and the
copy operation will append to *filename2* instead. All files
are treated as ASCII unless the /B switch is used.

COPY *ambig_name*+ Will *touch* the matching files. The content of the files aren't changed, but the file date and time
are updated to the current date and time, and the archive
attribute is set on. This will not work for files with the
read-only attribute on.

/V This option is used anywhere in the command to check
the copies against the original. This protection is usually
needed only in the presence of suspected hardware
malfunction.

/A The /A and /B options apply to the file specification immediately preceding the /A or /B and to all subsequent
file specifications unless another /A or /B overrides the
first. /A, when applicable to a source file, causes copying
of the file to cease when an end-of-file character (Ctrl-Z)
is encountered. The end-of-file character and all subsequent file data are not copied. /A, when applicable to a
destination file, causes an end-of-file character to be
added to the end of the copied material. /A, when applicable to a file to be appended to, causes appending to begin at the first end-of-file character within the file. If there
is no end-of-file character in the file, appending will begin
after the last character of the file. When appending is
complete, an end-of-file character will be added to the
end of the file.

/B When applicable to a source file, causes the entire file to
be copied regardless of any end-of-file characters. /B,
when applicable to a destination file, causes *no* end-of-file
character to be appended to the destination. Though not
documented, the /A or /B option may appear before any
filenames in the command. All copy operations that combine multiple files into one file have a default /A setting

for all files referenced in the command. All other copy operations have a default /B setting for all files referenced in the command.

Examples and Description

COPY B:F1.FFF Copies file F1.FFF from the default directory of drive B: to the default directory of the default drive.

COPY F1.FFF B: Copies the file F1.FFF from the default directory of the default drive to the default directory of drive B:.

COPY *.* B: Copies all files in the default directory to the default directory of drive B:.

COPY . B: Same as COPY *.* B:, but more elegant.

COPY B:. Copies all files in the default directory of drive B: to the default directory of the default drive.

COPY /B B:*.S + B:*.R SRFILES Copies files in the default directory of drive B: that have extensions .S or .R into the file SRFILES in the default directory of the default drive. SRFILES will contain all of the source files because the /B switch was used.

COPY . .. Copies all files in the default directory to the parent of the default directory. If the default directory is a root directory, this is an error (the root directory has no parent).

COPY B: \ DIR1 \ DIR1_2 \ *.DOC C: \ SUBDIR1 Copies all files in directory B: \ DIR1 \ DIR1_2 that have an extension of .DOC to directory C: \ SUBDIR1. The main names and extensions of the copies will be the same as the originals.

COPY F*.* G*.* Copies all files in the default directory that begin with the character *F* to corresponding files in the same directory with the same names, except that the first character in each name will be G rather than F.

COPY F*.* B:GG*.* Copies all files in the default directory that begin with the character *F* to corresponding files in the default directory of drive B: with the same names except that the first two characters of each name will be replaced by *GG*. If files with two-character names beginning with *F* (like F1, F2, and F3) exist in the default directory, B:GG will contain only the last of these to be copied, and no copies of the other two will remain. They will copy to the same file, namely B:GG, and overwrite each other.

COPY ALLFS + F1 + F2 + F3 Appends the files F1, F2, and F3 to the file ALLFS (all of these in the default directory). If F1, F2, or F3 contain data after an end-of-file character, that data will not be copied. After the command is complete, the last character in ALLFS will be an end-of-file character. If the file ALLFS did not exist before this command, F2 and F3 will be appended to F1, not ALLFS (presuming F1 existed before the command). See "Known Bugs," below. If ALLFS contains data after an end-of-file character (Ctrl-Z), that data will be destroyed.

COPY /B F1+F2+F3 ALLFS Copies the files F1, F2, and F3 to the file ALLFS. All of F1, F2, and F3 will be found in ALLFS regardless of end-of-file marks.

COPY .+ Causes all files in the default directory to have their modification time and date updated to the current time and date and their archive attribute set on. This is the *touch* operation.

One copy command may cause many, few, or no copies of files to be made. Frequently, one command will cause several copy operations. For each copy operation, COPY needs to know

- The source filename.
- The destination filename.
- Whether to treat the source file as an ASCII file.
- Whether to treat the destination file as an ASCII file.
- Whether to overwrite or append to any prior contents of the destination file.

If the source shown on the command line is a simple filename, COPY determines the full name of the file, including its directory path and drive, using the current default drive and directories as necessary. If the source is given as an ambiguous filename including * or ?, COPY uses the name as a pattern and steps through existing files to find those that match the pattern.

Once it finds a match, it carries out the remainder of the copy operation and then returns to search for any other matching files. It repeats this process until all matching files are processed. If the source shown on the command line is a directory, COPY performs the indicated copy operation for each file in the directory until all have been processed (except that it never sees nor processes hidden or system files).

In all cases, COPY has fully determined a single source filename (including directory path) before it determines the full name of the destination file. If you enter the destination as a simple filename, COPY extends it to a full name with drive and path as it would for a source file. If the destination supplied in the command is a directory, copy takes the name of the source file, strips it of its drive and directory information, then prefixes it with the destination drive and directories. This becomes the destination filename. If no destination is supplied in the command, COPY uses the default directory on the default drive as a destination and performs the same name manipulations as it would for any other destination directory.

However, there is a special case. If no destination is supplied, and + appears between file specifications in the command, COPY presumes the intent is to append the second and subsequent files to the first file. It therefore takes the first file named as the destination and prepares to append to it. (This doesn't always work. See the section "Known Bugs," below.) If the destination is ambiguous and includes * or ?, COPY develops a new destination filename. See the following paragraph for a discussion on ambiguous destinations.

Now that COPY has full source and destination filenames, it checks to see if they specify the same file. If they do, COPY issues an error message and continues with any remaining source files. If the source and destination files are not the same, COPY checks to see if the destination file exists. If it does, COPY must decide whether to write over and destroy the current contents or to append the new material to the end of the file. If this destination is the same as for the last copy operation called for by the command, then COPY will continue the copy operation where it left off in the same file, with the net effect of appending the source. In the first copy operation for the command, the destination file is always overwritten.

Next, COPY determines whether to handle the destination and source as ASCII files using the rules stated above for the /A and /B options. If the source is treated as ASCII, then COPY only copies until it sees an ASCII end-of-file character (Ctrl-Z). It then stops copying before sending the end-of-file character to the destination.

If the destination is to be treated as ASCII, then, when COPY is done copying, it adds an end-of-file character to the destination file. (If this destination is appended to in a later COPY operation of the same command, the appended material will overwrite this end-of-file character and another will be added to the new end of the file.) COPY continues until all source files are processed or a failure of some kind occurs (most often a full disk).

COPY notices if one of its former destination files in the same command turns up as a source file. If so, it issues an error that the contents were overwritten before the file became a source file and does not use it as a source file. This does no harm as long as you understand the meaning of the message.

Sequence to provide insurance of a good copy:

copy f1 f2 /v
comp f1 f2

The /V check is not entirely foolproof. Use this sequence if you suspect a bad disk drive.

Copying what you type to a file:

copy con file

Whatever you type goes into FILE. You must press Ctrl-Z and Enter to end the copying.

copy con prn
copy con lpt1
copy con lpt2
copy con lpt3

Each of the above commands copy what you type to a printer.
Again, the Ctrl-Z and Enter key sequence stops the COPY
command.

copy file prn
copy file lpt1
copy file lpt2
copy file lpt3

The above commands all copy a file to a printer. All of the
above use device files. See the material on the file system in
the concepts section.

The following command will prevent a message listing
files copied and prevent the *xx files copied* message from being
printed:

copy *.* >nul

By redirecting the message (standard) output of COPY to the
null device, this command makes it disappear. It doesn't sup-
press error messages from COPY (they go to standard error).
This command is handy in .CMD and .BAT files.

The following set of commands moves files from the default directory to the default directory on drive B:.

copy dir \ subdir \ *.fff b:
del dir \ subdir \ *.fff

The net effect of copying and then deleting the originals is to
move the files. If the new files will be in the same directory,
use the REN (RENAME) command instead.

Ambiguous destinations. If the destination specified is
ambiguous (includes * or ?), COPY builds a new filename from
the source filename and the destination pattern. It builds a
new filename by copying characters from the destination pattern until a * or ? is encountered. If it encounters a ?, it copies
the character in the corresponding position in the source file
into the new filename. (By *corresponding,* I mean in the same
character position counting from the beginning of the name
excluding any drive or directory information.) If it encounters
a *, it starts at the corresponding character in the source filename and copies all the rest of the source filename into the

new name until the source name is exhausted or the new name is full. It then performs the same type of operation on the extension of the new name. Finally, it prefixes the specified destination drive and directory to the new name to obtain the full destination filename.

Table 6-2 provides a few examples.

Table 6-2. Ambiguous Filename Examples

Source Name	Destination Pattern	Destination File	Comments
12345678	ABCDE?FG	ABCDE6FG	One character taken from source
12345678	ABCDE??G	ABCDE67G	Two characters taken from source
12345678	A*	A2345678	Seven characters taken from source
Z2345678	A*	A2345678	Same as for source 12345678
123.XYZ	A?CDE.P?R	A2CDE.PYR	Two characters taken from source
12345678.XYZ	A?CDE.P?R	A2CDE.PYR	Same as for 123.XYZ
12345678.XYZ	*.ABC	12345678.ABC	Just changes the extension

As the examples show, it's possible that multiple source filenames will generate the same new destination name. If this happens within one command, the same destination will be used repeatedly. Each time a copy is sent to it, the previous copy will be overwritten and destroyed. Watch out for this. Only use an ambiguous destination name if the source filenames involved follow a neat pattern and you can visualize the new names to be created. And, keep your destination patterns simple.

The touch operation. The command COPY *files+* causes *files* to be *touched* rather than copied. This means the file has its last modification date and time set to the current date and time, and its archive attribute is turned on. (See the command reference for ATTRIB, and see the section on file attributes in Chapter 2.) The file is not copied or even read in full. It is just touched to mark it as modified without really modifying it. You can use a filename, ambiguous file pattern, or directory name in the touch version of the COPY command. This operation is not documented, but it can be very useful.

Related Commands

XCOPY
MCOPY   The primary alternatives to the COPY command are
           the XCOPY and MCOPY commands. (MCOPY is a
           modified version of XCOPY. See the XCOPY com-
           mand reference.) Use XCOPY or MCOPY if you need
           to copy entire subtrees involving more than one level
           of directories. XCOPY and MCOPY are also preferable
           when you wish to copy only files that either have their
           archive attribute set (indicating they are in need of
           backup) or were modified after a specified date. Use
           XCOPY or MCOPY teamed with ATTRIB when many
           files are to be selected from a large group with a pat-
           tern more complex than the ambiguous file patterns
           used by COPY. The means of doing this is shown in
           the ATTRIB command reference. Finally, use XCOPY
           or MCOPY if you need an error level exit code from
           the copy operation.

RENAME   If you want to systematically change the names of files
           within a directory (for instance, COPY *.TXT *.DOC),
           use the REN (RENAME) command instead.

REPLACE   If you want to replace files in a directory with files of
           the same name in another directory, use the REPLACE
           command (especially if you want to confirm, file by
           file, that you really want to do the replacement). Simi-
           larly, if you only want to copy files from a source di-
           rectory which are not in a destination directory,
           REPLACE is more convenient. Note that TYPE F1 >
           F2 has the same effect as COPY F1 /A F2.

ATTRIB   Since COPY never alters a read-only file, you may
           need to use the ATTRIB command to unprotect a read-
           only file.

DELETE   The DEL (DELETE) command is often used with
           COPY to accomplish a move of files from one direc-
           tory to another without leaving the old originals be-
           hind.

COMP   Use COPY with the COMP (compare files) command
           to ensure that you have good copies.

Known Bugs

There is a bug in COPY in the latest version of OS/2 available at the time of this writing. If the command COPY F1 + F2 + F3 + F4 is invoked, the first file will only be used as the destination if it already exists. This is likely to be fixed in later versions of OS/2.

DATE
- Real (DOS) or protected mode.
- Network-compatible.
- Internal subprogram in COMMAND.COM and CMD.EXE.
- Occasionally used.

Purpose

DATE displays the current system date and asks if you want to change it. If you know in advance that you want to change it, you can specify the date you want on the same line with the date command. Most computers that will run OS/2 include a battery-operated realtime clock that runs even while the computer is shut off.

Format of Command

DATE Displays the date and asks if you want to change it. Just press the enter key for no change.

DATE *mm/dd/yy* Where *mm* is a valid month, *dd* is a valid day and *yy* is a valid year ranging from 80 to 99, for 1980–1999, and 00 to 79 for 2000–2079.

DATE *mm/dd/yyyy* Where *yyyy* is a year between 1980 and 2079.

Warnings

The DATE command may or may not set the date in that clock. You may or may not need a separate program to set that clock. If so, your computer manufacturer should supply it. OS/2 has a calendar, and it understands leap year. The date you enter must make sense. If you keep your computer on through midnight, the date might or might not roll over to the next day. It's a good idea to always check the date each morning. An incorrect system date can cause many unexpected problems. Keep it accurate.

DEL and ERASE

- Real (DOS) or protected mode.
- Network-compatible.
- Internal subprogram in COMMAND.COM and CMD.EXE.
- Can operate on entire directories.
- Frequently used.

Purpose

This command is usually called DEL, but ERASE works just the same (only it's harder to type). It deletes all files matching the file specification or path specified. It doesn't delete hidden, system, or read-only files. (See the ATTRIB command for information about these.) DEL will delete all files within a directory, but it will not remove the directory itself. You must use the RMDIR or RD command to do that. If DEL is about to delete all the files in a directory, it asks you if you are sure you want it to.

Formats of Command

DEL *filespec* *Filespec* may specify a drive and/or directory path and/or a filename or a file pattern using ? or *.

DEL *filespec filespec...* In protected mode, you may specify more than one file specification in one command.

Warnings

DEL deletes information and should be used with great care, particularly when used with ? and * or where only a drive or directory is specified. Always double- or triple-check your spelling when this command is used. Never count on an undelete utility to be able to recover deleted files.

Examples

DEL C: \ OLDDIR

ERASE C: \ OLDDIR \ *.* These commands are equivalent; they will delete all files in the specified directory after asking you if you are sure.

DEL C: Deletes all files in the current directory of C:.

DEL C: \ NEWDIR \ OLDFILE.OLD Deletes the single specified file.

DETACH

- Protected mode only.
- Network-compatible.
- Internal subprogram in CMD.EXE.
- Occasionally used.

Purpose

Used to run a process detached from the keyboard, mouse, and screen. The process may not communicate with the operator unless it's especially designed for detached use and it employs a pop-up window which the process must create when needed.

Format of Command

DETACH *command*   *Command* following DETACH may be any valid OS/2 command that doesn't require any further interaction with the user. (Unlike the CMD command, quotation marks are not needed after the DETACH keyword to keep redirection statements associated with the command following DETACH.)

Warnings

Once you have detached a process, you cannot reattach it. If for some reason the process asks for user input, it will wait forever and continue to use system resources even though it will never proceed. The only way to get rid of stalled, detached processes is to reboot the system.

Worse, if the process begins to do something undesirable, you have no way to stop it except to reboot. Don't detach a process unless you're very sure it will behave well.

It is a common error to detach a process which generally does not require any input, but which, under unusual situations, attempts to ask the user *Are you sure?* or *Press any key to continue....*

To avoid a process being blocked by such an attempt to get input, test it thoroughly before using it as a detached process.

Examples and Description

DETACH CHKDSK C: /V > C: \ FILELIST This command
will run CHKDSK to make a list of all files on drive C:
and place the result in a file called FILELIST. But, if
CHKDSK encounters any error in disk organization, it will
stop and ask the user *yes/no* questions. This would halt
the process and leave it suspended. Here's a solution:

```
copy con c: \ msg \ nos
n
n
n
n
n
n
n^z
detach chkdsk c: /v <c: \ msg \ nos >c: \ filelist 2>&1
```

In this sequence, the COPY command copies from the
console keyboard into the file C: \ MSG \ NOS. The lines with
N's go into the file. The ^Z (Ctrl-Z) ends input from the keyboard and completes the COPY command. The DETACH
command specifies that if CHKDSK asks for any input, it will
come from C: \ MSG \ NOS. Thus if CHKDSK asks any *yes/
no* questions, it will get N followed by a carriage return as an
answer (at least for the first seven times it asks). Output from
CHKDSK is again redirected to the file C: \ FILELIST, but the
2>&1 specifies that any error messages are to go to the same
file rather than to unsuccessfully try to go to the console.

However, there is still a rub. Some commands, like DEL,
ask *Are you sure?* questions in a special way. Just before they
ask the question, they read all pending input characters and
throw them away. This is to prevent an accidental answer to
the question from typing performed before the question was
asked. The answers to such questions cannot be redirected
into the command because it reads and exhausts the entire input file before it tries to read an answer to its question.

**DETACH (ATTRIB \ *.* /S > FLIST.TMP & REN
FLIST.TMP *.OUT)** In this command, ATTRIB \ *.* /S

produces a list of all files on the current drive. The segment that reads > *FLIST.TMP* causes the output from ATTRIB to go to FLIST.TMP. When ATTRIB is done, the segment that reads *REN FLIST.TMP *.OUT* will rename FLIST.TMP to FLIST.OUT. Since the ATTRIB command may take some time to complete, you can check on its progress by looking at the FLIST file. If its extension is .TMP, the ATTRIB command is still running. If its extension is .OUT, the ATTRIB command is done. This technique of renaming files to indicate progress is handy for any detached command which may take some time. The protected mode batch file FROMDOS.CMD uses this technique.

```
@echo off
:doagain
if not exist c:\dos2os2\*.cmd goto doagain
for %%f in (c:\dos2os2\*.cmd) do %%f /q
ren c:\dos2os2\*.cmd *.dne
goto doagain
```

If you run this fancy batch file with the command DE-TACH FROMDOS, you'll be able to create protected mode commands in real (DOS) mode and have them execute while you continue to work in real mode. Here is how it works:

@ECHO OFF Turns off echoing of the commands in FROMDOS.CMD as they execute. (The @ stops ECHO OFF from echoing itself.)

:DOAGAIN This is a label referred to later.

IF NOT EXIST C:\DOS2OS2*.CMD GOTO DOAGAIN This command causes control to return to the label DOAGAIN, if there are no .CMD files in the directory DOS2OS2. So, until a .CMD command is placed in DOS2OS2, FROMDOS just goes around in circles looking for a command.

FOR %%F IN (C:\DOS2OS2*.CMD) DO %%F /Q When a .CMD file is found in DOS2OS2, the FOR command causes it and any other .CMD files in DOS2OS2 to be executed. The /Q in the FOR command performs a batch file trick. If you make /Q the first argument of a .CMD batch file, it's the same as if you put @ECHO OFF at the beginning of the batch file. (Unfortunately, this only works for protected mode .CMD files, not real mode .BAT files.)

REN C: \ DOS2OS2 \ *.CMD *.DNE After all .CMD files in DOS2OS2 are executed by the FOR command, FROMDOS goes on to rename them so they all have the extension .DNE, which ensures that once the commands have been done, FROMDOS won't do them over and over again.

To use FROMDOS, launch it in protected mode with the commmand DETACH FROMDOS. Then, in real mode, put any protected mode commands you want executed into .CMD files in DOS2OS2. Even while you continue to work in real mode, FROMDOS will execute these commands in protected mode.

If any of the commands you place into a .CMD file in DOS2OS2 call for keyboard or mouse input or attempt screen output, FROMDOS will stop dead in its tracks. Since it's detached from the console, it can't correspond with the user. If it does stop, it will just sit until you reboot. If you don't mind it languishing there, you can remove the .CMD file in DOS2OS2 that caused the problem and again run FROMDOS from protected mode with DETACH FROMDOS. This will create another instance of FROMDOS just like the now-stalled first instance. The first one will still waste some system resources, but it won't interfere with the new copy.

If you put any .CMD files in DOS2OS2 while in protected mode, FROMDOS will do them as well, but there's no reason to do this. Look in Chapter 7, "How To," for other, more sophisticated ways of running protected mode from real mode. This is just one example.

DETACH causes a process to run independently of the session in which you are working. The detached command will start right away and run concurrently with all other sessions and tasks in protected and real modes. The command doesn't take up the full resources of the computer. It can do anything except use the screen, keyboard, or mouse of the console. Because it doesn't receive console access, OS/2 doesn't need to create and keep track of a copy of the screen associated with the process (as it does for full-blown sessions) resulting in a considerable savings in resources.

At first, a process that can't communicate with the user may seem useless, but this isn't always true. Many times, you only want to see the end result of a process. If this is the case, you can redirect the output of the process to a file and look at the file when it's done.

Some special processes designed to control system hardware may run in detached mode as well. Usually, the spool program supplied with OS/2 is run as a detached process. It manages printing and has no need to deal directly with the system operator.

It is possible for a detached process to communicate with the user directly through the console, but only if it is specifically programmed to do so. A programmer may include the capability to open a pop-up window from a detached process that allows it to use the console. Don't count on a program being able to do this unless its documentation specifically says it will.

A detached process ends like any other process. If you give the command DIR >AFILE, the DIR command will run to its end, and its output will go into AFILE. When the DIR is done, the process will vanish and no longer be in the system. However, a detached process will only end and be removed from the system if it runs to completion. The SPOOL program, for example, is designed to never end. If SPOOL is run as a detached program, the process containing it will not end until the system is rebooted.

The fact that you can't directly cause a detached process to end is sometimes a problem. If the process attempts to obtain keyboard input, it will wait forever, and there's no way for you to end it short of rebooting. That's why you should be careful that detached processes never try to use console input or output. Detached processes that are endlessly waiting for use of the console do no direct harm, but they certainly don't do any good, and they continue to use system resources. If your system becomes cluttered with zombie processes, it will run more slowly and you'll have less RAM available for other programs.

The DETACH command is worth practicing. It delivers one of the more useful abilities of multitasking: starting a process and forgetting about it until you want to see its results. You can do much the same with the START command, but considerably more of your computer's capability will be tied up in carrying out the process. DETACH is especially handy for long directory listings, sorting, compiling programs, and similar tasks where the computer works fairly hard but quietly.

You generally will want to have some idea of the progress of a detached process. To do this, it's handy to design the detached command so that it will send its output to a file and then rename the file when it's done. Then, with a quick DIR command, you can see if the process is working or if it is done. See the examples above.

Related Commands

START To start and run a process concurrently with your other work, use the START command if the process will need console input or output.

DIR

- Both real and protected modes.
- Network-compatible.
- Internal subprogram in CMD.EXE and COMMAND.COM.
- Very frequently used.

Purpose

DIR outputs a list of files that match the file specification you provide. It also outputs the volume label and directory name of the subject drive and directory. After listing files and directories, it shows the number of files found and the approximate disk space remaining unused. (Use the CHKDSK command for a more accurate estimate if you really care about a few hundred bytes.)

Formats of Command

DIR [*drive:*][*path*][*name*][*.extension*] [/P] [/W]

DIR [*drive:*][*path*][*name*][*.extension*]... [/P] [/W] The first form works in both protected and real modes. The second form (with more than one file specification) is recognized in protected mode only. Note that all parts of the file specification are optional. The /P option causes the directory to print until the screen is full, and then it waits for a keystroke before beginning a new screenful of output. The /W option produces a wide form of listing that places four files on a line, but it doesn't show file sizes or label directories as such.

DIR

DIR *.*

DIR . These three commands all do the same thing, they list the names of all files and subdirectories in the current default directory of the current default drive, with the exception of hidden and system files.

DIR C:

DIR C:*.*

DIR C:. All three list the names of all subdirectories and files in the current default directory of drive C:, with the exception of hidden and system files.

DIR C:*file*

DIR C:*file*.* These two commands list all files with the name *file* (regardless of their filename extension) that exist in the current default directory of drive C:. (DIR is unique as it is the only OS/2 command which recognizes that .* and a missing extension are synonymous.) These commands differ only if there exists a file or files with the same first name as a subdirectory (see example below).

Examples and Description

Say the current working directory contains FOO.DOC, a non-system, nonhidden file. FOO.BAK is also a nonsystem, nonhidden file. FOO is a directory containing the one file, BAR.FOO. The following commands (in bold) list the files shown:

DIR FOO.* FOO.DOC, FOO.BAK, and FOO. After FOO you will see <DIR> indicating that FOO is not a file but a subdirectory.

DIR FOO BAR.FOO (the entire contents of subdirectory FOO.

Now, delete and remove the FOO subdirectory with the command DEL FOO (when it asks if your are sure, answer *Y*) and remove the subdirectory with the command RD FOO. Now the commands shown above will provide different listings of files:

DIR FOO.* FOO.DOC and FOO.BAK.

DIR FOO FOO.DOC and FOO.BAK.

The way DIR FOO changes meaning depending upon the presence of a directory named FOO is just a quirk of DIR.

The following are common sequences that use the DIR command:

DIR I FIND /V "." Suppresses the . and .. (dot and dot-dot) listings.

DIR I FIND /V "o" (That's a lowercase letter *O* in the quotation marks. FIND is a rare command that is case-sensitive.) Suppresses the volume and directory name output lines.

DIR I FIND /V "e" Suppresses the volume, directory name, and file count lines.

DIR I FIND /V "." I FIND /V "e" Gives a simple list of files and directories without anything else but blanks.

DIR I FIND "<" Suppresses all but the directories listings.

DIR I SORT Lists files in alphabetic order, but the file count and disk space line appears at the top, followed by the volume line and the directory line. The remaining lines list the files and directories found.

DIR I FIND /V "e" I SORT Gives a fairly clean listing in alphabetic order.

DIR I FIND /V "e" I SORT /+10 Fairly clean and sorts output by file extension.

DIR I FIND /V "e" I SORT /+13 Fairly clean and sorts by file size.

DIR I FIND /V "e" I SORT /+24 Fairly clean and list files by date, except year is improperly handled.

DIR I FIND /V "e" I FIND /V "." I SORT Does what DIR should do. It gives a clean list in alphabetic order.

Except with the /W option, DIR notes which names are subdirectories and shows the sizes of files in bytes. DIR does not list files with the hidden or system attributes (see the ATTRIB command). DIR shows filenames with spaces between the primary name and the extension rather than the period used in every other command. The file length listed by DIR is the number of bytes contained in the file, not the disk space required to store the file. Most files use more bytes than they contain because OS/2 allocates disk space to files in chunks called *clusters* or *allocation units*.

When applied to a subdirectory, DIR lists . and .. (dot and dot-dot). These are synonyms for the current directory and its parent directory, respectively.

Related Commands

ATTRIB   The ATTRIB command offers a more compact listing that can span multiple subdirectories.

CHKDSK   The CHKDSK command produces a compact list of all files on a drive.

TREE   TREE produces a listing of all directories or all directories
          and files on a drive. This listing is neither compact nor
          aesthetically pleasing. The command FOR %%F IN (*.*)
          DO ECHO %%F lists files in one-by-one fashion.

DISKCOMP

- Both real and protected modes.
- Not network-compatible.
- External program.
- Rarely used.

Purpose

DISKCOMP compares two disks of the same type and format. The comparison is on a track-by-track, side-by-side physical basis and ignores all file boundries.

Formats of Command

DISKCOMP If the current default drive is a floppy disk drive, DISKCOMP will prompt you to insert the first and second disks to be compared alternatively. If the current default drive is not a floppy disk drive, DISKCOMP will complain and quit.

DISKCOMP *drive:* If the specified drive is a floppy disk drive, DISKCOMP will prompt you to insert the first and second disks to be compared alternatively. If the drive is not a floppy disk drive, DISKCOMP will complain and quit.

DISKCOMP *drive: drive:* If both drives specified are floppy disk drives, DISKCOMP will compare the disks in the drives.

Warnings

Two good disks containing identical files in identical order on them may differ, and their differences will not be discovered by DISKCOMP. A difference found by DISKCOMP may have nothing to do with the contents of any of the files on the disks.

Examples and Description

Here are come common command sequences using DISKCOPY:

DISKCOPY A: B:

DISKCOMP A: B: This sequence is for careful disk duplicators, but DISKCOPY is fairly reliable. It rarely lets errors get through. Note that two disks copied with DISKCOPY don't necessarily have the same volume label.

FORMAT A:

DISKCOMP A: You might do this to compare a newly formatted disk with a newly formatted disk made in a different drive to check for a bad or poorly aligned drive.

DISKCOMP is only useful for comparing disks copied with DISKCOPY or newly formatted blank disks. Generally, DISKCOMP is only used to check for disk drive problems or when manufacturing duplicate disks.

When DISKCOMP finds a difference, it reports its position by track number and side. (Which doesn't tell you much except that the disks are different, unless, of course you are a drive mechanic.)

When DISKCOMP is done comparing, it asks if you want to compare any other disks.

When DISKCOMP is using a drive, all other OS/2 processes are prevented from using the same drive. If the drive was the one from which the system was booted, this may not be allowed. You will have to use another disk drive or boot from a hard disk.

Related Commands

COMP   The COMP command compares the contents of files (what you really care about) and works with files on all types of disks and drives.

DISKCOPY   DISKCOPY makes a physical copy; DISKCOMP checks physical copies. All other commands that copy and compare deal with *logical* copies where physical placement and organization don't matter; only content is important.

DISKCOPY

- Both real and protected modes.
- Not network-compatible.
- External program.
- Rarely used.

Purpose

DISKCOPY makes a physical, track-by-track, side-by-side copy of a disk. This is not the same as copies made by the COPY or XCOPY commands.

Formats of Command

DISKCOPY

DISKCOPY *drive:*

DISKCOPY *drive: drive:* In the first form, if the current default drive is a floppy disk drive, DISKCOPY uses that single drive by prompting you to alternately insert the source and destination disks. Likewise, in the second form, you will be prompted to insert source and destination disks alternately in the drive specified. In the third form, DISKCOPY expects the source in the first drive listed and the destination in the second drive listed.

In all cases, all drives involved in the DISKCOPY must be floppy disk drives, or DISKCOPY will complain and quit.

If you attempt to copy from the drive where the system was booted, DISKCOPY will not work. You must use another drive or use the system drive as the destination drive only.

Warnings

If the destination disk is not formatted and is not designed for the same density of recording as the source disk, DISKCOPY will attempt to format it in the same way as the source disk. This may lead to errors in the copy or formatting processes, which DISKCOPY will report to you.

If the destination disk is formatted to a higher density than the source disk, DISKCOPY will attempt to reformat it and may generate errors in the format or copy processes.

Description

DISKCOPY copies the whole source disk, including all unused space on the disk. The one advantage of DISKCOPY over COPY is that DISKCOPY will also format the destination disk, if necessary. DISKCOPY quietly supplies a volume serial number which is not identical on the copy.

Related Commands

COPY
XCOPY   Generally, COPY or XCOPY are preferred to DISKCOPY unless you are in the disk-duplicating business. DISKCOPY is handy only if you are copying a series of identical new disks that all need formatting.

DISKCOMP Generally, you'll probably use DISKCOMP (rather than COMP) to check copies made with DISKCOPY.

DPATH

- Protected mode only.
- Network-compatible.
- Internal subprogram in CMD.EXE.
- Rarely used.

Purpose

Sets the value of the environment variable *dpath* to a list of directories.

Formats of Command

DPATH Shows the current setting of the *dpath* environment variable.

DPATH [*drive:*]*directory;*[*drive:*]*directory;...* Sets the *dpath* variable to the exact string following the command DPATH on the command line. This string must contain valid directory names with or without drive prefixes, separated by semicolons.

DPATH %DPATH%[*drive:*]*directory...* Appends the specified optional drive and directory (or drives and directories) to the current value of the *dpath* variable (just as would SET DPATH=%DPATH%...). This works because when OS/2's protected mode command processor program CMD.EXE sees the string *%word%*, it looks for an environment variable named *word* and puts its value in place of *%word%*.

DPATH ; Sets DPATH equal to a single semicolon, which programs recognize as meaning the same as no *dpath* variable.

Warnings

Don't count on a program paying attention to DPATH unless its documentation or your tests prove that it does.

Example and Description

DPATH C: \;C: \OS2;C: \OS2 \INSTALL This is the DPATH command executed by OS2INIT.CMD as originally set up by the installation process. OS2INIT.CMD is run as the first command in any copy of CMD.EXE started with the program selector.

DPATH is for use by programs that search the environment for a *dpath* variable and use it as intended. DPATH in no way alters the way the file system works (as does its real mode counterpart APPEND). The DPATH command keyword is entirely equivalent to SET DPATH=.

Programs that use the *dpath* environment variable are expected to look for their data files first in the default directory of the default drive, then in the directories listed in the *dpath* variable, in the order they are found in the *dpath* variable. (The directory names in the *dpath* variable are expected to be separated by semicolons.) Whether or not a program uses *dpath* at all or uses it correctly is up to the programmer of that program.

Related Commands

APPEND APPEND, in real mode, is intended for a similar purpose, but it changes the way the current directory appears to programs. DPATH doesn't change the way the current directory appears. It expects the program to figure out and use the *dpath* variable.

PATH   While PATH establishes the search path for commands, DPATH is used to set the search path for data files.

EXIT

• Both real and protected modes.
• Network-compatible.
• Internal subprogram in CMD.EXE and COMMAND.COM.
• Frequently used.

Purpose

Exits the current command processor program and returns control to the program that started it.

Format of Command

EXIT There are no options or arguments.

Description

In real mode, the command processor is COMMAND.COM. Giving COMMAND.COM the EXIT command will cause it to quit and return to the prior instance of COMMAND.COM by which the current instance was created. However, if the current instance of COMMAND.COM is the first one started when the system was booted, or if the current instance of COMMAND.COM was started with the COMMAND /P command, EXIT will do nothing. To get from real mode to the program selector, always use the Ctrl-Esc key sequence. EXIT in real mode won't take you to the program selector as it will in protected mode.

In protected mode, CMD.EXE is the command processor program. Giving CMD.EXE an EXIT command will always cause it to terminate and return control to the program which started it. This may be a prior instance of CMD.EXE in which the CMD command was given to start the child CMD.EXE, or it may be the program selector which is used to start new instances of CMD.EXE. No matter how long a copy of CMD.EXE has been running, it always remembers it parentage—when it exits, control returns to the parent CMD.EXE or the program selector.

FDISK

- Protected mode only.
- Not network-compatible.
- External program.
- Used only for system installation.

Purpose

The most fundamental division of a hard disk, from OS/2's point of view, is the partition. A hard disk may be broken into multiple partitions. Each partition is a logical boundry around a physical region of the disk. Partitions, once created, do not change size. Changing the size of a partition generally requires erasing all of its contents. Each partition is either a *primary partition* or an *extended partition.* Only a primary partition may be used to boot the system. At any time, there's at most one active partition which must be a primary partition. This is the partition used when OS/2 is booted from a hard disk. Each partition that is designated for OS/2 use is given a separate drive letter and is treated as if it were a physically distinct disk. Extended partitions (and only extended partitions) may be broken into multiple logical disk drives, each accessed with a different letter as if it, too, were a physically separate disk drive. Areas of a disk not included in a partition designated for use by OS/2 may be formatted differently for use by another operating system.

FDISK is a menu-operated program that allows you to create and destroy partitions, change partition sizes, create logical drives within an extended partition, and designate a primary partition as the active partition for booting. Generally, any use of FDISK other than setting the active partition will destroy all or a significant part of the data on the subject hard disk drive. Data destroyed in this way can only be retrieved with expert help and great difficulty.

Only use FDISK when you fully expect to destroy all data in your system. Even when you don't tell it to do anything, it can destroy all your data if the partitions you are using were created with a different version of FDISK. Since it's unlikely you'll find this situation desirable, FDISK is normally used only when installing a hard disk.

The need for partitions and FDISK stems from three factors:

- Some users want to be able to use their computers with an operating system other than OS/2 or DOS. If it weren't for partitions, to do so, they would have to physically install a different disk for the different operating system each time they switched.
- The File Allocation Table used as the basic indexing mechanism for all data on an OS/2 or DOS disk is inherently limited to keeping track of at most 32 megabytes of data. To deal with larger disks, the disks are broken into partitions, and extended partitions are broken down further into logical drives, each of which must be 32 megabytes or less in capacity.
- Partitions are used in the boot process to determine where on the disk you can obtain the system files needed to initially load the operating system each time it starts.

See the CHKDSK command and the concepts section on the file system for more information on partitions and disk organization.

After you create or alter the size of a partition with FDISK, you must use the FORMAT command to prepare it for use. (In general, FORMAT, too, destroys all data in its path.)

Some disk drives and controllers are distributed with programs designed to replace FDISK that allow more flexible installation of drives. If you use one of these (it's often worthwhile or necessary) and later invoke FDISK, you may destroy all information on the drive, even if you only used FDISK to check on the size of partitions, and even if you made no attempt to change the partitions.

In various versions of DOS and Xenix, FDISK programs with similar functions are included. Don't expect them to be compatible with OS/2's version of FDISK or the partitions it builds unless the documentation specifically says that they are. Microsoft and others have all sorts of versions of FDISK floating around, and some have very unfortunate incompatibilities.

Format of Command

FDISK There are no options or arguments for FDISK; it uses
    menus.

Warnings

Don't use FDISK unless you have literally nothing to lose on
the hard disk. If you don't understand it in detail, don't use
this program if you have any valuable data on your hard disk.
Use it either step by step from installation instructions or under the supervision of technical personnel.

Related Commands

FORMAT The FORMAT command is used to prepare a partition or
        logical drive created with FDISK.

FIND

- Both real and protected modes.
- Network-compatible.
- External program.
- Occasionally used.

Purpose

FIND searches its input for lines containing a specified string of characters. By default, it outputs all lines containing a match.

Format of Command

FIND [/V] [/N] [/C] *"string" file...* The /V, /N, and /C switches are optional. *String* is required and must be enclosed in quotation marks. The *file* or *files* for input are optional. If one or more files are specified, input is taken from the file(s) in the order shown on the command line. If no file is specified, input is taken from standard input.

/V Causes output of only those lines not containing a match.

/C Causes output of only a count of lines containing a match.

/V /C Causes output of only a count of lines not containing a match.

/N Causes each output line to be prefixed with its line number in the input stream or file.

Warning

Unfortunately, FIND is totally unaware that lower- and uppercase characters are related: It doesn't match *A* with *a*.

Examples and Description

FIND "SMITH" NAMES This will output the lines containing references to SMITH (but not Smith) in your NAMES file.

CHDKSK C: /V I FIND "LOSTFILE" This will output the full path name of every file on drive C: with the name LOSTFILE. Thankfully, CHKDSK uses all uppercase letters for filenames, so FIND's sensitivity to case doesn't cause a problem.

DIR I FIND " 2-" This will output the name of every file in the current working directory that was created or last modified in February (regardless of the year). Note the space before 2 so it won't be confused with 12. Use " 12-" for December (again with a leading blank) so it isn't confused with "1-12-89"—now you see why the string must be in quotation marks.

DIR I FIND /c " 2-29" Counts leap-day files.

FOR %%F IN (*.DOC) DO FIND "needle" %%F

FOR %%F IN (*.DOC) DO FIND "Needle" %%F

FOR %%F IN (*.DOC) DO FIND "NEEDLE" %%F These three find all reasonable references to *needle* in a haystack of document files. (But some word processors change characters just before or after special space characters. For these, you might search for *eedl* and *EEDL* and ignore any matches on *weedle*.)

With the /V option, it outputs all lines not containing a match. With the /C option, it outputs the count of lines with matches; with /V and /C, it outputs the count of lines not containing a match. Lines in the input are any character sequence ended with a carriage return/line feed character sequence. If the input contains a Ctrl-Z character, FIND will stop reading the input at that character. (Ctrl-Z is the end-of-file marker introduced with DOS 1.0. It has hung around well past its useful life. OS/2 and versions of DOS after 1.1 don't need it, but still respect it in commands intended to deal with text.)

FIND may get its input from a file or from standard input. Standard input is normally the console, but it can be redirected with a sequence like

dir I find "DOC"

in which the output from DIR is made the standard input to FIND via the I character.

See the DIR command reference for further examples of FIND.

Related Commands

There are many commercial and public domain programs that offer a more sophisticated version of FIND. Often (for historical UNIX-related reasons) these are named GREP, FGREP, or EGREP. Pick one up if you have a chance; FIND is brain-dead by comparison.

FORMAT

- Real (DOS) or protected mode.
- Not network-compatible.
- External program.
- Occasionally used for floppy disks. Rarely used for hard disks.

Purpose

The purpose of FORMAT is to prepare a disk for use by OS/2. In the case of a hard disk, FORMAT must be preceeded by FDISK to build partitions which are then individually formatted. For floppy disks, no such preliminaries are needed.

Formats of the Command

FORMAT /V:*label* Formats the disk in the default drive and gives it the specified label.

FORMAT *drive:* **/V:***label* Formats the disk in the drive specified and gives it the specified label.

/4 Formats a 5¼-inch disk at a lower capacity.

/N:*sectors* Allows you to specify the number of sectors on a formatted 3½-inch disk. Normally this would be 9 on the 720K disk and 18 on the 1.44MB disk.

/S The /S parameter allows you to prepare a disk partition or disk to be used as a boot partition or disk. This option allows certain necessary hidden files to be written to the newly formatted disk.

/T:*tracks* Allows you to specify the number of tracks on a formatted 3½-inch disk. The 720K disk has 40 tracks, and the 1.44MB disk has 80.

/V The /V option should always be used; it allows you to enter a name or label for the disk or partition to be formatted.

Warnings

FORMAT completely destroys all data on the floppy or hard disk partition formatted. Even if you stop the formatting process quickly, irrevocable damage will have been done. There are some utility programs available which attempt to undo the effects of a format, but don't rely upon them.

Missing partitions cause big surprises. If you attempt to format a hard disk that isn't partitioned (as with FDISK), FORMAT will go to the first partition it finds (generally on a second hard disk, if you have one) and format it. In other words, if you have two hard disks, and the first has not been partitioned or formatted, and the second one has, the command FORMAT C: will format the second disk. OS/2 doesn't even know the first disk is there until it is formatted.

Description

In the following table, 360K equals 360 × 1024, or 368,640 bytes; 720K equals 720 × 1024, or 737,280 bytes; 1.2MB equals 1.2 × 1024 × 1024, or about 1,260,000 bytes; and 1.44MB equals 1.44 × 1024 × 1024, or about 1,510,000 bytes.

Table 6-3. FORMAT Examples

Drive	Disk	Command	Resulting Capacity
Hard disk	N/A	FORMAT [/S] [/V:*label*]	Partition size
5¼-inch 360K	360K	FORMAT [/S] [/V:*label*]	360K
5¼-inch 360K	1.2MB	FORMAT [/S] [/V:*label*]	360K
5¼-inch 1.2MB	360K	FORMAT /4 [/S] [/V:*label*]	360K
5¼-inch 1.2MB	1.2MB	FORMAT [/S] [/V:*label*]	1.2MB
3½-inch 720K	1MB	FORMAT [/S] [/V:*label*]	720K
3½-inch 720K	2MB	FORMAT [/S] [/V:*label*]	720K
3½-inch 1.44MB	1MB	FORMAT /N:9 [/S] [/V:*label*]	720K
3½-inch 1.44MB	2MB	FORMAT [/S] [/V:*label*]	1.44MB

In general, the resulting capacity will be the lower of the disk and drive capacities. You do not need any special options unless the disk is to be formatted at less than the drive's capacity. A 5¼-inch 360K disk formatted in a 1.2MB drive may not work in a 360K drive. In all cases, the /S and /V:*label* options are just that, optional.

A disk may be formatted at any time, even after it has been used. Generally, disks are sold unformatted and must be formatted before use. Hard disks are sometimes formatted before delivery. If you have any question about whether a disk is formatted, try to read it with the DIR command. If the disk can't be found by OS/2, or if a general failure results, you will need to format (or run FDISK and FORMAT) the disk. If the disk works—for example, the DIR command comes back finding no files, but it doesn't cause any other error message—then you don't need to format the disk.

You can think of FORMAT as laying down a road map used by OS/2 in finding its way around a disk surface. There are many forms of the FORMAT command for the various disks and disk drives available. You have only been shown the most useful ones. Don't experiment with option combinations different from those shown here; they'll only lead to trouble. The only options that are really optional are the /V and /S options.

The /V option should always be used. It allows you to enter a label for the disk or partition to be formatted. Use a name that describes the disk itself rather than its content. In other words, be general in your disk name rather than specific. For instance, if you use a disk to store all your files relating to your class action suit against a major corporation, call the disk LEGAL_NOTES rather than naming it after the corporation in question. That way, when you are working on another class action suit against another corporation, the label will still apply. Remember, the content will generally change without the need for reformatting, and very few users are good about using the LABEL command to change the name given to a disk when they change its contents. If you use a general, descriptive name, you won't have to give it another thought.

Labels may contain any of the characters allowed in a filename except there is no period in a label, and the label may be up to 11 characters long. It's often handy to use the underline character where you would like to use a space (not allowed) in a volume label.

Typical labels are:

MINSCRB40_1 Indicating partition 1 of a 40MB Miniscribe drive
144M_104 Indicating a 1.44MB 3½-inch disk, (standard 1.44MB disks are all 3½-inch disks), which bears the serial number 104.

The /S parameter allows you to prepare the disk partition or disk for use in booting the system. To be a boot disk, the disk must contain in a particular location the two hidden system files that contain the guts of the operating system and several auxilliary files that become part of the operating system, or it must control the boot process. FORMAT /S will place these needed files on the newly formatted disk or partition. The list of needed files will change with different versions and upgrades of OS/2. For this reason, boot disks normally contain a file named FORMATS.TBL, which FORMAT reads to determine all of the files needed for a boot disk. FORMAT must be able to find these files to copy them to the new disk.

If the root directory of the current default disk is bootable, FORMAT will find the system files there and look for the other files as well. If the default disk is not bootable, FORMAT will ask you to put a bootable system disk in drive A: (or in the current default drive if it uses floppy disks). If FORMAT can't find any files listed in FORMATS.TBL, it will list the ones still needed on the new disk. You can copy them to the new disk with the COPY command. However, you cannot simply copy the two hidden system files.

Related Commands

FDISK   FDISK is used on a newly formatted hard disk to establish partitions.

GRAFTABL

- Real (DOS) mode only.
- Network-compatible.
- External program that loads and leaves part of itself in memory.
- Rarely Used.

Purpose

In some graphics modes, the IBM Color Display Adapter, Enhanced Graphics Adapter, and Video Graphics Adapter don't normally have character shapes assigned for those characters with ASCII codes over 127. These characters are called *extended ASCII characters* because standard ASCII does not include them. GRAFTABL provides access to these characters.

Formats of Command

GRAFTABL 437 Loads extended US IBM PC character shapes for use in graphics display modes.

GRAFTABL 860 Loads extended Portugese character shapes for use in graphics display modes.

GRAFTABL 863 Loads extended Canadian-French character shapes for use in graphics display modes.

GRAFTABL 865 Loads extended Nordic character shapes for use in graphics display modes.

GRAFTABL ? Outputs the current extended graphics code page in use, if any, and describes the GRAFTABL command and the code pages available for it.

GRAFTABL /sta Outputs the name and number of the current extended graphics code page in use, if any.

Warnings

As GRAFTABL runs and loads part of itself into memory to stay until the next boot, it will reduce the amount of real mode (DOS) memory available to other programs. Like other "terminate-and-stay-resident" programs, GRAFTABL should not be run from within another program; it should be run directly by COMMAND.COM (not with the BASIC SHELL command), or from the DOS window of a word processor, or from a command shell that provides menus. If you find you need GRAFTABL frequently, put it in your AUTOEXEC.BAT file.

Description

Normally, these characters are accented and otherwise modified Romance language characters, line drawing characters, the Greek alphabet, and various math and engineering symbols like the integral sign, the radical, and the degree mark. Without stored tables of the shapes for these characters, the display adapter cannot show them on the screen in graphics modes.

Running GRAFTABL loads a table of symbol shapes for the display adapters to use and sets the necessary pointers to it in memory to cause the display adapters to recognize the table. In video modes 4, 5, and 6, the display adapters will use the character shape table loaded by GRAFTABL. In other modes, the table does no good.

If you find that while running graphics applications some characters are not seen, try running GRAFTABL before the application program and see if the characters appear. If the program you are running is a professional product, you will probably not have this problem. However, with your own programs, or amateur offerings (especially those written in BASIC), you may find GRAFTABL is a prerequisite to full use of the character set.

When you run GRAFTABL, you may select from one of four language-specific code pages. You may also use GRAFTABL to inquire about the code page in use, if there is one, and about the selection of code pages available.

Remember that changing code pages with GRAFTABL only alters the rendition of characters in graphics modes within real mode. In protected mode, the usual code page mechanism handles the tasks performed by GRAFTABL in real mode. In summary, don't use GRAFTABL unless you find you need it to see all the characters used by one or more of your programs that use screen graphics.

Related Commands

COUNTRY   Changes currency and time/date formats to conform to those used in various foreign countries and the US.

CHCP   Changes the current code page for the command processor.

HELP

- Real (DOS) or protected mode.
- Network-compatible.
- External program.
- Occasionally used.

Purpose

The HELP command provides needed information.

Formats of Command

HELP Displays a message telling you what keypresses will take you from one session to another, how to end a session, and how to get more help.

HELP ON Gives you a long prompt that shows how to change sessions and how to go to the program selector.

HELP OFF Reverses HELP ON.

HELP SYS*nnnn* Where *nnnn* is an error number. This command gives some extra information about the error and how to avoid it in the future.

HELP *nnn* Where *nnn* is an error number with or without leading zeros; does the same as HELP SYS*nnnn*.

Description

There are three ways in which the HELP command may assist you.

- HELP ON causes a line about how to jump from one session to another and how to end a session to be part of your command prompt. (With the PROMPT command, you can do the same thing or better.) HELP OFF gets rid of this long prompt.
- The unadorned command HELP will display a message about how to jump between sessions and how to get more help.
- When you receive an error message from OS/2, it starts with an error identifier of the form SYS*nnnn* where *nnnn* is a number (usually with several leading zeros). If you enter the HELP command with this identifier, it will copy the error message again and follow it with a brief explanation.

When using the last form of the HELP command, you don't need to type the SYS or leading zeros—just type HELP and the error number. Programmers can use the same HELP facility. Since HELP just looks up the message in a file, programmers need only supply the necessary messages in a file and install it in the right place with the right name for HELP to use it. If you use a program with such a facility, it may show error identifiers that don't begin with SYS. In such cases, you will probably need to type the entire error identifier for HELP to find the appropriate message. Also, other programs can use the same help messages as OS/2 uses for its commands. If you see *** in an error description, it's a hole in the basic error message used to contain some variable word, like a filename, when the message is first issued.

JOIN

- Real (DOS) mode only.
- Network-compatible.
- External program.
- Occasionally used.

Purpose

JOIN allows two or more disks to appear as one in real (DOS) mode.

Formats of Command

JOIN   Outputs the attachment of drives caused by existing joins, if any.

JOIN *drive1: drive2:\ directory*   Makes *drive1* appear to be the specified *directory* of *drive2*. Note that there must be a subdirectory of the root directory of *drive2*. The directory must not contain any files if the join is to succeed. If the directory doesn't exist, it's created and the join is completed.

JOIN *drive1:* **/D**   If *drive1* is joined as a subdirectory of some other drive, this command will undo the join and *drive1* will subsequently appear as a normal, separate drive.

Warnings

JOINs are nearly perfect. They make a whole disk appear to be a subdirectory, and they allow you to combine multiple disks into one directory structure so that you almost never have to refer to a meaningless drive name. Rather, you can use more meaningful directory names. The only practical rub is that a drive cannot expand and contract like a directory, so you have to do some planning about how your disk space usage will match your directory structure before you build a super directory tree containing multiple drives.

FORMAT and several other commands ignore joins, and CHKDSK cannot process a joined drive.

Examples and Description

JOIN E: C: \ BIN This command causes drive E: to become
known as C: \ BIN and no longer as E:.

JOIN E: /D This command undoes the first command.

JOIN This command outputs any active joins.

JOIN allows two or more disks to appear as one in real
(DOS) mode. A drive can be joined to another so that the first
drive appears as a subdirectory of the root directory of the second. Thereafter, the first drive is no longer known to the system and explicit references to it will fail.

JOINs are handy, especially if you have multiple hard
disk partitions and most especially if you have some small
partitions left over from drives slightly larger than the 32-
megabyte range of a partition or logical drive. If you use JOIN,
it's generally best to include it in your AUTOEXEC.BAT file so
that it's always created when you start real mode. This will
eliminate confusion about the status of your joined drives.
And, after all, avoiding confusion is what an operating system
is all about.

Related Commands

SUBST While JOIN makes a drive look like a directory, SUBST
makes a directory look like a drive.

KEYB

- Must be issued in protected mode, but it alters keyboard in both modes.
- External program.
- Rarely used.

Purpose

KEYB, in combination with the DEVINFO and COUNTRY commands in your CONFIG.SYS file, allows you to change the meaning of some keys on your keyboard.

Warnings

Don't use KEYB lightly. There is nothing more unnerving than a keyboard that changes. If you normally use a language other than American English and care about accent marks, currency symbols, and the like, you may want to experiment with the KEYB command.

If you want foreign language support, you should ask your dealer or a technician to assist in setting your system up for the language you want to use. Even then, you will have frustrations. The means of supporting non-US characters and keys in OS/2 is messy, it isn't comprehensive, and it's not supported by all major software developers.

Format of Command

KEYB *layoutcode* Various layout codes are supported. Before you can use a layout, however, it must be described to OS/2 in a DEVINFO command in your CONFIG.SYS file.

Description

You must issue the KEYB command in protected mode, but it alters the operation of the keyboard in both protected and real modes. However, some DOS programs may not respect the changes.

Related Commands
COUNTRY
CHCP
GRAFTABL
DEVINFO   Before you can use a layout, however, it must be described to OS/2 in a DEVINFO command in your CONFIG.SYS file.

LABEL

- Real (DOS) or protected mode.
- Not network-compatible.
- External program.
- Occasionally used.

Purpose

Each floppy disk and hard disk partition may have a volume label. You can create volume labels with the LABEL command or with the FORMAT command. Since the FORMAT command destroys all the data on a particular disk or partition, it's a bit drastic for just changing a label. That's what the LABEL command is for.

Formats of Command

LABEL [*drive:*] Shows current label and asks if you want to enter a new one. If you don't specify a drive, the current default drive is used. If you only want to see the volume label and don't want to be asked if you want to change it, use the VOL command.

LABEL [*drive:*] *newlabel* This command replaces any existing label with *newlabel*. If you don't specify a drive, the current default drive is presumed.

You may see the label of a disk or partition by using the VOL, DIR, CHKDSK, or LABEL commands. Labels consist of 11 characters. You may use in a label any character that is legal in a filename, except that no period may be used in a label. It's handy to use the underline character where you might want to use a space (spaces are not allowed).

It's good practice to label disks, partitions, and logical drives. Generally, the label should explain something about the disk or partition. The volume label is stored in the root directory as if it were a file or directory name, except that it has a special marker. There should never be more than one label in a root directory. If you see more than one label, or you see a label that changes by itself, run CHKDSK because the organization of your disk has been damaged.

Related Commands

FORMAT   FORMAT and LABEL make labels.
VOL
DIR
CHKDSK   These three commands display the label.

MD and MKDIR

- Real (DOS) or protected mode.
- Network-compatible.
- Internal subprogram in COMMAND.COM and CMD.EXE.
- Frequently used.

Purpose

MD and MKDIR have exactly the same effect. MD allows you
to create multilevel directories. The file system is organized
into files within directories within directories and so on. Without directories, a significant file system can become confused
beyond usefulness.

Directories should be made, used, and deleted frequently
to keep your file system a proper reflection of the logical
structure of your programs and data. (See the concepts section
on the file system for more information about directories.)

Format of Command

MD [*drive:*] *directorypath* The directory specified in
directorypath must not already exist; if it does, MD will do
nothing but alert you to your error. Within the *directorypath* specified, all directories except the last mentioned
must exist. If *drive* is not specified, the current default
drive is presumed.

If the directory starts with \, it's found by OS/2 by trac-
ing the directory names from the root directory until the new
part of the directory is encountered. If the directory does not
begin with \, it's found by OS/2 by searching within the current default directory of the subject drive through each directory until the new directory to be added is encountered. If a
file with the same name as the new directory exists, MD will
fail and the new directory will not be created.

Examples and Description

Presuming the current default drive only has a root directory:

MD LTLLEAG
MD LTLLEAG \ PLAYERS
MD LTLLEAG \ PLAYERS \ NEW

MD LTLLEAG \ PLAYERS \ OLD
MD LTLLEAG \ COACHES
MD LTLLEAG \ COACHES \ FRESH
MD LTLLEAG \ COACHES \ TIRED
MD LTLLEAG \ COACHES \ RETIRED

This sequence of commands will build a small directory structure or tree for use in keeping track of your little league. It forms the bones of a structure in which to include individual files. When typing a sequence like this, the command editing keys (especially F3) can be very handy.

MD LTLLEAG
CD LTLLEAG
MD PLAYERS COACHES
CD PLAYERS
MD NEW OLD
CD .. \ COACHES
MD FRESH TIRED RETIRED

This sequence does the same as the last. In protected mode only, you can make more than one directory with a single MD command. Note that the several directories need not all have the same parent as they do here, but it tends to keep things simple for the operator if they do. Note that CD .. \ COACHES changes directories by moving to LTLLEAG, the parent directory of PLAYERS, and then to LTLLEAG's subdirectory COACHES. The dot-dot (..) in the sixth line is just a nickname for the parent directory of the current default directory. Notice that again the command editing keys can be very handy in a series of commands like this.

MD LTLLEAG && CD LTLLEAG
MD PLAYERS COACHES && CD PLAYERS
MD NEW OLD
CD .. \ COACHES
MD FRESH TIRED RETIRED

The shortened sequence above does the same as the last in protected mode.

MD LTLLEAG | CD LTLLEAG
MD PLAYERS COACHES | CD PLAYERS
MD NEW OLD

CD .. \ COACHES
MD FRESH TIRED RETIRED

This sequence does the same in real mode. Note that the vertical line (|) is supposed to redirect output from the first command to the second and then execute the second. There is no output from MD, and CD takes no input, so the only result of using | is that both commands are executed. Try making a batch file called MDCD.BAT which uses this trick (but you must do it in one line).

Related Commands

CD   CD (or CHDIR) changes the default directory.
RD   RD (or RMDIR) removes a directory (but only after all of the files in the directory have been deleted).

MODE

- Real (DOS) or protected mode, but with differences in usage.
- Network-compatible.
- External program.
- Occasionally used.

Purpose

MODE has always been the kitchen sink for various unrelated controls of your computer's hardware. In OS/2, it is best viewed as five separate commands, and that's how it is treated here. The five functions of MODE are:

- Setting serial communications port parameters in protected mode.
- Setting serial communications port parameters in real mode.
- Setting video display mode for a particular session.
- Setting parallel printer characteristics.
- Turning disk-write verification on and off.

Each of these will be dealt with as if it were a separate command because the fuctions are so dissimilar.

Notes on serial port control. Serial communications ports are designed to conform to one of the most widely used standards in the computer world. This standard is "Recommended Standard Number 232" of the Engineering Department of the Electronic Industries Association.

The standard spells out in detail how a modem (modulator/demodulator) that sends data over a telephone line is to be controlled. Unfortunately, the vast majority of serial communications applications are not for modems. RS-232 employs many interlocking controls that deal with when to hang up, when to go *off hook*, waiting for dial tones, waiting for rings, and so on. Obviously, when a serial port is used to connect a printer to a computer, it doesn't make good sense for the computer to wait for a dial tone.

Time and events have seriously bent the RS-232 standard into many areas for which it was not intended. Today, in all but strict telephone applications, RS-232 is no longer a standard as much as it is a group of techniques. As a result, just plugging two RS-232 ports together won't make them talk to each other. A variety of settings must be made to make them work at the same speed, with the same characters, and to make sure each port talks into the other's ear rather than ear to ear and mouth to mouth.

In addition, most serial devices cannot receive data continuously. They have to take a breather from time to time to eject a page, write to a disk, or wait for a keystroke from a human. The RS-232 tradition allows a variety of ways to throttle communications. You just have to be sure that both communicating devices will be using the same technique. The MODE command provides a way to control how serial ports under OS/2 are set up. Their speed of operation, type of character, throttling method, and other parameters can be set with MODE.

Unfortunately, being able to set them does not tell you what setting is proper for a given device attached to your computer. You have to determine this from the documentation for your device, whether it's a printer, modem, terminal, plotter, or cash register. If your attached device is not too bizarre, there is likely to be a page about connecting to DOS or OS/2 computers that provides a MODE command to copy. By all means, copy it and forget the rest of this section.

However, there is yet another nest of problems for serial communications under OS/2. Since multiple concurrent processes run under OS/2, there is a risk that two or more programs will attempt to exercize control over a single serial port at the same time.

Within protected mode, OS/2 handles such contentions nicely. However, since DOS offers minimal support for serial ports, nearly all DOS programs that do any serious serial communications must manipulate the serial port hardware directly.

Protected mode programs must use OS/2 functions to access ports; therefore, they're prevented from affecting the hardware settings directly. But if a DOS program resets the parameters of a serial commmunications control circuit, OS/2's own functions will not work. Microsoft's answer to this problem is to leave to you the responsibility for letting a DOS program control a port. If you do, you must be sure that no protected mode program will also access the port until the DOS program is done and you have turned control of the port back to OS/2's communications functions. You use the command SETCOM40 to give and take away control of a serial port by real mode DOS programs.

Recall that two communicating serial ports must have compatible settings before they'll work properly together. You may alter port settings in either real or protected mode. However, you have more choices and better control in protected mode, so you should use MODE while in protected mode to establish port settings. Since the settings are ultimately stored in hardware chips, which are oblivious to real versus protected mode, the settings you make in protected mode apply to real mode as well. But, if you give control of a port to a DOS program with the SETCOM40 command, there is a good chance that the program will alter the settings. Therefore, if you will be using the port in protected mode, you should repeat the MODE command to set port parameters just after releasing the port from DOS control with SETCOM40.

OS/2's control of serial ports in protected mode doesn't come free. To provide this support, a device driver program must be installed when the operating system is booted. This program is started with the CONFIG.SYS file statement DEVICE=COM01.SYS for IBM ATs and compatibles and DEVICE=COM02.SYS for PS/2-compatible computers. If neither of these statements are in the CONFIG.SYS file, OS/2 can't manage serial ports, but DOS programs still can. And since OS/2 doesn't commandeer them, you no longer need to use SETCOM40 to turn DOS access to the ports on and off. But then you can't use the ports at all in protected mode. Generally, the appropriate DEVICE statement for your computer should be used if you will be using any serial devices, but when the COM0X.SYS device driver program is loaded, it takes away some memory that would normally be available in real mode.

Finally, DOS telecommunications programs for modem communications generally won't work under OS/2 at all. These programs must respond to data as it arrives at the serial port. If some protected mode process is running when a burst of data comes into the port, the DOS program will not be able to respond in time to avoid missing some of the data. If you want to run OS/2 and communicate over the phone, you will need an OS/2 protected mode communications program.

MODE for Protected Mode Serial Ports

• Protected and real (DOS) modes, but options differ.
• Network-compatible.
• External program.
• Occasionally used.

Purpose

Sets parameters of operation for COM serial communications ports. This command only works if your CONFIG.SYS file contains a DEVICE command that loads a serial port device driver program when OS/2 is booted. For AT-compatible computers, the CONFIG.SYS file command is DEVICE=COM01.SYS. For PS/2 computers, the command is DEVICE=COM02.SYS.

Many of the parameters set by this command have to do with the details of serial communications. Their proper settings depend upon the devices attached to the serial ports. Look in the documentation for the device you want to attach to your computer for the proper settings.

The COM0X.SYS device driver program for ATs and compatibles can only handle two serial ports, named COM1 and COM2. The version for PS/2 compatibles handles COM1, COM2, and COM3.

The protected mode version of this command is more capable than the real mode. It's generally recommended that you use the protected mode version, though either version sets parameters for both modes.

Formats of Command

MODE COM*n*   Where *n* is 1 or 2 for an AT compatible and is 1, 2, or 3 for a PS/2. This command outputs the current settings in the same form as they are set by the following form of the MODE command.

Examples

MODE COM*n:baud* [*parity*] [*, databits*] [*, stopbits*] [*, TO=ON/OFF*] [*, XON=ON/OFF*] [*, IDSR=ON/OFF*] [*, ODSR=ON/OFF*] [*, OCTS=ON/OFF*] [*, DTR=ON/ OFF/HS*] [*, RTS=ON/OFF/HS/TOG*]   Protected mode version (all on one line).

MODE COM*n:baud* *[parity]* [*, databits*] [*, stopbits*] [*,P*] Real
mode version. COM*n* is COM1, COM2 or, for PS/2
compatibles, COM3. The remaining variables are ex-
plained at length below.

Baud is the data transmission rate. (The word *baud* is derived from Emile Baudot's name.) Valid values are shown in
Table 6-4.

Table 6-4. Valid Baud Values and Their Abbreviations

Valid Values	Valid Abbreviations
110	—
150	15
300	30
600	60
1200	12
2400	24
4800	48
9600	96
19200	192

Parity indicates how a check bit (the parity bit) is set for
each character sent or received. Valid values are shown in Table 6-5.

Table 6-5. Parity Values

Value	Meaning
N	No parity bit.
O	Odd: The bit is set so the number of bits is always odd.
E	Even: The bit is set so the number of bits is always even (the default).
M	Mark: Parity bit is always 1.
S	Space: Parity bit is always 0.

Real mode option P causes timeouts of less than 30 seconds to be ignored, but it issues an error after about 30 seconds of no response from the attached device. (In DOS 3.X,
the P option causes indefinite timeouts to be allowed as the
protected mode TO option does in OS/2.)

The variable *databits* sets the number of data bits in each
character sent or received. Valid values are 5, 6, 7, or 8. The
default is 7 (5 and 6 are almost never used today).

The variable *stopbits* sets the number of bits sent after a
character to mark its ending. Valid values are: 1, 1.5, and 2.

The value 1.5 is only valid if *databits* equals 5. Default is 2 for 110 baud, 1 for other rates.

If the TO option is on, when the attached device doesn't respond for long periods, OS/2 will not give up on it. When off, if the device does not respond in a reasonable time, OS/2 treats it as an error, which makes sense, depending upon the device. Printers, for instance, may wait a long time for you to load more paper. The default is Off.

If the XON option is on, XON/XOFF throttling of communications is used. This scheme causes each side to send an XON character when it is ready to receive and an XOFF when it needs a rest. The default is Off. The other throttling methods below use special wires in the communications cable rather than special characters sent over the main wires.

If the IDSR option is on, the attached device will only send data when the computer sends a *Data Set Ready* signal over a particular wire in the cable to the device. The default is On.

If the ODSR option is on, the attached device must send a *Data Set Ready* signal over a particular wire in the cable before the computer will send data. The default is On.

If the OCTS option is on, the computer will only send data to the attached device while the device sends a *Clear to Send* signal over a particular wire in the attaching cable. The default is On.

If the DTR option is HS, the attached device will only respond if the computer sets the *Data Terminal Ready* line in the cable on. The computer is set to turn this line on and off to control the activity of the attached device. If on, the computer always asserts *Data Terminal Ready*. If off, the computer never asserts *Data Terminal Ready*. The default is On.

If RTS is on, the computer always asserts *Request to Send*. If off, the computer never asserts *Request to Send*. If HS, the computer asserts *Request to Send* when it wants to send data, and only sends it when the attached device asserts *Clear to Send*. If TOG, the computer asserts *Request to Send;* then, when the device asserts *Clear to Send,* the computer ends the *Request to Send* assertion until the next transmission. (This is almost never used and is intended for half duplex systems.) The default is On.

Warnings

When it comes to setting communications parameters, don't give up easily. It almost never works right the first time. Experiment with multiple settings. When you get it working, make sure you note the proper values and use them in the future, preferrably from a batch file. If you can't get it working, the cable used to attach the serial device may not be appropriate. (There are various standard cables as well as standard settings.)

Examples

MODE COM1:12N,8,1,TO=ON,DTR=ON In this example, COM1 is set for 1200 baud, no parity, eight bits of data per character, one stop bit after each character, timeout errors suppressed, and Data Terminal Ready enabled. This isn't an unusual setting if COM1 is attached to a daisy-wheel printer. For a laser printer, the baud is typically around 9600 baud.

Related Commands

The MODE command for serial port settings in real mode offers some, but not all of the same options.

MODE for Display Control
• Real (DOS) or protected mode.
• Network-compatible.
• External program.
• Occasionally used.

Purpose
Within the limits of the display hardware attached to your system, you can change the display mode (color graphics or black-and-white, 40 or 80 characters wide on the screen, and monochrome mode for monochrome display adapters). For some display systems, you can also set the number of lines of text displayed on the screen. When you set these parameters, they only apply to the session in which the MODE command is given.

If you enter a command that causes your display to misbehave, use MODE BW40 to get it back to something you can read (if that doesn't work, use MODE MONO). Then, again experiment.

Format of Command
MODE [*displaymode*][, *lines*] *Displaymode* may be 40, 80, BW40, BW80, CO40, CO80 or MONO. The values 40 and 80 refer to the number of characters displayed across a full screen line. BW means use black-and-white. CO means use color. MONO means make the display compatible with a Monochrome Display Adapter. Valid values for *lines* are 25, 43, and 50, but only certain adapters are capable of 43 or 50. (Try it on yours to see if it works.) If no value is specified for *lines*, 25 is assumed.

MODE for Parallel Printer Control

- Real (DOS) or protected mode.
- Network-compatible.
- External program.
- Rarely used.

Purpose

This command lets you set the rendition of characters from printers attached to parallel printer ports LPT1, LPT2, or LPT3. This command will only work with some printers, and it doesn't alter how programs with special printer control features and drivers deal with the printer. To see if these settings work on your printer, try them. If they don't work, you can send *escape sequences* directly from your files to the printer with the COPY command to set particular features.

Format of Command

MODE LPT*n width* **[,** *chars_per_inch*] [*,P*] LPT*n* may be LPT1, LPT2 or LPT3. But, if you don't have a printer attached to LPT3, using LPT3 won't cause much to happen. PRN may be used in place of LPT1. The *width* specification may be 80 or 132 characters per line. (The default is the last value given in a MODE LPT... command, or, if a value isn't given, 80.) The *chars_per_inch* specification may be 6 or 8. It refers to the number of text lines printed per inch of paper. (The default is the last value given in a MODE LPT... command, or 6, if a value isn't given.) Finally, the P option causes OS/2 to treat delays in the printer responding to commands to be accepted as non-errors. Without the P option, such delays cause an error message to be issued.

Examples

MODE LPT1 80,6 A common setting.

MODE LPT1,,P Doesn't change the width and character height, but suppresses timeout errors.

MODE for Disk Verification

• Real (DOS) or protected mode.
• Network-compatible.
• External program.
• Rarely used.

Purpose

This command turns special disk-write verification on and off.
It's normally off. If on, every disk-write operation includes a
reread of the written portion to be sure it's accurate. This reread slows operation. Don't use this command unless you
think you have problems with a disk or drive. This form of
verification is not foolproof. Some types of errors can escape
this test. Note that verification caused by the VERIFICATION
command affects all drives, not just disk drives.

Formats of Command

MODE DSKT Outputs whether disk verification is on.
MODE DSKT VER=ON Turns disk-write verification on.
MODE DSKT VER=OFF Turns it off.

MORE

- Real (DOS) or protected mode.
- Network-compatible.
- External program.
- Frequently used.

Purpose

If you have ever started reading something on the screen only to have it zoom past and off the top, you'll understand the need for the MORE command. MORE is designed to read from the standard input and output to the standard output, but it stops the text when the screen is full. Then it waits until you indicate with a keypress that you are ready to move on.

   Since MORE takes no options or arguments, you must use input/output redirection as shown below to send a file through MORE to the screen.

Formats of Command

MORE Accepts input (from the keyboard by default) and prints it to the output (the screen by default) until the screen has been filled. Then it prints —*More*— and waits for another keypress before proceeding.

MORE *<file* This types a file onto the screen until the screen is filled. Then its behavior is like the previous format.

program I **MORE** This accepts output from the program until the screen is full, and then it behaves like the previous two formats.

Warnings

If you use MORE in a batch file and redirect the output of MORE to a file, make sure you know to press a key from time to time so it doesn't wait for you forever.

Examples

MORE *<*TEXTFILE Prints a file one screen at a time.

DIR I **MORE** Sends directory to the screen one page at a time.

PATCH

- Both real and protected modes.
- Network-compatible.
- External program.
- Rarely used.

Purpose

PATCH allows you to change individual bytes (the basic
eight-bit unit of information used in microcomputers) and particular bits within them. It is a rudimentary binary editor. The
term *patch* in programming means a small after-the-fact alteration to a program to fix a problem. The PATCH command
makes such alterations possible if somewhat cumbersome.
That is how you will generally use PATCH—under the direction of a technician telling you what to do in one way or another. This is an very advanced feature and far beyond the
scope of this book.

PATH

• Both real and protected modes.
• Network-compatible.
• Internal subprogram in CMD.EXE and COMMAND.COM.
• Frequently used.

Purpose

The PATH command simply displays or sets the *path* environment variable in the current environment. This variable tells OS/2 where to find programs. Proper PATH settings are essential to the proper operation of OS/2 and many programs.

Formats of Command

PATH When used by itself, the PATH command displays the current command path for the active session. This is the second thing to do when you type a command and OS/2 cannot find it. (The first thing is to make sure you spelled the command properly.)

PATH *string* Whatever string of characters follows the command PATH becomes the value of the *path* environment variable for the current session. (This is identical to SET PATH=*string*.) A space in *string* ends it, so spaces cannot be entered into the *path* variable.

PATH ; By convention, when you have no PATH, the *path* environment variable is set to a semicolon with no directory name before or after it. OS/2 will ignore such a path.

PATH *%path%dirname;* In protected mode, this will add the directory named *dirname* to the current path. In real mode, this will not work in a regular command (because the percent signs are not interpreted as having the meaning that they contain a variable name), but it will work in a batch file where *%path%* will be properly expanded into the current value of the *path* variable. Note that this command presumes that the old value ends with a semicolon to separate it from the newly added directory name.

Warnings

An invalid path is easy to enter, but it won't work. The PATH command doesn't check to see that the directories exist and are properly spelled.

To avoid hard-to-find problems, always include the drive for each directory in the *path* value.

Example and Description

PATH C: \ PALIAS;C: \ CMD;C: \ PBIN;C: \ BIN;C: \ OS2;

This command is from the how-to section on organizing your hard disk. Its design presumes that C: \ PALIAS contains a few short .CMD files that implement any aliases you are using (read Chapter 7, "How To" for information about aliases; they aren't part of OS/2), C: \ CMD contains your protected mode batch files, C: \ PBIN contains .COM and .EXE program files for programs especially for protected mode, C: \ BIN contains .COM and .EXE program files for programs which work in both protected and real modes, and C: \ OS2 contains the programs which implement OS/2 commands.

When you type a command for OS/2 to execute, it takes these steps:

- First, it checks to see if the command is an internal command. If so, the command is executed and that's it.
- If the command is not an internal command, OS/2 looks for a program of the same name. It looks in the current directory of the default drive for a program with the same first name as the command and an extension of .COM.
- If the program is found, OS/2 runs it.
- If not, it looks for a file with the same first name and an extension of .EXE.
- If OS/2 finds the program, it's run.
- If it doesn't find the program, it looks for a batch file of the same first name and the extension .BAT if you are in real mode or an extension of .CMD if you are in protected mode.
- If OS/2 finds a matching batch file, it takes its commands from there until the batch file is finished.

- If it doesn't find an appropriate batch file, OS/2 looks at the *path* variable in the current environment. It scans the *path* variable value for semicolons. It expects that each part of the *path* variable value is a directory name and that the semicolons separate the directory names from each other.
- For each directory name, in the order given, OS/2 searches for a file matching the command it's trying to execute in the same way it searched the default directory: first for a file with the extension .COM, then for .EXE, and finally for .BAT or .CMD.

OS/2 begins searching for a program or batch file in the current directory and continues through each directory specified in the *path* variable. The order of this search is important. You may have more than one program or batch file that matches the command specified. The first one found is run, according to the search sequence described above.

Normally your *path* variable (your *current path*) is set in a batch file. For protected mode, the batch file OS2INIT.CMD is run every time a new session using CMD.EXE as a command processor is started from the program selector. This is the logical place to put a PATH command to set the command search path for that session. In real mode, the batch file AUTOEXEC.BAT is automatically run when you start the DOS session. This is the logical place for your real mode PATH command. (OS2INIT.CMD and AUTOEXEC.BAT, as initially built by the OS/2 installation process, each contain a PATH command that lets OS/2 find the programs that are part of OS/2 itself.)

Determining the proper real and protected mode paths for your system is a major consideration in organizing your hard disk. See Chapter 7, "How To," to read about organizing your hard disk.

Don't write overly complex paths. We all type commands incorrectly from time to time. If you include many directories in your path, it may take OS/2 an inconveniently long time to search all of the directories just to find that there isn't a match for a command.

Related Commands

SET To set the *path* variable, the command SET PATH= will work just like PATH. Also, you can see the current path, along with all your other environment variables, with the command SET by itself.

PRINT

- Real (DOS) or protected mode.
- Not always network-compatible.
- External program.
- Frequently used.

Purpose

The PRINT command sends a file to a selected parallel printer. Though not necessary, generally PRINT is used in conjunction with the SPOOL program to send files to a printer through the SPOOL program. This procedure allows you to go on with another task while the file is being printed.

Formats of Command

PRINT [/D:LPT*n*] [/B] *filename [filename...]* The square brackets indicate the /D and /B options are not required. The filename may include drive and directory. Multiple filenames may be used. The *n* in LPT*n* may be 1, 2, or 3, indicating output to parallel printer LPT1, LPT2, or LPT3. (You may also use PRN in place of LPT1—they mean the same.) If the /D:LPT*n* option is not used, it is the same as specifying /D:LPT1. If the /B option is used, Ctrl-Z characters are not interpreted as the end of the file to be printed.

PRINT [/D:LPT*n*] /C The /C switch allows you to cancel printing of the file currently printing on the printer labeled LPT*n* (where *n* = 1, 2, or 3). If /D:LPT*n* is not specified, LPT1 is presumed. If other files are awaiting printing on the same printer, this command does not cancel them, it only cancels the currently printed file. (Requires that SPOOL be running and handling the specified printer.)

PRINT [/D:LPT*n*] /T Like the /C form, except all files printing or awaiting printing on the specified printer are canceled and all printing to that printer is stopped. (Requires that SPOOL be running and handling the specified printer.)

/C Kills the current printing job and goes on to the next.

/T Kills the entire list of printing jobs.

/B Allows you to adjust the size of the printing buffer.

Description

In order to use PRINT to send a file to a serial printer, you must use the SPOOL program to redirect parallel printer output to a serial printer and trick the PRINT command into thinking it is dealing with a parallel printer.

The SPOOL program is designed to run in protected *detached* mode, that is, detached from the console, quietly running in the background unnoticed. When you want to send a file to the printer, you need some way to contact the SPOOL program and tell it what you want to do. PRINT does this by sending the file to a specified printer while the SPOOL program intercepts this shipment, copies it to a disk file and then sends it to the printer in the background while other programs continue on. The SPOOL program also sends whole files to printers without allowing print streams from more than one program to become intermixed while printing.

As you need the PRINT command to tell SPOOL to print a file, you will also need to tell SPOOL to stop printing a file. You will sometimes have the frustrating experience of printing a long file which is in some way incorrect. To avoid waiting for the file to complete printing, you can use the PRINT *filename* /C command to stop the process. (In fact, you may want to include the PRINT /C command in batch files named KILLPRN.BAT and KILLPRN.CMD. It's hard to remember the /C switch when your printer is spewing paper all over the room or banging its printhead back and forth.)

The PRINT command allows an option /B, which causes OS/2 to send Ctrl-Z characters to the printer. Without this command, if OS/2 sees a Ctrl-Z character, it presumes it marks the end of the print file. This is a holdover from old DOS 1.1 and is no longer needed for most modern programs. When in doubt, it is best to use the /B switch because formatted printing often includes binary graphics values which may happen to contain the code for a Ctrl-Z. If you see printouts that are inexplicably truncated, especially in an area of fancy formatting or graphics or line drawing, be sure to use the /B option to print the file.

PROMPT

- Real (DOS) or protected mode.
- Network-compatible.
- Internal subprogram in COMMAND.COM and CMD.EXE.
- Occasionally used.

Purpose

The PROMPT command sets the string of characters output by the command processor program when it's ready for a command.

Formats of Command

PROMPT By itself, with no arguments, the PROMPT command removes the current prompt string, which causes the command processor to use a default prompt string. In the case of COMMAND.COM, this default is the current drive and directory followed by a greater-than sign (>), indicating that it is the operator's turn to give a command. An example of this is C:\USR\YOU>. In protected mode, CMD.EXE uses a default prompt that includes the current drive and directory within square brackets, for instance, [C:\USR\YOU].

PROMPT *string* The *string* becomes the prompt for the current session.

The *string* may include any of the special codes listed in the following chart.

String	Result
$$	Places $ into the prompt.
$_	Dollar sign followed by an underline character places a return in the prompt making it split into two lines.
$A	Places & into the prompt.
$B	Places I into the prompt.
$C	Places (into the prompt.
$D	Places the date into the prompt.
$E	Places an escape character into the prompt.
$F	Places) into the prompt.
$G	Places > into the prompt.
$H	Places a backspace into the prompt.

$I   Places the help line (showing session-changing keys) into the prompt.
      (See the HELP command.)
$L   Places < into the prompt.
$N   Places the default drive into the prompt.
$P   Places the default directory of the default drive into the prompt.
$Q   Places = into the prompt.
$S   Places a space into the prompt (needed for leading spaces).
$T   Places the time into the prompt.
$V   Places the OS/2 version number into the prompt.

Warnings

A confusing prompt can lead an operator into serious errors.
An overly long prompt can frustrate an operator (there's never
enough screen space). Avoid overly complex and distracting
prompts.

Examples and Description

PROMPT [$P]$G Makes the protected mode prompt look
  more like the real mode.
PROMPT $T $P> Includes the time in the prompt. This is
  usually more of an annoyance than a help.

In protected mode, the command processor is CMD.EXE,
and in real mode, it is COMMAND.COM. When ready to accept a command, each of these programs looks in the current
environment for a variable with the name PROMPT. If it's
found, the value of this variable is sent to the console to tell
the operator it's time to enter a command. In normal use of
the system, it's beneficial to have the prompt tell the operator
something about the current state of the system.

Helpful prompts indicate the current default drive and directory so the operator knows where he or she is in the file
system. The prompt should also indicate whether the operator
is in real or protected mode. (See the HELP command for an
easy way to make a helpful, if verbose, prompt.)

Since the PROMPT command is entered like any other
command, OS/2 has to use some tricks to allow characters
that have a special meaning to get past the processor and into
the prompt string. To accomplish this, characters that would
normally be acted upon by the command processor are given

special codings that begin with the dollar sign. OS/2 allows limited special variable parts of the prompt string which will be interpreted at the time the string is output. In this way, things like the current working directory and current time may be included in the prompt.

Remember that the *prompt* variable is an environment variable and it behaves like other environment variables. It is known only within the current session. Any child program started by the command processor, including another instance of the command processor itself, will inherit the prompt string. But if the child changes it, when control returns to the parent, the change will be forgotten.

Generally a PROMPT command is included in OS2INIT.CMD and AUTOEXEC.BAT to cause your standard prompt to be set each time a protected mode session is begun with the program selector and when the single real mode session begins. (Note that the PROMPT command you put in these two batch files should be different so you can easily tell whether you are in real or protected mode each time the prompt is issued.)

If you have turned on ANSI console support in protected mode with the ANSI command or in real mode with the CONFIG.SYS command DEVICE=ANSI.SYS, then you can include console control escape sequences in the prompt. This can allow you to change colors, make the prompt show up different places on the screen, and so on. You can even change the meaning of some keyboard keys, but this can get tricky and may surprise users. To include the escape character needed in such sequences, use $E in the PROMPT command as described above.

Batch files may sometimes use the prompt to express a message, or they may set the prompt off so that echoing from the batch file is neater. Menu batch files often set the prompt to something like: *Enter Your Selection:*.

Related Commands

SET You can set the *prompt* variable with the SET command as well, but the PROMPT command is generally more convenient.

RECOVER
• Real (DOS) or protected mode.
• Not network-compatible.
• External program.
• Can operate on single files or entire drives.
• Rarely used.

Purpose
RECOVER eliminates bad sectors from a file in order to make
the rest of the file readable. This can save the bulk of a large
text file, but it will make most binary (program) files
unworkable.

Formats of Command
RECOVER *filename* Recovers the specified file. *Filename* may
    contain drive and path specifications.
RECOVER *drive:* Recovers all files on the specified *drive*.
    Another way of saying this is that this command poten-
    tially deletes portions of all files on the specified drive.

Warnings
Use RECOVER C: (or any other hard disk drive) only as a last
resort before reformatting or throwing away the disk drive.
You may experience large losses of data which may have been
otherwise recoverable with technical assistance or nontechnical
persistance.

Description
Many disks and most hard disks have flawed areas on their
surfaces that prevent accurate data storage at these locations.
Since OS/2 always reads and writes disks in chunks (called
sectors), a sector containing a flaw will not work properly. The
drive hardware and low-level software built into your machine
automatically check that each sector read is an accurate rendition of what was saved. A *cyclical redundancy check* value (or
CRC) calculated from the bytes written in the sector is appended to each sector. When the file is read, this number is
recalculated. If it does not match the CRC read from the disk,

something has gone wrong. The error is reported to OS/2.

When OS/2 detects a read error, it normally tries the read again several times. If it can't read successfully, it issues an error message to the console or to the program performing the read. In many cases, this will cause the rest of the file to be difficult to access. The RECOVER command makes a copy of a file that contains a flawed sector. It allows the process to continue through the read error, but the copy does not contain the sector containing the disk flaw. The information from the flawed sector or sectors just disappears from the file. For some files, like documents, this is better than losing the entire file. For binary files, like programs, it does little good because part of the file has about as much value as no file at all.

Since disks commonly have flaws on their surface, OS/2 includes a provision to avoid bad sectors, and it never uses them in a file. In such cases, the bad sectors do no harm except to reduce the total disk space available. What causes problems is when previously good sectors turn bad. That's when you need the RECOVER command. Not only does RE-COVER remove bad sectors from the subject file or files, it also marks any flawed sectors in the file or files as bad and never again to be used by OS/2. The initial list of bad sectors is created by the FORMAT command and is stored as settings in the FAT (File Attribute Table). New bad sectors scanned by the RECOVER command are marked as bad in the FAT. The FAT is the master index to the contents of the disk.

If you run the RECOVER command on an entire disk, it will remove all bad sectors from any files on the disk and mark them bad. This can cause a substantial loss of data if your disk is failing.

Often, some of the information discarded by RECOVER could have been recovered by multiple attempts to copy the file. Some bad sectors are bad only some of the time, and repeated efforts to read them are often justified. (If you are really willing to expend some effort at retrieving the data stored in a bad sector, try copying it when the computer is at different temperatures and is tilted at different angles. Although this rarely works, it's worth a try.) Once a sector has

been discarded by RECOVER, it's not likely you will ever recover the data contained in that sector. Thus, RECOVER recovers files by discarding the information in bad sectors. It
doesn't recover the information near a disk flaw.

OS/2 reads and writes in sectors. Sector sizes are different
for different disk formats. A sector with a flaw is lost entirely.
So, the amount you stand to lose from a surface flaw varies
with the sector size. Normally, the larger the disk, the larger
the sectors tend to be. Also, OS/2 does not add sectors to disk
files one by one as the file grows. They are added in clusters
or allocation units, each of which may contain one or more
sectors. If a bad sector is discovered, the FAT record of the
bad spot makes the entire cluster unavailable.

Thus, a two-byte-wide flaw may make 2K unavailable
when the cluster containing it is marked as bad.

Related Commands

CHKDSK CHKDSDK will straighten out problems relating to what
         information is in what file.
FORMAT FORMAT will mark bad sectors for an entire disk as part
         of its normal operation.

REN and RENAME

• Real (DOS) or protected mode.
• Network-compatible.
• Internal subprogram in COMMAND.COM and CMD.EXE.
• Frequently used.

Purpose

Note that RENAME and REN mean the same thing. RENAME renames a file. It changes the name of a file or files to some new name.

Format of Command

RENAME *oldname newname*

REN *oldname newname* Causes the file named *oldname* to be named *newname*. These two commands are the same to OS/2. The old name may include drive and directory specifications, but the new name may not, as RENAME doesn't change the directory in which a file resides. If the new name includes * or ? characters, the corresponding characters from the old name are not changed. If the old name contains * or ?, all matching files will be renamed and the new name must contain * or ? to avoid an attempt to give several files the same name.

Examples and Description

REN C: \MY \OLDFILE NEWFILE This is a correct example. If the file exists in the current drive and directory it will be renamed.

REN C: \MY \OLDFILE C: \MY \NEWFILE This command generates an error because the new name must not contain drive or directory information.

REN C: \MY *.DOC OLD.DOC This example also generates an error because it attempts to rename more than one file to the same name.

REN C: \MY *.DOC *.OLD This command renames all files in C: \MY with the .DOC extension so they have the extension .OLD.

Note that RENAME and REN mean the same thing. RE-NAME renames a file. It changes the name of a file or files to some new name. If you think of the directory path of a file as part of its name, you might think REN could be used to move a file from one directory to another. It can't. (Some utilities, commercial or public domain, can do this. They typically are called MV or MOVE utilities.)

If you're renaming multiple files, you can specify a file-name with * or ? in it for the old filename and then use a name containing * or ? in the new name. In such cases, the characters in the old name corresponding to the * or ? in the new name remain the same, and the other characters of the old name are changed to the new pattern. Renaming is not the same as copying and deleting the original. RENAME does not copy the file, it renames the file in place.

REPLACE

- Real (DOS) or protected mode.
- Network-compatible.
- External program.
- Can operate on entire directories.
- Occasionally used.

Purpose

REPLACE copies files from a source disk to a destination disk, replacing those files on the destination whose names match specified files on the source disk. This is especially handy for software updates. REPLACE can also be used to add only those files which do not match filenames on the target disk.

You may use REPLACE to copy only into a selected directory of the destination disk, to copy to all subdirectories of a specified directory, or to copy to all directories on the destination disk.

Formats of Command

REPLACE *source_drive:filename* [*destination_drive:*] [*destination_directory*] [/A] [/S] [/P] [/R] [/W]
    Source_drive: and *filename* must be specified. *Filename* may optionally include a directory specification. *Filename* may include the * and ? characters. *Destination_drive:* is optional and, if not specified, is taken to be the current default drive. *Destination_directory* is optional; if omitted, the current default directory for the destination drive is presumed.

/A /A causes REPLACE not to replace but to add files to the destination which are on the source but not in the destination directory. You may not use /A if the destination is to include subdirectories as specified.

/S /S causes REPLACE to scan all subdirectories of the destination and to replace all files found in those directories that match source files. Using this with the destination being the root directory of the destination disk causes all matching files on the entire disk to be replaced. (Watch out for files with similar names from different software systems.)

/P /P causes REPLACE to ask for confirmation from the console before each replacement. It's a good idea for extensive replacements—but it's easy to answer incorrectly, so don't rely too heavily on this.

/R /R allows REPLACE to replace files which have the read-only attribute set (see ATTRIB for more about read-only files). Such files are not normally allowed to be altered unless the read-only attribute is removed.

/W /W causes REPLACE to wait for you to change floppy disks before starting. It's only needed if the REPLACE program itself is on a floppy disk. Rarely used.

Warnings

It's easy to replace files unintentionally because many software systems use similar filenames. Watch your use of the /S switch, especially in commands of the form REPLACE A: C: \ /S, which may replace files all over a hard disk.

Examples and Description

REPLACE A:*.* C: \ /S /R For each file in the current directory of A:, REPLACE will search all of C: for files with the same name, and, wherever they're found, it will replace them with the A: file of the same name. This command is powerful but dangerous.

REPLACE A:*.EXE C: \ BIN For each .EXE file on A:, replaces the corresponding .EXE file in C: \ BIN.

REPLACE A:*.EXE C: \ BIN /A For each .EXE file on A: which is not found in C: \ BIN, REPLACE copies the file to C: \ BIN. The combination of the last example and this one is the same as COPY A:*.EXE C: \ BIN.

SET

- Both real and protected modes.
- Network-compatible.
- Internal subprogram in CMD.EXE and COMMAND.COM.
- Occasionally used.

Purpose

SET sets the value of environment variables.

Formats of Command

SET *name value* Sets the variable called *name* to have the value *value*. No spaces or command characters are allowed in either string.

SET *name=value* Does the same as the last command, but makes more sense.

SET *name* If a variable called *name* exists, it's deleted.

SET *name=* Same as the last command.

Examples and Description

> **SET TMP=D: **
> **SET RAMDISK=D:**
> **SET USER=JOE**
> **SET HOME=C: \ USR \ JOE**
> **SET DISPLAY=VGA** These are typical of the sets one might find handy in batch files.

SET sets the value of environment variables. These variables each have a name and a value. The name and its value may be any string of characters that don't have a special meaning to the command processor. These variables and values are accessible to any program or batch file and to the command line in protected mode. In batch files and on the protected mode command line, %*name*%, where *name* is the name of a currently defined environment variable, will be read by OS/2 as the current value of the variable. If there isn't a variable with a matching name, %*name*% is treated as if it were not there.

The current names and values of all environment variables are inherited by each program from the program which

starts it. This includes the command processor programs
COMMAND.COM and CMD.EXE. So, if you run a child command processor started by the current (now parent) command
processor, the child will inherit all the variables known to the
parent. However, a program cannot change the environment
variables or their values for its parent. Therefore, if the child
command processor changes variable values, deletes variables,
or adds new ones, these alterations will disappear when the
child processor exits and control returns to the parent. In other
words, if any program changes, deletes, or adds variables,
those acts will only be known to that program and any other
programs it starts.

Many programs rely on environment variables to set options or to indicate where certain files should be found. To
prepare for such programs, use the SET command to set the
needed variables. This applies to COMMAND.COM and to
CMD.EXE as well. The variables *path, prompt,* and *append*
mean something special to COMMAND.COM (though *append*
is a bit odd—see the APPEND command). The variables *path*
and *prompt* influence how CMD.EXE behaves (where it looks
for programs and what prompt it displays while waiting for a
command), and DPATH is presumed to be used by programs
looking for data or auxilliary files in protected mode. You can
change these variables with the PATH, PROMPT, and DPATH
commands, but you can also change them with SET.

In protected mode, each instance of CMD.EXE in each
session has a different set of environment variables. These are
often initialized by the OS2INIT.CMD batch file executed
whenever the program selector is used to create a new session.
(And, of course, real mode has its own set of environment
variables.)

In real mode, environment variables are often created and
given initial values in AUTOEXEC.BAT, the batch command
run whenever the real mode session is started.

In real mode, if you have problems with *out of environment
space* messages, put the command SHELL=COMMAND.COM
/P /E:*n* in your CONFIG.SYS file on the drive from which you
boot. The *n* may be set to the number of bytes you need in

your environment to avoid this message (1024 is a good starting point). Then reboot. This is a permanent solution. The temporary solution is to give the real mode command COMMAND /P /E:1024. This will expand your real mode environment until your next boot. You won't have problems like this in protected mode, as the environment space is elastic. In real mode, the size is fixed by COMMAND.COM and stays the same until a new instance of COMMAND.COM with a different E: option replaces the currently running COMMAND.COM. (See COMMAND.)

After SET has done its job, the names of variables are displayed by SET as all uppercase (%*name*% may be in lowercase, but OS/2 doesn't care), but the values always retain the capitalization used when the variables were set.

Related Commands

PATH   Sets the *path* variable.
PROMPT Sets the *prompt* variable.
DPATH   Sets the *dpath* variable. SET can set any of them.
APPEND Sets the *append* variable (if you use the /E option), and does some other things as well.

SETCOM40
- Real (DOS) mode Only.
- Network-compatible.
- External program.
- Rarely used.

Purpose
To allow real mode access to ports normally under exclusive control of protected mode.

Formats of Command
SETCOM40 COM*n*=ON

SETCOM40 COM*n*=OFF For AT compatibles, *n* in these commands may be 1 or 2. For PS/2 machines, *n* may be 1, 2, or 3. (Some AT clones may allow you to use COM3. If yours does and you are using the standard IBM serial device drivers, you won't need to use SETCOM40 for COM3 because protected mode programs don't even know it exists. Your DOS programs can have COM3.

Description
As discussed under the MODE command, OS/2 serial port communications are normally handled through a special program called a *device driver*, which is linked into OS/2 when it starts. One side effect of the OS/2 serial communications device drivers is that they hide the serial ports from DOS programs and make it appear that there are none. This is to keep DOS programs from toying with the ports while protected mode programs are trying to use them. SETCOM40 overrides this hiding of ports and makes them available to real mode DOS programs. It can also be used to hide them again.

So, if the usual OS/2 device drivers are installed, you must use SETCOM40 to make the serial ports COM1, COM2 and, for PS/2 machines, COM3, available to DOS programs. You need this switch, because OS/2 cannot control conflicting accesses to these ports from protected mode and real mode programs. OS/2 leaves it to you to be sure that no protected mode program will use the ports while they are accessible to a real mode program.

To use a serial port in real mode, you must first make sure that there are no protected mode programs using the desired port and then give the command SETCOM40 COM1=ON (presuming it's COM1 you want to use). Then you run the DOS program that needs the port. When it's done, give the command SETCOM40 COM1=OFF to return the port to the exclusive control of the driver that serves protected mode.

If this seems a clunky way to do things, blame it on the design of the Intel 80286 processor, not on Microsoft or IBM. (But, if OS/2 were built for the 80386, this wouldn't be such a problem area.)

If you're using a serial printer, you don't normally need to worry about using SETCOM40 to make it work. The whole job of printer management is handled by the SPOOL and PRINT programs. In fact, if you have a serial printer installed in the usual way (see the section in the next chapter on installing serial printers), you should never use SETCOM40 to refer to the port to which that printer is attached.

If you have serial ports to spare, you may decide to dedicate one to real mode and the others to protected mode. To do this, pick your ports, then include the needed SETCOM40 command for the port given to real mode in your AUTOEXEC.BAT file and make sure your protected mode programs always use another port.

Contention over ports is not often a practical problem because communications programs for modems and the like won't work right in OS/2 real mode anyway. There are timing problems related to multitasking in addition to port access problems. Plan on doing your communicating with programs written especially to run in OS/2 protected mode. (But if you use a serial mouse, you might have a problem.)

Related Commands
See the MODE command.

SORT

- Both real and protected modes.
- Network-compatible.
- External program.
- Occasionally used.

Purpose

SORT is a utility program that sorts the lines in text files alphabetically.

Formats of Command

SORT [/R] [/+nn] <*file* SORT gets its input from *file* and sends its output to the screen. To send the output to a file, add >*outfile* (using the name of the file you want). SORT may also send its output to another program (rarely useful) if you add | *otherpgm* to the command instead of the > clause.

otherpgm | **SORT [/R] [/+nn]** Same as the last form, except SORT gets its input from the output of some other program. Again you can redirect the output of SORT to a file with > (or >> to append to a file), or to another program with |.

Description

See the DIR command for examples. SORT is a utility program that sorts the lines in text files alphabetically. In this case, the definition of a *line* is any string of characters terminated by a carriage return and a line feed. In this case, *alphabetically* means in order of the ASCII codes for the characters in the lines. If you don't use any options, SORT sorts a file's lines by comparing them character by character, starting with the first character of each line and continuing until it can figure out which line should come first.

SORT is a bit unusual: The file it sorts cannot be specified as part of the SORT command. SORT gets its input from stdin (standard input) and sends its output to stdout (standard output). You must use I/O redirection command characters to get something into SORT, and you must use them to put SORT's output anywhere except on the screen.

SORT allows you to specify that it should skip some number of characters at the beginning of each line before beginning its comparison, and you may tell it you want the output in reverse order. SORT treats the upper- and lowercase of a given letter as the same value. It ignores case for all letters. It alters the order of special characters if foreign language support is implemented.

SORT will be unable to process input longer than about 63K, and it's slow as SORT programs go. If you do much sorting, buy a SORT program or get one from the public domain. Programmers have a special fascination for sorting, so there are many inexpensive ones from which you may choose.

SPOOL
- Runs in protected mode only, but serves both modes.
- External program.
- Network-compatible.
- Frequently used.

Purpose
SPOOL receives output and reroutes it through a temporary file to the printer of your choice.

Format of Command
SPOOL [*drive:*][*directory*] [/D:LPT*n*] [/O:LPT*n*]

[/O:COM*m*] The drive and directory tell SPOOL where to put its temporary files. If not specified, the default-drive directory \SPOOL is presumed. You should make this directory and forever stay out of it. More than one copy of SPOOL can use the same directory.

/D The /D option specifies from which parallel printer port SPOOL is to steal its input. This is the port to which you should tell your programs to send their output. It may or may not be where SPOOL actually sends the material. If you do not specify /D, LPT1 is presumed. (You can use PRN for LPT1, but it's old-fashioned.)

/O The /O option specifies either the parallel port (LPT1, LPT2, or LPT3) or the serial port (COM1 or COM2 for AT-type machines and COM1, COM2, or COM3 for PS/2 machines or others with serial device drivers supporting COM3). If you don't specify the /O option, output is sent to the same port from which input is stolen. Remember that once a copy of SPOOL starts it runs without further interaction with you until you reboot or turn off the computer. So get the command right before you execute it.

Examples and Description
DETACH SPOOL C:\SPOOL /D:LPT1 /O:COM1
DETACH SPOOL C:\SPOOL /D:LPT2 /O:LPT1
DETACH SPOOL C:\SPOOL /D:LPT3 /O:LPT2 These three commands set up a system with one serial printer

attached to COM1 and two parallel printers, one attached
to LPT1 and the other to LPT2. Programs that print will
see these as LPT1, LPT2, and LPT3. When a program
sends output to LPT1, in reality it will be printed on the
printer attached to COM1. Output sent to LPT2 will end
up on the printer attached to LPT1, and output sent to
LPT3 will go to the printer attached to LPT2. Note that
additional CONFIG.SYS and regular commands will be
needed to set up the COM1 port for use with a particular
printer.

RUN SPOOL C: \ SPOOL /D:LPT1 /O:COM1
RUN SPOOL C: \ SPOOL /D:LPT2 /O:LPT1
RUN SPOOL C: \ SPOOL /D:LPT3 /O:LPT2 These commands do just the same as those above, but they are intended for inclusion in the CONFIG.SYS file on the root
directory of the boot drive. As OS/2 finishes its loading
process, the spoolers begin operating.

Spool is an old computer term originating from Simulta-
neous Peripheral Operation Off-Line (also known as Simulta-
neous Printer Operation Off-Line). The idea of spooling is to
free your computer from having to wait for the printer to catch
up before it goes on to another task. SPOOL in OS/2 is a program you almost always use and almost never see. It is normally run detached from the console so doesn't generate any
screen output, nor does it need any keyboard or mouse input.

SPOOL does three jobs.

- It spools. That is, it takes output sent by a program to a
printer and reroutes it into a temporary file.
- From the temporary file, it periodically sends out characters
at a rate that won't get ahead of the printer. It also allows
output designated by a program as going to one output port
to be sent to another.
- Finally, it keeps print output from different programs separate. If it were not there to manage this separation, lines of
printing from different concurrent programs would come out
intermixed.

The SPOOL program needs to know three things when it is running.

- It needs to know which printer's output it is to reroute and place in a file.
- It needs to know a directory in which it can keep its temporary files without getting in your way.
- It needs to know the printer to which it is to send the data.

If you don't tell it otherwise, it steals output designated for parallel printer port LPT1, puts its files in the \SPOOL directory of the default drive, and sends its output to the same printer port from which it's stealing.

There are three ways to run the SPOOL program.

- You can start a session for it and give the SPOOL command, but it will never end and the screen for that session will never change. It will be wasted.
- You can preceed the SPOOL command with the DETACH command, to cause SPOOL to run by itself without a screen attachment.
- Finally, you can use a CONFIG.SYS file command which is executed when OS/2 starts.

The appropriate CONFIG.SYS command is RUN followed by an otherwise normal SPOOL command. The CONFIG.SYS RUN command does the same job as a DETACH command. It only does it automatically when the system starts up. Once your SPOOL commands are correct for your printer arrangement, it's best to put them into CONFIG.SYS RUN commands and forget about them until you buy a new printer.

The input device (the printer SPOOL steals from) must be a parallel printer: PRN, LPT1, LPT2, or LPT3 (PRN and LPT1 are the same). But, SPOOL can send its output to any of these or COM1, or COM2, or, if you have a PS/2 compatible, to COM3. This is how OS/2 supports serial printers attached to a COM port. Unfortunately, SPOOL doesn't do the whole job for serial printers. The COM port must be managed by a loaded device driver and it must be set to the proper communications parameters for your printer before it will work for

SPOOL. See the section in the next chapter on installing serial printers for the rest of the story.

If you have more than one printer, you can run more than one copy of SPOOL. In fact, you can run one SPOOL for each printer. Just make sure that none of your SPOOL commands list the same input device and that none list the same output device. (But it's all right to have an input device for one SPOOL as the output device of another.)

In real mode, there's one problem with SPOOL: It doesn't know when to quit. Remember that one of SPOOL's jobs is to keep output from different programs separate. Part of the way it does this is to collect all printer output from a program in a file until the program tells it that the batch is complete and the file is ready for printing. DOS programs don't do this because they were built before SPOOL was offered. As a result, the print output from most DOS programs will continue to go to the file and not start actually printing until the program ends.

If the program doesn't tell SPOOL where the end of a print run is, you can. You do this by holding the Ctrl and Alt keys and pressing the PrtSc key (don't hit Del by accident). This tells SPOOL that what it already has from this program is a logically connected whole and to go ahead and print it. It also means that output from other programs may be printed immediately after this batch goes through.

If you hit Ctrl-Alt-PrtSc at the wrong time, you might find that your DOS program output will go in two batches with output from some protected mode program in between. Since many programs, especially word processors, do some spooling of their own, at first you might find it tricky to know when your program has finished sending a lump of material to the printer, but practice will quickly make it clear.

When in doubt, wait and don't press Ctrl-Alt-PrtSc. At the worst, you'll have to wait a little longer until your output is printed.

Related Commands

PRINT   The PRINT command is used to send files to the SPOOL
        program for printing.

START

- Protected mode only.
- Network-compatible.
- Internal subprogram in CMD.EXE.
- Occasionally used.

Purpose

The START command is an alternate way of starting new sessions.

Format of Command

START [*"session description"*] [**/C**] [*"command"*] The *session description*, if specified, must appear in quotation marks. It will be shown in the program selector to describe the session created. The /C option specifies that when the command that follows is completed, the session will be closed. *Command* may be a full OS/2 protected mode command with its own I/O redirection and command combinations. The session created will begin execution of this command immediately. If no command is specified, the command processor CMD.EXE is presumed to be the program you want run at the start of the session. If the command contains the redirection or command combination characters <, >, |, or &, it must be enclosed in quotation marks. Otherwise the quotation marks are optional (but recommended). Finally, if the command is contained in quotation marks, the session description must be specified even if it's only a blank in quotation marks.

Example and Description

START *"FAVORITE WORD PROCESSOR"* /C *"WP"*
Starts a session running your favorite word processor. When the word processing program is exited, the session will be ended (because /C was specified).

The START command is an alternate way of starting new sessions. Usually you do this with the program selector, but by using START, you can perform the same operation automatically from within a batch file. Usually START commands are

227

included in your STARTUP.CMD batch file. This batch file is run in protected mode when OS/2 is started. START commands in STARTUP.CMD are a way to start automatically all of the sessions with which you normally work. You may also place start commands in .CMD files to start several sessions which you tend to use together.

The START command allows you to specify a string that will be shown describing the new session in the program selector. You may also use START to specify the program or a .CMD file to be run in the session when it begins (just as you would manually from the program selector). Finally, you have the option of using START to begin a session with a .CMD file or program and then end the session as soon as that batch file or program is completed. This is a way to build a session for use with a particular program and then make the session disappear when the program is complete. It avoids the housekeeping effort usually required to remove inactive sessions.

Note that, like the CMD command, START potentially contains a command within a command. As for the CMD command, if the command the new session is to execute includes any I/O redirection or command combination characters such as <, >, |, or &, the entire command that the new session is to perform should be enclosed in quotation marks to keep all of its parts together. Also, since the character string you provide is normally in quotation marks, if you place the command in quotation marks, you must provide a session description string so OS/2 doesn't think the command is a session description. The best practice is to provide a session description string in quotation marks (even if it's just a blank) and always include the entire command for the new session in quotation marks. This not only avoids misunderstandings between you and OS/2, but also makes the commands easier to read when you've forgotten what they do.

When writing batch files to be used as the starting command for a session, keep in mind that your batch file will not know what the current drive or directory is, and it must refer to directories and files with full path specifications until the batch file sets the current drive and directory for itself. Also, such startup commands (like the program selector's startup

batch file OS2INIT.CMD) are usually used to set up *path*,
prompt, *dpath* and similar environment variables for the session to use.

In addition to using START to run your commonly used
sessions, it can be a handy alternative to DETACH for processes that may need console interaction. You can even use it
as a test for processes you plan to run detached. If, under any
circumstances, the command requires console input or output,
it's not a suitable candidate for use with DETACH.

Related Commands

You can use the program selector for the same job, but not a
batch file.

DETACH   DETACH runs a program outside of the session where it
was started, as does START. The difference is that
START gives the program a different session with its
own virtual console, while DETACH runs the process
outside any session and with no virtual console.

CMD.EXE   CMD.EXE, when it runs a program, runs it in the current session, not a different session. CMD as a command, runs as a subprocess to the current session, not a
different session.

SUBST

• Protected mode only.
• Not network-compatible.
• External program.
• Rarely used.

Purpose

SUBST allows you to define a drive letter as referring to a directory on another drive.

Formats of Command

SUBST Lists any currently active substitutions.

SUBST *drive1:* *[drive2:]directory* Causes future references to *drive1:* to actually refer to the specified *drive2:* and *directory* following. If *drive2:* is omitted, it's presumed to be the current default drive. The directory specification may be a full or partial path name (one starting with \ from the root directory or one starting at the current default directory). Either way, SUBST converts it to a complete drive and directory specification before defining *drive1:* as its alias.

SUBST *drive1:* /D Removes the previous substitution of *drive1:* for some directory.

Warnings

Any command like SUBST that makes the file system appear other than it really is can lead to confusion and operator error—sometimes with serious results. Avoid such confusing redefinitions of file-system component names.

To help avoid confusion, it's best to select drive letters for substitutions that are very unlikely to be real drives. Using drive letters like T:, U:, and so on, tends to clarify that these are not real drives.

Examples and Description

CD C:\USR\JOE
SUBST J: C:\USR\JOE
SUBST J:. Following the CD command shown above, the two SUBST commands say the same thing.

SUBST J: /D J: Returns to its normal meaning which is probably an invalid drive specification.

SUBST allows you to define a drive letter as referring to a directory on another drive. After SUBST is used to define such a mythical drive, the directory specified will appear to programs to be the root directory of the newly created mythical drive. All subdirectories of the directory aliased to the new drive name will appear as subdirectories of the mythical drive. You can also use the SUBST command to list active substitutions and to delete an active substitution.

There's rarely a compelling need for the SUBST command when using modern programs. It's only required when some program requires that certain files be on a drive with a certain name and you have them elsewhere or simply don't have a drive by that name at all.

There's also a deceptive use of SUBST. If you specify a drive that really exists as being an alias for a directory on another drive, most commands and programs will not be able to access the real drive. It is effectively hidden. This is generally not a favorable condition. The usual selection of a drive name is some letter not normally used in your system.

Related Commands

ASSIGN ASSIGN makes a drive letter refer to another drive.

JOIN   JOIN makes a drive look like a subdirectory. SUBST makes a subdirectory look like a drive.

SYS

- Real (DOS) or protected mode.
- Not network-compatible.
- External Program.
- Rarely Used.

Purpose

SYS copies the special operating system boot file IBMIO.COM and IBMDOS.COM (or alternative names with different editions of OS/2) from the current default disk to another disk.

Format of Command

SYS *drive:* Copies system files to the specified drive.

Warnings

Always test disks on which the SYS command has been used before relying on them.

Example and Description

SYS A: Copies the system files from the current default disk to the floppy disk in drive A:.

SYS copies the special operating system boot file IBMIO.COM and IBMDOS.COM (or alternative names with different editions of OS/2) from the current default disk to another disk or floppy disk. You cannot use COPY to do this, as these special hidden system files must be in a special position in the disk's root directory for your hardware to be able to load them when the system boots. At the time these files are loaded, your computer does not yet have the necessary programming loaded to access files in the usual way.

SYS only copies these files, not all the files copied by FORMAT with the /S option. The destination disk must not have any other processes using its files and it must be newly formatted or already contain boot files from OS/2 or DOS. Otherwise, SYS will not find the location it needs for these files.

For new disks, it's generally easier to use the FORMAT command with the /S option because it does the whole job of transferring all the needed operating system files to the disk, and you need to format new disks in any event. SYS is normally used only when converting from one version of DOS or OS/2 to another.

TIME

- Both real and protected modes.
- Network-compatible.
- Internal subprogram in CMD.EXE and COMMAND.COM.
- Occasionally used.

Purpose

The TIME command is no mystery. It displays or allows you to set the time of day known to your system.

In the typical microcomputer design, there are two clock systems. One is a *realtime clock,* which is a silicon chip driven by a battery, much like a digital watch. As it is battery operated, it doesn't forget the time (it doesn't stop working) when the system is turned off or unplugged.

The second clock system is built into the normal operation of the computer. In the typical PC- or AT-compatible design, while the computer is operating, a chip is set to count electrical cycles until a certain number is reached. This number is chosen so that the count is exhausted 18.2 times every second (about every 55 milliseconds). When this happens, the counter chip sends a signal to a chip capable of interrupting the processor. When the processor is interrupted, it runs a small piece of program called an *interrupt handler.* This program simply maintains memory locations for the current year, month, day, hour, minute, second, and decimal part of a second. On each interruption, these counters are updated to keep track of the time of day. (The system knows about leap year and how many days are in each month.)

When a program asks OS/2 the time of day, it gets this system time from the program-operated clock. But since this clock relies upon memory, which is destroyed when power to the computer goes off, there is no guarantee that it was set accurately when the computer last started. That's what the battery-operated clock is for: Whenever OS/2 starts, it reads the battery-operated clock to set the system clock to its initial value. Even though the timing of certain events within your computer is accurate to billionths of a second (nanoseconds) as in 120-nanosecond RAM, sometimes your system clock will slip a bit. (Usually this is due to the processor being unable to answer a clock interrupt from time to time and dropping a count. Also, real mode program errors can scramble the current time and date setting.)

You can use the time command to make sure your machine is set to the right time. When you set your system time and date (see the DATE command), you don't set the battery-operated clock. Usually you need a separate program supplied by your computer manufacturer to set the battery-operated clock.

The TIME command displays and optionally sets the current system time as maintained by the program. The setting you make will be lost when you boot or turn off the computer, but the time should be set properly from the battery-operated clock as OS/2 is loaded.

The cost of even the least expensive clone is a bit steep for an alarm clock, so should you care about the accuracy of the time it maintains? Well, yes. First, remember those time and date parameters in the BACKUP, RESTORE and XCOPY commands. They are available so that you can keep different versions of the same file straight. If your system clock is significantly off, you cannot tell which of two files is more recent. In database and programming systems as well as in ordinary file-system housekeeping, this can become a serious problem.

As a rule of thumb, every time you reboot your system or start a new day, whichever is first, run the time and date commands to check the system clock.

Formats of Command

TIME This simple form of the command displays the current system time and asks if you want to alter it.

TIME *hh*[*:mm*][*:ss*][*.cc*] In this form, the command sets the system time to the time you specify. Note that 24-hour time is used so that *hh* may range from 0 through 23 hours, *mm* is for minutes, *ss* is for seconds, and *.cc* is for hundreths of a second. If you leave out one parameter, you must also leave out all of those that follow. No spaces should appear within the time value specification. All parts of the time not specified are taken to be 0. If your system is set for a country other than the U.S., the colons and periods may be replaced by other characters commonly used in the country for which your system is set.

Related Commands

DATE The DATE command is similar to the TIME command.

TRACE and TRACEFMT

- Protected mode only.
- Network-compatible.
- External program.
- Very rarely used.

Purpose

These two commands allow the creation and maintenance of a *trace*, which indicates what the computer has been doing. These commands are only useful under the direction of a technician.

TREE

• Both real and protected modes.
• Network-compatible.
• External program.
• Rarely used.

Purpose

The TREE command displays all directories on a specified disk and can list all files in each directory. TREE output may be very long for a large, heavily used hard disk.

CHKDSK with the /V option and ATTRIB with the /S option can each produce a list of all files on a disk. For some purposes, you may prefer the output from ATTRIB or CHKDSK (especially if you are planning to sort the list with the SORT command).

Formats of Command

TREE [*drive:*] [/F] The optional drive specification indicates which disk's directories are to be output. If no drive is specified, the current default drive is presumed. The /F option causes TREE to output the names of all files, directory by directory, intermingled with its usual directory output.

Examples

TREE C: /F Lists all directories and files on drive C:.

TYPE

- Both real and protected modes.
- Network-compatible.
- Internal subprogram in CMD.EXE and COMMAND.COM.
- Frequently used.

Purpose

TYPE copies a file or, in protected mode, files, to stdout (standard output), which is the screen if you do not use I/O redirection to send it somewhere else. TYPE is intended to display text files, but there is nothing to prevent you from typing other files. Nontext files will appear as gibberish on your screen and make your console beep if there happen to be any bell character codes in the file (ASCII value of 7).

The only processing or conversion TYPE does is to expand tabs to spaces in such a way that tab row positions are eight characters apart. (This can be handy if you want to convert the tabs in a file to spaces and can get along with the standard eight-column tab positions.)

In real mode, you may only specify one file in a TYPE command. In protected mode, you may specify multiple files and you may use file patterns containing ? and *.

Formats of Command

TYPE *filename* For use in real mode. In real mode, the *filename* may include drive and directory, but must refer to a single file and may not use ? or *.

TYPE *filespec* [*filespec...*] For protected mode. In protected mode, *filespecs* may include drive and directory specifications and the wildcard characters ? and *, and there may be multiple *filespecs* separated by spaces.

Examples and Description

FOR %%F IN (C: \ USR \ *.DOC C: \ USR \ *.BAK) DO
    TYPE %%F For use in real mode. It does the same as the following protected mode command.

TYPE C: \ USR \ *.DOC C: \ USR \ *.BAK TYPE TEXT.TAB >
TEXT.NTB This command will make TEXT.NTB a copy
of TEXT.TAB with all tabs expanded to eight-character tab
stops.

Related Commands

If you don't want tabs expanded, use COPY *filespec* CON instead of TYPE. If you really want a binary file to be sent to
the console, it's better to use COPY *binfile* /B CON. This will
preset the console to not treat certain character codes specially.

VER

• Both real and protected modes.
• Network-compatible.
• Internal subprogram in CMD.EXE and COMMAND.COM.
• Rarely used.

Purpose

VER simply outputs the currently running version name for OS/2 or DOS. It can be handy, especially when using a computer your are not familiar with.

Format of Command

VER

VERIFY

• Both real and protected modes.
• Network-compatible.
• Internal subprogram in CMD.EXE and COMMAND.COM.
• Rarely used.

Purpose

VERIFY sets extra verification tests for all hard disk and floppy disk write operations on or off. With verification off, writes to disk are still checked fairly thoroughly by the disk subsystem hardware. It's rare for the verification added by VERIFY to unearth a fault which would not be caught by OS/2 even if VERIFY were off.

Programs may also set verification on or off but rarely do so.

VERIFY ON slows the operation of your disk system. Use VERIFY ON only if you suspect unreported errors are being written to your disk. If you never use the VERIFY command, it will always be off. If you specify VERIFY ON, it stays on for the session in which it is set until it is reset with the VERIFY OFF command. Each session's verification setting is independent of all other sessions.

The MODE DSKT VER=ON command sets verification on, but only for floppy disk writes. VERIFY applies to both floppy disks and hard disks.

Formats of Command

VERIFY ON
VERIFY OFF

VOL

• Both real and protected modes.
• Not network-compatible.
• Internal subprogram in CMD.EXE and COMMAND.COM.
• Rarely used.

Purpose

VOL displays the volume label for the disk.

Formats of Command

VOL [*drive:*]
VOL *drive:* [*drive:*] In both forms, *drive:* is of the form A:. If
    a drive is not specified, the current default drive is pre-
    sumed. In protected mode, you may specify more than
    one drive as shown in the second form above (separate
    them with spaces). VOL will report on each drive.

Description

VOL displays the volume label for the disk or floppy disk in a
drive. (Why it is a separate command from the LABEL command which sets the volume label is a mystery.) Since the DIR
command outputs volume labels annoyingly often, the VOL
command is rarely used.

The only option or parameter to the VOL command is the
drive to report on. In protected mode, you may specify more
than one drive in one VOL command.

Sometimes VOL can be handy in batch files working with
floppy disks. For example, if you want to maintain a list of all
floppy disks which have been subject to a particular batch file,
you might include a command like VOL A: >>BATCH.LOG
in the batch file.

XCOPY

- Real (DOS) or protected mode.
- Network-compatible.
- External program.
- Can operate on entire directories and directory trees.
- Occasionally used.

Purpose

XCOPY is an extended COPY command. It adds the abilities to create directories, copy entire file trees including multiple subdirectories at any depth, select files to copy based upon their modification date, and limit the files copied to only those marked as modified with the archive file attribute. (See the ATTRIB command for more about attributes.)

Format of Command

XCOPY [*drive1:*][*dir1*][*filepat1*] [*drive2:*][*dir2*][*filepat2*] [**/S**] [**/D:**mm-dd-yy] [**/E**] [**/P**] [**/V**] [**/A**] [**/M**] Either *drive1:*, *dir1*, or **filepat1** must be specified as the source of files to copy. If you omit *drive1:* or *dir1*, the current default drive and directories are used as usual in OS/2. If *filepat1* is not specified, all files in the source directory are presumed (that is, no *filepat* is the same as *.*.) The *filepat1* source file pattern may use the ? and * wildcard characters. You must specify one of *drive2:*, *dir2*, or *filepat2* as a destination. Again, standard defaults apply. If the destination is valid but doesn't exist, XCOPY can't tell whether it should be a file or a directory, so it asks you.

/A The /A option causes XCOPY to copy only files from the source that have their archive attribute set to On—files marked as modified since they were last backed up (however, don't count on the validity of this attribute as ATTRIB and XCOPY itself as well as other programs can turn this attribute on and off).

/D The /D option means to include only files with a modification date equal to or later than that specified are to be included in the copy (the - characters in the date may be replaced by other characters if you are using country support).

/E The /E option causes XCOPY to create copied directories on the destination even if they will be empty (usually it is best to set this option when using the /S option).

/M The /M option has the same effect as the /A option, except that just after a file is copied, the source copy has its archive (modified) attribute set off.

/P The /P option causes XCOPY to ask for confirmation before copying each file.

/S The /S option means all of the source's subdirectories and the files and subdirectories they contain are to be included in the copy.

/V The /V option sets disk-write verification on (as with the VERIFY command) for the duration of the XCOPY; use this option if you think your destination disk may be failing.

Warnings

If a file on the destination has the same name as a file copied from the source, it will be overwritten and destroyed by the new copy from the source.

Examples and Description

XCOPY C: \ D: \ /S /E This will copy all directories (including empty ones) and files on C: (except hidden and system files) to drive D:.

XCOPY C: \DATA A: \ /E /M /S This will copy every modified file in C: \DATA and all of its subdirectories to drive A:. You may repeat this command multiple times as it fills floppy disks.

XCOPY is an extended COPY command. It adds the abilities to create directories, copy entire file trees including multiple subdirectories at any depth, select files to copy based upon their modification date, and limit the files copied to only those marked as modified with the archive file attribute. (See the ATTRIB command for more about attributes.)

XCOPY behaves somewhat differently, depending upon whether its source and destination file specifications refer to files or directories.

If the source specified is a directory, all files in the directory are copied to the destination. With the /S option, not
only are all files copied, but all subdirectories and all of the
files they contain are also copied to the destination. This is
one way in which XCOPY will create directories on the target
disk.

If the destination is a directory and /S is specified, the
source files and directories will be copied into the destination
directory. (As above, using the /S results in subdirectories of
the destination directory being created). If the destination is a
file, the source files will be copied into the file, but, of course,
subdirectories of the destination file cannot be created. If the
destination does not exist, XCOPY asks you if it is to be a file
or directory. (Watch out for this question. Your decision may
cause problems, if you run XCOPY detached.) If you indicate
that the destination is a directory, it will be created when the
first file is copied to it.

Generally XCOPY will only create a directory on the target if it has some files to put into the directory. You can use
the /E option to force creation of directories even if they will
be empty.

With the /A and /M switches, XCOPY can be limited to
copying only files with the archive attribute on, that is, files
marked as having been changed since they were last backed
up. With the /M option, this attribute for the source is turned
off after the copy is made. In this way, XCOPY behaves like
the BACKUP command. Using the /M option, XCOPY and
ATTRIB can be used to create a multiple floppy disk copy of a
directory or a file tree.

As an example, assume you have a directory named
DATA and you want to copy all its files to floppy disks. You
realize that this will require more than one floppy disk. To do
this, make DATA the current default directory and give the
following commands:

attrib +a *.*
xcopy . a: /m.

The ATTRIB command will mark all of the files as modified. As XCOPY copies the files to the floppy disk in A:, it will

mark each file it copies as no longer modified. When XCOPY runs out of floppy disk space, it will fail with an error message. Then you can insert another floppy disk and press F3 and the ENTER key to repeat the last command; XCOPY will then start copying again. It will not recopy the same files because they've been marked as no longer modified. You can continue this process through an unlimited number of files and floppy disks.

When you're done, you should usually issue the command ATTRIB +A *.* to again set all of the files as modified. If you don't do this, the next time you perform a routine BACKUP, these files might not be included in the backup. The safe course is to mark files as modified when you are in doubt about their status.

You may notice that XCOPY used in this way does much the same job as BACKUP. In fact, you can often use XCOPY as a substitute for BACKUP. However, BACKUP can do one trick that is beyond XCOPY. BACKUP can copy one large file to span multiple floppy disks. XCOPY can only copy files that will entirely fit on one destination floppy disk. (By the way, if you have a file larger than a floppy disk, you should consider breaking it down into smaller files. You probably won't be able to do this with database files, but for other files, OS/2 works best with files of moderate size.)

If you think about it, there are probably many situations in which XCOPY, especially with the /S, /A, and /M options, can help you in file system housecleaning. Since XCOPY is not often used in other everyday operations, the trick is to remember what XCOPY can do and to use it when appropriate.

Related Commands

COPY and MD With repeated COPY and MD commands, you can do anything XCOPY can do. It just involves more typing.

COPY COPY will copy files, but it will not create directories and it ignores the modification date and archive attribute of files.

BACKUP   BACKUP will do what XCOPY does as well as copy
              large files across multiple floppy disks; however,
              the copies it makes are not in normal form and can
              only be usable after they have been processed with
              the RESTORE command to go back to the same di-
              rectories from which the BACKUP was made.

Chapter 7
How To

Chapter 7
How To

This chapter is broken into sections designed to give you assistance with specific problems. The discussion will be limited to the subject at hand and complete unto itself so far as is possible, given the subject matter.

How to Install OS/2 the First Time

Installing OS/2 is not difficult. The hard part is making sure you can still use DOS if OS/2 fails you or if one of your programs doesn't get along with OS/2. It's assumed that you have a hard disk named C: and that it currently has DOS 3.3 installed.

First, boot the computer with DOS. Then insert a blank, formatted floppy disk into drive A: and perform the command SYS A:. This will place the boot files on your floppy disk. You still have a bit more to save. Copy your AUTOEXEC.BAT file to A:, as well as your CONFIG.SYS file and COMMAND.COM. You're through with the floppy disk for the moment.

Now comes what might be the hard part. Your DOS commands must be neatly segregated from other programs in a directory of their own. Make a directory C:\DOS33 and copy all of your DOS command files and DOS .SYS files (including COMMAND.COM) to it. (If you have your original DOS floppy disk, you can copy them from it.)

Make sure none of your DOS programs are anywhere but in C:\DOS33. The problem is that some DOS command programs from one version are not compatible with other versions of DOS, let alone OS/2. If they are executed in OS/2, they will not work and may even prevent you from using the OS/2 version that does work. Other programs usually aren't a problem. Most programs require a minimum version of DOS, but they work on it and all later versions of DOS, including OS/2 real mode. Only DOS programs like FIND, SORT,

CHKDSK, and so on, will cause compatibility problems with versions of DOS after the one for which they were intended.

While you are separating out your DOS files, remember to include all DOS .SYS files in your effort. They need to be segregated as well.

When you have contained all of your DOS programs and .SYS files, modify your AUTOEXEC.BAT file to install a path that includes C: \DOS33 (usually as the last item in the path). (Remember to copy this upgraded version to your floppy disk.) Now rename AUTOEXEC.BAT (on both your hard disk and your floppy disk) to be AUTOOLD.BAT. Finally, create a new AUTOEXEC.BAT file on your floppy disk with these commands:

echo c: > a:autoexec.bat
echo autoold.bat > a:autoexec.bat
set comspec=c: \dos33 \command.com

Finally, edit your CONFIG.SYS file on A: to specify the new home of any .SYS files you have moved. Wherever you find a DEVICE command in CONFIG.SYS, change it to have this form: DEVICE=C: \DOS33 *filename*.SYS. Finally, add or change the SHELL command in your CONFIG.SYS. It should now read SHELL=C: \DOS33 \COMMAND.COM /P /E:1024. (You may want even more than 1024 bytes for environment variables, but 1024 bytes is usually enough.) You may now discard your old C: \CONFIG.SYS; the system will never use it again.

Your new floppy disk should now boot the system. Be sure to test that the new DOS floppy disk will boot successfully.

Now install OS/2. Turn off your computer. Insert the OS/2 Installation disk into drive A: and turn the power back on. Wait for OS/2 to boot. Be patient. If you're accustomed to booting from your hard drive, booting from a floppy will seem very slow by comparison. Once OS/2 is up, follow the instructions shown.

That's about all there is to getting it started. A great deal of customization is possible. Some of it is covered in upcoming sections. If you don't plan to read all of this book and all of the OS/2 manuals, it's a good idea to run the program called *Introducing OS/2*, which is distributed with the IBM version of the system. It's a good introduction. If you have it, you'll see it in the program selector on your first boot after installation is complete.

How to Organize Your File System

There are many factors in designing your file system. Some are aesthetic and convenience matters; others determine whether your system will work or not. Here the emphasis will be on the customization required to make the system work.

As you know by now, most commands merely tell OS/2 to start a program. Where it finds the program file is a bit tricky. Since OS/2 has two modes of operation, and you probably want to be able to boot DOS and use it as well, there are several compatibility issues involved. Table 7-1 is a taxonomy of program compatibility.

Table 7-1. The Taxonomy of Program Compatibility

Program Type	Works in DOS	Works in OS/2 Real Mode	Works in OS/2 Protected Mode
Mixed Mode	Y	Y	Y
Real Mode	Y	Y	N
DOS Only	Y	N	N
DOS Version-Specific	3.3 Only	N	N
OS/2-Specific Real Mode	N	One version only	N
OS/2-Specific Protected Mode	N	N	One version only
OS/2-Specific Mixed Mode	N	One version only	One version only
Protected Mode	N	N	Y

Mixed mode programs offer one program file (perhaps with support file) that works in all modes. These programs are rare. Real mode programs are normal programs written for DOS that don't have compatibility problems with OS/2. DOS-only programs are real mode programs that are incompatible with OS/2. Nearly all communications programs for DOS fall into this group.

DOS version-specific programs are mostly the command programs distributed with DOS. They have a built-in test that stops them from running under any operating system version other than the one with which they were sold. OS/2-specific real mode programs are typically OS/2 command programs sold as a part of OS/2 that will only work in real mode and again have a test included to keep them from working on other DOS versions (for example, SUBST, and JOIN).

OS/2-specific protected mode programs won't work in real or DOS mode, and they, too, have a built-in test that keeps them from running on different versions of OS/2 (for instance, SPOOL and KEYB). OS/2-specific mixed mode programs include most of the programs for OS/2 commands. Most work in both real and protected modes but require the operating system version with which they were packaged. Generally, protected mode programs should work on current and future versions of OS/2, but in protected mode only.

You will want to arrange your program files on the disk so that it will be rare that an incompatible program will be invoked. To accomplish this, separate them into directories and select that directories are active as sources of programs by altering the PATH variable. In addition, you will have two versions of batch files: .BAT files for real mode and .CMD files for protected mode. You will want to be able to override program names with batch files. This gives you a chance to make a batch file with the same name as a program, but that performs some extra task before or after invoking the program of the same name. Here's a suggested scheme:

C:\OS2	Command programs part of OS/2
C:\PBIN	Other protected mode programs
C:\RBIN	Other real mode programs
C:\BIN	Mixed mode programs not from OS/2 proper
C:\BAT	.BAT files for real mode OS/2 or DOS
C:\CMD	.CMD files for protected mode OS/2
C:\DOS33	DOS version-specific programs and device drivers
C:\ALIAS	Not necessary, but handy

The directory C:\ALIAS contains very short batch programs made on the fly. They are intended to be handy one-liners and the like. Here is what your path would be like in various modes of operation:

Under DOS 3.3:   PATH=C: \ ALIAS;C: \ BAT;C: \ RBIN;C: \ BIN;C: \ DOS33;
OS/2 Real Mode: PATH=C: \ ALIAS;C: \ BAT;C: \ RBIN;C: \ BIN;C: \ OS2;
OS/2 Protected Mode: PATH=C: \ ALIAS;C: \ CMD;C: \ PBIN;C: \ BIN;C: \ OS2;

In addition to directories in the path, there should be directories for other special-purpose files. At boot time, OS/2 loads several device drivers and code-page description files. These go nicely in the directories:

.SYS FILES (Device Drivers):   C: \ BOOT \ SYS
.DCP FILES (Codepage Files):   C: \ BOOT \ DCP

There are a few .SYS files that almost have to be in the root directory of the boot drive. These are:

AT and Compatibles
CLOCK01.SYS
COUNTRY.SYS
DISK01.SYS
KBD01.SYS
PRINT01.SYS
SCREEN01.SYS

PS/2 and Compatibles
CLOCK02.SYS
COUNTRY.SYS
DISK02.SYS
KBD02.SYS
PRINT02.SYS
SCREEN02.SYS

These device drivers are loaded automatically before CONFIG.SYS is read, so there isn't an easy way to tell OS/2 where to find them. It looks for them in the root directory of the boot disk. Keep your other .SYS files in C: \ BOOT \ SYS to reduce the clutter in the root.

In addition to .SYS files used at boot time, OS/2 protected mode programs rely upon *dynamic link library* files. They go nicely in C: \ DLL, but you must make the LIBPATH command in the CONFIG.SYS file look like this: LIBPATH=C: \ DLL;C: \ OS2 \ INSTALL. The *install* part is no longer needed when you're through installing and using *Introducing OS/2*.

255

While it's running, OS/2 puts material it can no longer fit
into memory into a file called SWAPPER.DAT. It also makes
temporary copies of files when printing them. To keep these
out of the way (and to keep you out of *their* way), it's wise to
make a directory for them. Make directories named C: \ SYSTMP
(for SWAPPER.DAT) and C: \ SYSTMP \ SPOOL (for spool
files). To tell OS/2 where to put SWAPPER.DAT, use the
CONFIG.SYS command SWAPPATH=C: \ SYSTMP. To tell it
where to send the spool files, use the CONFIG.SYS command
RUN=C: \ OS2 \ SPOOL.EXE C: \ SYSTMP \ SPOOL /D:LPT1
/O:LPT1. Here we are interested in the C: \ SYSTMP \ SPOOL
part of the command. The other parameters are covered in sections on installing a serial printer and installing multiple
printers.

If you want to get good at using OS/2, you'll have to
make and use batch files. There are a few directories that can
be very handy when working with batch files:

C: \ ALIAS For on-the-fly batch files (in the command path).
C: \ DEL   For copies of deleted files.
C: \ LIB   For libraries of files needed by complex applications
          programs.
C: \ TMP   For temporary files; may be placed on a ramdisk.
C: \ MSG   A place to keep standard messages and file fragments
          used by batch files.
C: \ ETC   A place for things with no other place.

You probably won't need all of these directories all the
time, but they're handy to have. They're familiar to programmers, and they don't take much disk space.

Finally, you need a place for yourself and the work you
do. You need a directory or directories in which to do your
work. By convention, the tree of directories in which you do
your work is planted at C: \ USR. As subdirectories to \ USR,
you should have the primary areas of your work. It's best not
to organize your work areas by what programs you use on the
files in them—it's better to do it by subject and bring in the
tools needed to do a job. If your tools are installed properly,
there's usually no effort needed to bring them to bear in almost any directory. While you're at it, you should create a directory in \ USR that is your home directory. You'll start out

in the home directory and keep in it desktop items like a phone list, a log of messages, and so on.

As an example of \USR directories, let's examine a lawyer's disk organization. He or she would probably have directories like

C:\USR\PAM	Home directory.
C:\USR\CLIENTS	Contains clients.
C:\USR\CLIENTS\BIGBUCKS	Contains general activity with Bigbucks Industries.
C:\USR\CASES	Full-blown cases might get too complicated to keep under a client directory.
C:\USR\BILLINGS	Billings might be separated as here or as a subdirectory for each client.
C:\USR\PROSPECTS	For those clients considering her services.

To summarize, a structure like the following would be reasonable:

C:\ALIAS	For on-the-fly batch files (in the command path).
C:\BAT	.BAT files for real mode OS/2 or DOS.
C:\BIN	Mixed-mode programs not from OS/2.
C:\BOOT	Files used at boot time only.
C:\BOOT\DCP	Code-page description files.
C:\BOOT\SYS	Device driver files.
C:\CMD	.CMD files for protected mode OS/2.
C:\DEL	For copies of deleted files.
C:\DLL	Dynamic link libraries.
C:\DOS33	DOS version-specific programs and device drivers.
C:\ETC	A place for things with no place.
C:\LIB	For libraries of files needed by complex applications programs.
C:\MSG	A place to keep standard messages and file fragments used by batch files.
C:\OS2	Command programs part of OS/2.
C:\PBIN	Other protected mode programs.
C:\RBIN	Other real mode programs.
C:\SYSTMP	Temporary files created by the system (especially SWAPPER.DAT).
C:\SYSTMP\SPOOL	Temporary print files.
C:\TMP	Temporary files; may be placed on a ramdisk.

This scheme suffers from having a cluttered root directory, especially when you consider all the other files the installation process places there, but there's a slight performance penalty for placing program directories in deeper subdirectories.

How to Improve Your OS/2 Installation

You will benefit from a review of the previous section before reading this section.

Four files are critical to the installation process. The first is CONFIG.SYS, which must reside in the root directory of the boot drive. It tells OS/2 how to load itself, where critical parts are stored, and what device drivers are needed to operate your hardware.

The second file is AUTOEXEC.BAT. This batch file is run the first time the real mode session is run after a boot. It works like AUTOEXEC.BAT for DOS. The third is STARTUP.CMD that is the protected mode batch file run just before the program selector starts. Finally, there's OS2INIT.CMD (the name may be different, but this is the standard name).

In summary,

CONFIG.SYS Runs while OS/2 is loading. Uses special commands. Sets capabilities and basic parameters of the operating system.

AUTOEXEC.BAT Runs once at the beginning of real mode session. Initializes variables for real mode operation.

STARTUP.CMD Runs once at the beginning of protected mode operation. Usually used to set serial ports and to start standard sessions automatically.

OS2INIT.CMD Runs at the beginning of every protected mode session started by the program selector (by not by the START command). Usually used to set variables for use in session.

Both AUTOEXEC.BAT and OS2INIT.CMD are largely occupied with setting variables used by batch files and with environment variables having commands like like PATH, DPATH, and PROMPT. They also typically change the default directory to the user's home directory.

STARTUP.CMD doesn't usually do much variable setting

because it starts in one session and environment variables are local to each session. STARTUP.CMD, as the name implies, generally contains START commands to automatically start other sessions you normally want at hand when the system starts.

CONFIG.SYS

CONFIG.SYS is quite different. It's actually a blueprint for how the variable portions of OS/2 are assembled to create a complete operating system tailored to the hardware and applications at hand. Since it is the first to be used when the system boots, we will start with CONFIG.SYS in our customization process.

It's possible to do many things with CONFIG.SYS—most of them bad. Here, we'll cover only the practical highlights.

First, edit your CONFIG.SYS file to add the command PAUSEONERROR at the beginning. This statement will pause operation whenever an error is encountered, and it will display a message so you can see what happened. After noting the error, you can usually cause CONFIG.SYS processing to proceed. Without this command, it may take many boots and much frustration to find a minor error.

You may use EDLIN to edit CONFIG.SYS, or you may use any editor. Just be certain that the editor or word processor will not insert strange characters into the file. Use the editor in programming mode or nondocument mode, if you have the option. To check that your editor is behaving as desired, simply type the CONFIG.SYS file. If it doesn't contain any Greek characters, smiling faces, or the like, your CONFIG.SYS is all right. Also, remember that CONFIG.SYS is processed before the system has a *path* or *dpath* variable set. Therefore, all filenames should specify drives and directories. There are no current defaults that can be relied upon in all cases.

Next, look for a BREAK command in CONFIG.SYS. If you don't find BREAK=ON, add it. This applies only to real mode and has the same effect as the regular command of the same name. It simply gives you better control over runaway programs in real mode, with a very small performance loss.

Now look for BUFFERS=; it should be there. Buffers are memory areas of 512 bytes, each used to store information temporarily as it moves to and from the disk. Having too few buffers causes mechanical activity in the disk system to be slower than necessary. Having too many buffers wastes time managing the buffers themselves. The standard number of buffers is about 30, but no one seems to know an optimum setting.

If you have some time on your hands, develop a sample session with the computer that reflects your usual mix of activities. Run it with several different settings of BUFFERS and see which is the fastest setting. Make sure you reboot the machine between tests, and make the tests absolutely uniform. If the number of buffers is anywhere within a reasonable range, say from 25 to 100, the differences to overall system performance should be minor.

If you're using an American machine (that is, a machine built in the Orient, but designed for use in the U.S.) with an American keyboard, and you don't think you'll be using foreign character sets, delete any CODEPAGE statement in CONFIG.SYS. If you don't need it, it only confuses matters.

Related to the CODEPAGE statement is the COUNTRY statement. If there is no COUNTRY command in your CONFIG.SYS, OS/2 requires the file COUNTRY.SYS in the root directory of the boot disk. If there is a COUNTRY statement, it merely serves to tell OS/2 where to find COUNTRY.SYS or a future replacement for it. For each choice of country, the system supports two codepages. The CODEPAGE statement specifies that to use, but if the CODEPAGE specifies a page that isn't supported for the country specified, it's an error. It's a good idea to use the COUNTRY command simply to put COUNTRY.SYS in a directory other than the root directory and to avoid use of the CODEPAGE statement. This causes the system to default to the most common codepage for the country specified.

Associated with the CODEPAGE and COUNTRY CONFIG.SYS statements are a variety of DEVINFO statements specifying different keyboard layouts, screen character sets and printer fonts for IBM daisywheel and dot-matrix printers. In practice, again the best course is to avoid use of this feature. The inflexibility of these facilities, the opportunity for trivial errors, and the fact that no word processors (or other programs of significance) pay any attention to code pages makes this a feature ahead of its time. Perhaps in a few years it will come into its own.

Device drivers. Device drivers are specialized chunks of programming designed to interface particular hardware devices with OS/2. Since OS/2 runs with a variety of hardware, device drivers are added to customize it for a particular situation without requiring the capability to run all possible devices loaded all of the time. Basically, you need device drivers for the realtime clock, keyboard, screen, printer, disk drives, and mouse. A limited number of device drivers are offered with the standard IBM edition of OS/2, and more will be offered by other vendors and customizers of OS/2. The drivers from IBM tend to come in two flavors: those for the AT and compatible machines and those for the PS/2 and compatible machines. Driver files ending in 01 tend to be for ATs, those ending in 02, for PS/2s (this doesn't hold true for mouse drivers). During the installation process, the questions you answered caused the installation program to pick certain drivers. Generally, you won't have to change these.

When OS/2 boots, it expects to find drivers named CLOCK0x.SYS, DISK0x.SYS, KBD0x.SYS, SCREEN0x.SYS, and PRINT0x.SYS (x is 1 or 2). These are presumed to be in the root of the boot disk.

In addition to these default, standard drivers, you might want OS/2 to install the following drivers in order to improve its capabilities.

EGA.SYS. One of these is the EGA.SYS driver. To install it, add the CONFIG.SYS command DEVICE=*path* \ EGA.SYS, where *path* is the full drive and directory path specification for EGA.SYS. This makes some of the bare hardware of the EGA display system available to DOS programs. Most DOS programs that use an EGA to its full advantage need this access.

So, if you have an EGA, install the EGA.SYS driver. It will allow DOS programs to perform tricks that OS/2 cannot undo. This will cause odd display behavior when you leave the real mode session and go into a protected mode session or the program selector. The solution is to get back into real mode and have the program that reset the display get it back to normal. This may require stopping the program.

Mouse drivers. If you plan to use a mouse, you must load two drivers to support it. The first is a general driver called POINTDD.SYS. Again, the CONFIG.SYS command is DEVICE=path \ POINTDD.SYS. In addition, you need a driver specific to your brand of mouse. The drivers available support bus, parallel, serial and *In-Port* mouse interfaces for Mouse Systems– and Microsoft-brand mice. The formats of the CONFIG.SYS command are DEVICE=*path* \ MOUSEA0*x*.SYS where *x* is 0, 1, 2, 3, or 4 and DEVICE=*path* \ MOUSEB0*x*.SYS where *x* is 0 or 1. After any of these commands, you may add these options: MODE=*x* with *x* being *P* for mouse use in protected mode, *R* for use in real mode and *B* for both (the default). The QSIZE=*nn* option sets the number of bytes of mouse input buffered during delays in processing. The value of *nn* may range from 1 to 100. The default is 10. Changing this parameter will change the way your screen behaves during rapid mouse activity. For serial mice, there is the option SERIAL=COM*n* where *n* is 1 or 2 on ATs and 1, 2, or 3 for PS/2s. This specifies the serial port to which the mouse is attached. Once you specify this, the port will not be accessible for other uses or other device drivers. The mouse device hides the port from all others.

Ramdisks. If you want to use some RAM for a ramdisk, use the command DEVICE=*path* \ VDISK.SYS *b,s,d* where *b* is the number of K in the ramdisk, *s* is the sector size in bytes (128, 256, 512, and 1024 are valid), and *d* is the maximum number of directories allowed in the root directory of the ramdisk. If you set the sector size small, files will be saved with a minimum of wasted space. If you set it high, reading and writing speed will be improved. Generally, small or medium sector sizes are best. In fact, after the *b* option, it's probably just as well that you let the other options take their default values (128 bytes per sector, 64 directory entries). If you use a VDISK, its drive letter will be the next in sequence after all of your real drives.

If you have any external floppy disk drives, you may let OS/2 know about them with the DEVICE=*path* \ EXTDSKDD.SYS command in your CONFIG.SYS. This command takes obscure options. You should consult the supplier of the drive for the correct settings. If you use EXTDSKDD.SYS and VDISK.SYS, include the VDISK commands after the EXTDSKDD.SYS command(s) in CONFIG.SYS.

COM serial Ports. OS/2 doesn't automatically know about COM serial ports. There's a good reason for this: You might not want it to.

You might want to leave all COM port control to real mode programs. Usually, though, you'll want to include DEVICE=*path* \ COM0*x*.SYS with *x* being 1 for ATs and 2 for PS/2s. This allows protected mode programs (including SPOOL.EXE, which controls printers) to use the ports. If you want to return control of a port to a real mode program, use the real mode command SETCOM40. Note that if you have installed a serial mouse before installing COM0*x*.SYS, one of the ports will fail the installation. This is because the mouse driver has already hidden it. In general, you should include serial mouse drivers in CONFIG.SYS before COM0*x*.SYS. To set the parameters for serial communication over a COM port to values matching the connected hardware, you should use the MODE command.

Disk caching. If you have a PS/2 machine, the CONFIG.SYS command DISKCACHE will improve disk performance significantly. It has only one option, the size of the cache (in K) is entered as a number after the DISKCACHE keyword. The optimal size depends on your disk drives and your available memory. Minimums for big performance gains are 64 for a 20MB drive and 128 for larger drives. Experiment with this setting. Increasing the size makes disk activity faster but more frequent as there is less memory available to OS/2 and it must swap material in and out of memory more often.

As mentioned under disk organization, you can use the LIBPATH=*path;path* command to tell OS/2 where to find the .DLL dynamic link files many protected mode programs rely upon. Similarly, SWAPPATH=*drive:path* tells OS/2 where to put the SWAPPER.DAT file it uses for shuffling material in and out of memory.

Miscellaneous CONFIG.SYS commands. The CONFIG.SYS SHELL command relates only to real mode and is identical to the same command in DOS. Here's an appropriate form: SHELL=*path* \ COMMAND.COM /P /E:*n* where *n* is the number of bytes available for storage of environment variables (1024 is a good number to begin with). You need the /P option. The /E option specifies the maximum number of bytes for environment variables. If you get *Out of Environment Space* errors in real mode, increase the number after /E:. Again, make sure the path specified includes the drive and directory for finding COMMAND.COM.

The RUN command is covered under the section on installation of a serial printer. For data processing applications, the other CONFIG.SYS commands available are generally best left as they are set by the installation program.

AUTOEXEC.BAT

Once your CONFIG.SYS file is squared away, the next task is to build AUTOEXEC.BAT. Basically, the AUTOEXEC.BAT file should set a path for programs and batch files and should set a prompt (though the default prompt isn't bad). In addition, it's an ideal place to set a variety of environment variables handy for use in batch files. Those will be covered with OS2INIT.CMD in the next section. You probably have a good starting point for your AUTOEXEC.BAT in your old one from DOS. Many programs expect to find certain environment variables, and you may find some in your old AUTOEXEC.BAT. You can copy it, but remember to change the path so that DOS programs aren't called by OS/2 and so that OS/2 programs can be found in the path.

OS2INIT.CMD

OS2INIT.CMD is the batch file the program selector runs first in each session it starts. You may notice in your CONFIG.SYS file a PROTSHELL= command that mentions OS2INIT.CMD. This is where the program selector program (DMPC.EXE) is told about OS2INIT.CMD. You could change the name, but there's no reason to do so. Put OS2INIT.CMD into your \ CMD directory where it belongs, modify CONFIG.SYS so

that OS2INIT.CMD is changed to C: \ CMD \ OS2INIT.CMD
and DMPC.EXE can find it. Like AUTOEXEC.BAT,
OS2INIT.CMD is the place to define your path and environment variables. Here is an example:

```
@echo off
set dd1=c:
set dd2=d:
set dd3=e:
set os2=%dd1% \ os2
set alias=%dd1% \ alias
set cmd=%dd1% \ cmd
set pbin=%dd2% \ pbin
set tmp=%dd1% \ tmp
set msg=%dd1% \ msg
set del=%dd1% \ del
path=%alias%;%cmd%;%pbin%;%os2%;
set user=TED
set home=%dd1% \ os2usr \ %user%
set cdpath=%home%;%cmd%;
cd %home%
call help on
cls
```

The @ECHO OFF command makes the file run quietly
without echoing each command as it's executed. Environment
variables *dd1* through *dd3* make known the drives available to
batch files. When the file is run, OS/2 expands the variable
%dd1% to C:. The *os2, alias, cmd, pbin, tmp, msg, del* and *home*
variables tell batch files where directories of special interest
are to be found. Placing these into variables allows you to put
the directories on different drives and still have them found by
batch files. The *user* variable is handy for batch commands
like ECHO HAVE A NICE DAY %USER%. The CALL HELP
ON command uses a batch file included with OS/2 that
changes the prompt to remind you that Ctrl-Esc gets you back
to the program selector. The CLS command simply clears the
screen for neatness. The *cdpath* variable is used by some of the
batch files described in other sections that follow. The line CD
%HOME% causes the new session to start out in the home directory. You may change this if you like, but it tends to keep
things less confusing if sessions always start from the same
place.

STARTUP.CMD

STARTUP.CMD is a batch file automatically run in the first protected mode session created after boot-up. It doesn't do much good to set environment variables here because they will not be known to other sessions. This is a good place to include START commands that begin other sessions you like to find available when your system starts. Here is an example:

```
@echo off
call c: \ cmd \ os2init
mode com1:96,n,8,1,TO=ON >nul
echo COM1 set to 9600,N,8,1,TO=ON for LaserJet.
echo LPT1 redirected to COM1 as primary printer.
start "C: Rolling Directories" "call c: \ cmd \ os2init && rolltree c:"
start "D: Rolling Directories" "call c: \ cmd \ os2init && rolltree d:"
exit
```

Again @ECHO OFF makes STARTUP.CMD run quietly. In this example, OS2INIT.CMD is called to set up a path simply for convenience for the rest of this batch file. The MODE command prepares a serial port for use by a LaserJet printer, and the ECHO commands that follow tell the user about it.

The START commands each include a description of the programs run that will appear in the program selector. Then each starts a session with two combined commands. The first is OS2INIT.CMD, so the session has the usual environment variables (though OS2INIT.CMD is automatically called by the program selector, it is not automatic for the START command). The second is ROLLTREE.CMD, a batch file described below that continuously shows a list of directories for a specified drive.

You will notice that the last command is EXIT. It's not necessary to exit and end this session, but doing so causes the next screen displayed to be the program selector, which is a good place to start a session. Without EXIT, you would simply see the CMD prompt waiting for a command when STARTUP.CMD ended. You could then get to the program selector with a press of Ctrl-Esc.

In place of or in addition to the START commands shown, you could add START commands for your favorite programs. But it's wise to include OS2INIT.CMD in each of these because you don't know what the session may be used for in the future. This will ensure that any process running later in that session will have a proper set of environment variables.

With a little creativity and careful stewardship of your system resources, the combination of CONFIG.SYS, STARTUP.CMD, OS2INIT.CMD, and AUTOEXEC.BAT can be simple and an effective tool in making your computer use more convenient.

How to Install a Serial Printer

When you print using OS/2's normal printing facilities with a serial printer, your data goes from the program originating the printing (often the PRINT program), to SPOOL.EXE (which is running quietly in the background), into a temporary disk file, back through SPOOL.EXE to a serial port driver, to the physical serial port, along a cable and into your printer (Figure 7-1).

Figure 7-1. Serial Printing Data Flow

PROGRAM ▶ SPOOL.EXE ▶ COMO*x*.SYS ▶ COM*n* ▶ PRINTER
                              (Device Driver)   (Port)
             Temporary File

First, in your CONFIG.SYS file, place the command RUN=C: \ OS2 \ SPOOL.EXE C: \ SYSTMP \ SPOOL /D:LPT1 /O:COM1. This starts the SPOOL.EXE program running detached in the background without a screen attached. It also tells SPOOL to use the directory C: \ SYSTMP \ SPOOL as the directory for its temporary files. It further tells SPOOL to get input by trapping any output destined for LPT1. Finally, it tells SPOOL to send its output to COM1. You can change the location of SPOOL.EXE and the temporary files—this just follows the disk organization suggested above.

Be sure that the path to SPOOL.EXE is right and that the directory for temporary files exists. Also, you can change the input device to LPT2 or LPT3 and the output device to any of these LPT's (parallel ports) or to COM2, or, on PS/2s, to COM2 or COM3. But you cannot make the input device a

COM port. Whatever device you choose for SPOOL's input is the device programs will think they are printing to. Whatever output device you specify will be the real physical port where the signals are sent. There had better be a printer attached there to catch them.

To get the serial port working, you need to put the command DEVICE=C: \ BOOT \ SYS \ COM0x.SYS in your CONFIG.SYS file. Again, you can change the location of COM0x.SYS, but it has to be where you say it is. The x in COM0x.SYS is 1 for ATs and 2 for PS/2s. Loading this device driver gives OS/2 the means of dealing with a serial port, but it doesn't tell it what settings to use. Use the MODE command to communicate the settings.

In STARTUP.CMD, place the command MODE COM1:96,N,8,1,TO=ON to set the serial port for a speed of 9600 baud, no parity check bit in characters, 8 data bits per character, 1 stop bit after each character, and time out processing that will wait for the printer without squawking while you change paper, clear a jam, or untangle your ribbon. You can change the baud to 110, 150, 300, 600, 1200, 2400, 4800, or 19200 (you may abbreviate any of these to the first two numerals, except for 19200, which is abbreviated 192).

You can also change the parity to O for odd, E for even, M for mark, or S for space (these are all more or less standard modes of operation). You can also change the data bits to 7 (or even down to 5, but no normal printers work with 5-bit characters), and the stop bits may be changed to 2 (rare today).

The right settings will depend on how your printer is configured. You will have to look in your printer manual to find the answer. The parameters for the OS/2 mode command dealing with baud, parity, data bits, and stop bits are the same as for DOS so you can take them from an example for DOS. The difference is that TO=ON is new and replaces the P option in DOS. (P is still allowed in real mode, but it doesn't work the same way as in DOS.) Again, you can specify COM1 or COM2 for ATs and COM1, COM2, or COM3 for PS/2s, but it had better be the same port the /O: device communicated to SPOOL, and there must be a printer attached to that port.

Finally, if you want to send a file to the printer, use the PRINT command. If your SPOOL /D: device is LPT1, just say PRINT *filename;* if you're using another LPT input to SPOOL, use PRINT /D:LPT*n* where the *n* matches the LPT in the SPOOL /D option.

Once all of these commands are in place, you must reboot the computer to make them effective. If your printer does strange things or won't show its on-line light, first try turning it off and back on again. If it prints gibberish, your MODE command needs to be matched between the serial ports of the computer and printer. If nothing happens or OS/2 complains about an invalid device, one of your LPT or COM commands is wrong. Remember the device specified in SPOOL /D must be the one the program thinks it is printing to. The SPOOL /O device must match the mode COM port. The COM port for an AT must be COM1 or COM2, and for a PS/2, COM1, COM2, or COM3.

While testing, it's best to start by using the PRINT command to print small files. Then, when everything is running in harmony, print some large files and check over the entire printout. Some serial communications errors only appear in small portions of long runs. Remember to put a PAUSEONERROR single-word command at the beginning of your CONFIG.SYS file so you can see if an error is detected in it. Write the error messages down for later reference.

How to Install Multiple Printers

If you have several printers, simply RUN SPOOL.EXE more times in your CONFIG.SYS file. See the previous section on serial printers for some background. Say you have three printers attached, to ports COM1, LPT1, and LPT3. The COM1 printer is serial, the others are parallel (or the plugs won't match). The port names to which your programs can print are LPT1, LPT2, and LPT3. Generally LPT1 is presumed to be your main printer. LPT2 and LPT3 are usually specialty printers. If you want your COM1 printer to be your primary printer, followed by the one attached to LPT3, and finally the one attached to LPT1, here are the commands needed (pre-suming your COM1 printer matches the MODE communications parameters shown):

In CONFIG.SYS.

device=c: \ boot \ sys \ com01.sys
run=c: \ os2 \ spool.exe c: \ systmp \ spool /d:lpt1 /o:com1
run=c: \ os2 \ spool.exe c: \ systmp \ spool /d:lpt2 /o:lpt3
run=c: \ os2 \ spool.exe c: \ systmp \ spool /d:lpt3 /o:lpt1

In STARTUP.CMD
mode com1:96,n,8,1,to=on

The DEVICE= and MODE commands prepare COM1 for proper operation. The RUN= commands run three copies of SPOOL.EXE. These don't interfere with each other because they each steal input from different devices and send output to different devices. The first routes output destined for LPT1 to COM1, the second sends output labeled for LPT2 to LPT1, and the last sends LPT3 output to LPT1. Your programs see only LPT1, LPT2, and LPT3; they aren't aware that output actually goes somewhere else.

Of course, the file paths shown may differ from those you use, but make sure they're accurate. Each should begin with a drive followed by a complete path from the root to the target directory. There isn't a default directory or drive in the usual sense when CONFIG.SYS is processed. Remember, these commands will not take effect until you reboot your system. Also remember to include the command PAUSEONERROR at the top of your CONFIG.SYS file so you can see any errors found in it.

How to Install Applications Programs

If you simply use the installation routines that come with most commercial programs, your file system is likely to become a mess. Too many programs presume too much. They create directories right and left and put them where they want them, not necessarily where you want them.

The rationality of your file system is important. Putting some effort into program installations can be well worth the effort. Here are some rules of thumb about what you want in an application installation:

- You want the program to be able to deal with files in any directory.
- You want to be able to start the application from any directory.
- You don't want the application program to put files into your root directory, nor do you want it to build its own directory as a subdirectory of the root.
- You want it to use your display system to its full capability (EGAs emulating CGAs are a vision-straining waste).
- You want it to have attractive output on your printer, and you want to be able to send output to the printer of your choice.

The problems with applications program installations are largely due to a lack of standards or sloppy programming.

The first problem for a large applications program is finding its own support files. These files typically contain configuration information; they may contain a part of the program that is loaded only when needed (an *overlay*); they may contain font tables; or you may not be able to figure out what they contain.

There are several ways a program can find its support files. The simplest is for the program to presume the support files are in the current default directory of the current default drive when the program is started. This requires that you always start the program from one directory or have extra copies of the files in several directories. Many programs that make the presumption also have other means of finding their files if they are not in the current directory. Unfortunately, these other means are often only mentioned in a footnote or an obscure appendix. Common means of finding support files not in the current directory are

- To presume the files are in a directory listed in the PATH variable.
- To look for a variable of another name that tells where they are (like BPATH, or LIB, or INCLUDE).

Some programs presume their support files are in a directory of a particular name, but this is of little help. When preparing to install a complex application, read the documentation thoroughly. Find out as much as you can about how it finds its support files.

- If it uses an environment variable with an uncommon name, initialize the variable in AUTOEXEC.BAT or OS2INIT.CMD.
- If it uses a common name that might conflict with other programs, build a batch file to set the variable, run the program, and, after the program exits, set the variable back to its old value.
- If the program uses the *path* variable and has many support files, use such a batch file to alter temporarily the *path* variable and set it back to its original setting so your command processor doesn't have to sort through all those files every time it looks for a command program.

For example:

Normal system path:
C: \ ALIAS;C: \ BAT;C: \ RBIN;C: \ BIN;C: \ OS2;
Program: SUPRUPR.EXE in C: \ RBIN
Support files in: C: \ LIB \ SUPRUPR
Program uses *path* variable to find support files.

Batch file to run program SUPRUPR.BAT in C: \ BAT
@echo off
set oldpath = %path%
set path = c: \ lib \ suprupr;%path%
%rbin% \ suprupr
set path = %oldpath%
set oldpath =

Note: Because \ BAT is before \ RBIN in the path, the batch file will run instead of SUPRUPR.EXE.

In this example, when SUPUPR.BAT runs, it saves the current path in *oldpath*. Then it adds the location of the SUPRUPR support files to the beginning of the path so they will be found quickly while SUPRUPR is running. Finally, SUPRUPR.EXE is invoked with *%rbin%* \ SUPRUPR to make sure the batch file doesn't call itself again. The variable *%rbin%*, according to an earlier how-to, is set to C: \ RBIN,

where SUPRUPR.EXE is. After SUPRUPR.EXE runs,
SUPRUPR.BAT regains control and restores the path to its ear-
lier setting. It also clears *oldpath* to keep the environment neat.
The same effect could be achieved with:

```
@echo off
setlocal
path=c:\lib\suprupr;%path%
%rbin%\suprupr.exe
endlocal
```

In this form, you rely on the fact that variable changes
bracketed by SETLOCAL and ENDLOCAL are temporary and
forgotten after the ENDLOCAL command.

If you get a stubborn real mode program that insists on
finding its support files in the current directory at startup, use
this approach:

```
@echo off
append c:\lib\suprupr
%rbin%\suprupr
append ;
if not exist suprupr.cnf x
copy suprupr.cnf c:\lib\suprupr
del suprupr.cnf
```

The APPEND in real mode makes the contents of the appended directory appear to be in the current directory. There
is one flaw in this: If the program makes a new copy of one of
its support files rather than modifying the file in place, that
new copy will appear in the current directory rather than the
appended directory. Experience with the program will tell you
with which files it might do this. As shown in the last three
lines of the last batch file, you can look for such files and put
them where they belong, if found.

Usually, if a program can find its support files, it will use
the proper display and printer drivers and modes because it
will remember them from initial configuration. Often, you
need to make the first run of a program from its home directory so that it can save any configuration information you
supply.

Unfortunately, there's no simple way to redirect printer

output on the fly in OS/2. You can redirect it with SPOOL.EXE, but once set, the redirection is hard to change. But most programs use LPT1 unless told otherwise, and SPOOL.EXE can be run in your CONFIG.SYS file to send this to virtually any printer you want.

As for display modes, some programs will use EGA displays in a way that will cause OS/2 problems if you jump from the program to another session or the program selector. There is no simple cure for this. It's a weakness in the EGA design. If your screen is scrambled upon leaving real mode, press Alt-Esc until you get back to real mode and run the program to completion to restore the display to its normal state.

Don't expect any printed output from a real mode program until after it completes. SPOOL keeps collecting printer output until the program ends. You can force it to print with Ctrl-Alt-PrtSc, but when you do this, make sure it is at a logical boundary in the printer output.

Appendix

Often-Used Commands and Examples

Appendix
Often-Used Commands and Examples

These are short examples, not command descriptions. In the examples, A: and B: are example floppy disk drives; H: and I: designate hard disk drives. If the command applies to a floppy disk or a hard disk, D: and E: are used.

File System
This category includes all commands dealing with disk data storage.

Physical Media Management
These commands deal primarily with disks as a storage medium rather than as a set of files.

Media Initialization. These commands prepare disks for use.

FORMAT D: /S /V:DISK_1	Formats and labels a bootable disk.
FDISK H:	After formatting, prepares a hard disk for use.
SYS H: /S	Makes disk bootable (usually).

Tracking. These commands help keep track of disks.

LABEL D: DISK_2	Labels a disk.
VOL D:	Outputs label of disk.

Duplication.

DISKCOPY A: A:	Copies an entire floppy disk track by track.

Testing. Most testing of disk media performance is done quietly and automatically whenever a disk is used. These commands provide additional tests of disk integrity.

CHKDSK D:	Checks disk for invalid file connections.
DISKCOMP A: A:	Compares two floppy disks, track by track.
FORMAT D: /S /V:DISK_3)	While formatting, checks for bad spots.
VERIFY ON	Causes more rigorous checking during disk operations.

Fault recovery.

RECOVER D: Attempts to isolate bad spots on disk.
CHKDSK D: /F Attempts to fix invalid file linkages.

File Tree Management

These commands deal with the file tree system of naming and categorizing files. They emphasize the grouping and naming of files rather than the content of files.

Tracking and cataloging. These commands aid in keeping track of files and groups of files.

DIR D: \DIR1 \SUBDIR1   Lists files in directory.
TREE D: Lists all directories on disk D:.
CHKDSK D: /V   Lists all directories and files on disk D:.
ATTRIB D: \DIR1 /S   Lists all files descended from D: \DIR1

Tree alteration. These commands create and destroy directory groupings of files.

MD D: \DIR2 \SUBDIR7   Creates subdirectory SUBDIR7 in D: \DIR2.
RD D: \DIR2 \SUBDIR7   Removes SUBDIR7 which must be empty.
XCOPY D: \ E: \DH /S/E Copies all files and dirs on D: into dir
                            E: \DH.

Testing. This command checks the file tree for improperly formed directories and files.

CHKDSK D: Checks D: for invalid file linkages.

Fault Recovery. These commands deal with protecting the file tree from damage.

BACKUP H: \ A: /S /F /L Makes backup copy of all on current drive.
RESTORE A: H: \ /S   Restores backup made in last command.
RECOVER D: \DIR \FILE Attempts to remove bad sectors from file.

File content management. These commands deal with the content and attributes of individual files. Even though most of these commands may operate on multiple files in one run of the command, they deal with them one by one.

Attribute control.

ATTRIB +R −A D:FILE3 Marks FILE3 as read-only and unmodified.

Duplication. These commands duplicate the contents of a file(s). They differ in the convenience of applying them to multiple files selected in different ways.

COPY D: . E: \DIR5   Copies files in current DIR of D: to \DIR5
COPY D: . E: \DIR5 /S /E Same, except copies SUBDIRS as well
REPLACE D: . E: \DIR5 /S Same, but only copies files not on E:

Deletion.

DEL D: .   Deletes all files in current directory of D:

Alteration. These commands alter the internal content of files.

EDLIN D:TEXTFILE   Allows you to edit text in TEXTFILE.
PATCH D:PGM.EXE   Allows you to edit nontext bytes in PGM.EXE.

Testing. These commands check the contents and integrity of individual files.

COMP D: \D1 E: Compares all files in D: \D1 and E: \D1 byte by byte.
CHKDSK FILE   Checks file validity and tells if scattered on disk.

Text file management. These commands deal primarily with text in files.

EDLIN D: \D1 \TEXTFILE   Allows you to edit text in the file.
TYPE D: \D1 \TEXTFILE   Outputs contents of file.
FIND "needle" D:HAYSTACK   Outputs lines containing "needle".
SORT <WORDS >DICTION   Outputs lines of input file in alphabetical order.
MORE <TOME   Outputs long text file one screen at a time.

I/O Device Management

These commands deal with control of input/output devices.

Console Management. These commands control the operator's screen and keyboard.

ANSI ON   Makes screen respond to special codes for color, and other parameters.
CHCP 860   Makes screen and keyboard handle Portuguese characters.
GRAFTABL   Makes unusual characters displayable when in graphics modes.
KEYBFR   Sets up your keyboard for typing in French.
PROMPT $P-$G Makes prompt show current drive, directory, and an arrow.
CLS   Clears console screen.

Printer Management. These commands control the use of printers.

PRINT /D:LPT3 D: \ DITTY	Prints DITTY on printer 3 while you go on with another task.
SPOOL H: \ SPOOL /D:LPT1	Straightens out printing from multiple tasks.
MODE LPT1=COM1	Sends output intended for LPT1 to COM1 instead.

Communications port management. This command controls how serial communications ports are used.

MODE COM1:9600,N,8,1,P	Sets up COM1 port to talk to a fast printer.

Process Management

These commands influence what the computer is to do and when.

CMD /C MYBAT	Runs MYBAT.BAT in a child command processor.
START "MY BATCH" "MYBAT > MYBAT.OUT"	
	Starts new session running MYBAT
COMMAND /C MYBAT	Same as last example.
DETACH ORPHAN	Runs program ORPHAN in background.
EXIT	Exits child command processor to parent.
EXTPROC MYCMD	In batch file, this command will send commands to
MYCMD.EXE.	
FOR %F IN (*.DOC *.TXT) DO FIND "needle" %%F	
	Runs FIND several times.
GOTO LINEBELOW	In batch file, processor jumps to line labeled
:LINEBELOW.	
PAUSE	In batch file, waits for a keystroke.
BREAK ON	Makes it easier for Ctrl-C to stop a program.
CALL SUBBAT	In a batch file, runs SUBBAT.BAT and returns to next line on completion of that batch file.
:LINEBELOW	In a batch file, place for GOTO to go to.

Program Environment Management

These commands alter what programs and commands see
when they run. This includes temporarily altering the appearance of the file system.

APPEND D: \STUFF;E: \THINGS	Files in STUFF and THINGS seem to be in the current directory on the default drive.
ASSIGN D:=E:	Makes drive E: look like drive D:. (Use SUBST instead.)
BREAK ON	Makes it easier for Ctrl-Break to stop a program.
CD \HOME	Makes \HOME the current default directory.
D:	Makes D: the current default drive.
SETLOCAL	In a batch file, saves default drive, path, and environment.
ENDLOCAL	In a batch file, restores that saved by setlocal.
JOIN D: E: \FAKED	Makes drive D: \ look like subdirectory E: \FAKED to programs.
SET USER=JOE	Environment variable USER lets programs know about JOE.
SUBST E: \FAKED D:	Makes E: \FAKED look like D: \ to programs.
TIME 13:00:00.00	Tells system it's 1:00 PM and sets the clock.
DATE 04-01-90	Sets date in system clock.
SHIFT	In batch file, shifts %1 to %0, %2 to %1, and so on.
VERIFY ON	Tells OS/2 and programs to check disk-writes carefully.

Operation Information

These commands provide information to the computer user.

HELPMSG DOS1809E	Expands on obscure error message with a longer obscurity.
VER	Tells the operator which version of OS/2 is running.
REM COMMENT	Lets you put a do-nothing comment line into a batch file.
:COMMENT	Neater way to put a comment line into a batch file.

Table A-1. Quick Command Chart

Key

Column A: Full command name
Column B: Alternate command name

Column C:

R   Real mode
P   Protected mode
B   Both modes

Column D: Invalid on network drive

Column E:

Program resides

CMD   In CMD.EXE file
C.C   In COMMAND.COM file
C&C   CMD and COMMAND files
EXE   An .EXE file
COM   A .COM file

Column F:

Performs setting or action:

SET   Changes OS/2 operation
ACT   Performs and immediate act
INFO   Outputs information only

Column G:

Where usually used:

C   On command line
B   In a batch file
1   On setup of system or a disk
A   In AUTOEXEC.BAT
S   In STARTUP.CMD
O   In OS2INIT.CMD
D   For diagnosis

Column H:

!   Can destroy data or confuse operator into destroying it.

Table A-1. Quick Command Chart, continued

Column I: Type of action or setting

A	B	C	D	E	F	G	H	I
ANSI		P			SET	S		SETS CONSOLE
APPEND		R			SET	B,C		SETS SEARCH
ASSIGN		R			SET	N	!	SETS NAMES
ATTRIB		B		EXE	ACT	C,B		FILE MAINT
BACKUP		B	Y	EXE	ACT	B,C	!	FILE MAINT
BREAK		R		COM	SET	A		SETS CONSOLE
CALL		B			ACT	B		FLOW CONTROL
CHCP		B		C&C	SET	A,S		SETS CONSOLE
CHDIR	CD	B		C&C	SET	C,B		SETS NAMES
CHKDSK		B	Y		ACT	C	!	TEST
CLS		B		C&C	ACT	B,C		SETS CONSOLE
CMD		P		EXE	ACT	B,C		FLOW CONTROL
COMMAND		R		COM	ACT	B,C		FLOW CONTROL
COMP		B		COM	INFO	C		FILE MAINT
COPY		B		C&C	ACT	B,C	!	FILE MAINT
DATE		B		C&C	SET	ASC		INITIALIZE
DEL	ERASE	B		C&C	ACT			FILE MAINT
DETACH		P		CMD	ACT	B,C		FLOW CONTROL
DIR		B		C&C	INFO	C		FILE MAINT
DISKCOMP		B	Y	COM	INFO	C		FILE MAINT
DISKCOPY		B		COM	ACT	C	!	FILE MAINT
DPATH		P		CMD	SET	O		SETS NAMES
ECHO		B		C&C	INFO	B		INFO
ENDLOCAL		B		C&C	SET	B		ENVIRONMENT
EXIT		B		C&C	ACT	C,B		FLOW CONTROL
EXTPROC		P		CMD	ACT	B		FLOW CONTROL
FDISK		B	Y	EXE	ACT	1		SETS NAMES
FIND		B		COM	ACT	C,B		TEXT TOOL
FOR		B		C&C	ACT	B,C		FLOW CONTROL
FORMAT		B	Y	COM	ACT	C	!!	INITIALIZE
GOTO		B		C&C	ACT	B		FLOW CONTROL
GRAFTABL		R		COM	SET	A		SETS CONSOLE
HELP		B		EXE	ACT	C		INFO
IF		B		C&C	ACT	B		FLOW CONTROL
JOIN		R		EXE	SET	A,C		SETS NAMES
KEYBxx		B		C&C	SET	S,A		SETS CONSOLE
LABEL		B	Y	COM	SET	C		SETS NAMES
MKDIR	MD	B		C&C	ACT	C		FILE MAINT

Table A-1. Quick Command Chart, continued

A	B	C	D	E	F	G	H	I
MODE		B		COM	SET	A,S		SETS COMM
MORE		B		COM	ACT	B,C		TEXT TOOL
PATCH		B		COM	ACT	C	!!	MISC
PATH		B		C&C	SET	A,S		FLOW CONTROL
PAUSE		B		C&C	ACT	B		FLOW CONTROL
PRINT		B		COM	ACT	C		PRINT CONTROL
PROMPT		B		C&C	ACT	C	!	SETS CONSOLE
RECOVER		B	Y	C&C	ACT	C	!	FILE MAINT
REM		B		C&C	INFO	B		MISC
RENAME	REN	B		C&C	ACT	C		FILE MAINT
REPLACE		B		EXE	ACT	C,B	!	FILE MAINT
RESTORE		B	.	COM	ACT	B	!	FILE MAINT
RMDIR	RD	B		C&C	ACT	C,B		FILE MAINT
SET		B		C&C	SET	ABC		ENVIRONMENT
SETCOM40		R		EXE	SET	A,B		SETS COM
SETLOCAL		B		C&C	SET	B		ENVIRONMENT
SHIFT		B		C&C	SET	B		ENVIRONMENT
SORT		B		EXE	ACT	B,C		TEXT TOOL
SPOOL		B			ACT			PRINT CONTROL
START		P		CMD	ACT	SOCB		STARTS SESS
SUBST		B	Y	EXE	INFO	ASCB		SETS NAMES
SYS		B	Y	COM	ACT	C		INITIALIZE
TIME		B		C&C	SET	ASC		INITIALIZE
TRACE		P		EXE	INFO	C		DIAGNOSTICS
TRACEFMT		P		EXE	INFO	C		DIAGNOSTICS
TREE		B		COM	INFO	C		FILE MAINT
TYPE		B		C&C	INFO	C,B		FILE MAINT
VER		B		C&C	INFO	C		INFO
VERIFY		B		C&C	SET	C		MISC
VOL		B		C&C	INFO	C		FILE MAINT
XCOPY		B		EXE	ACT	C,B		FILE MAINT

Table A-2. File Specification Parts and Terms

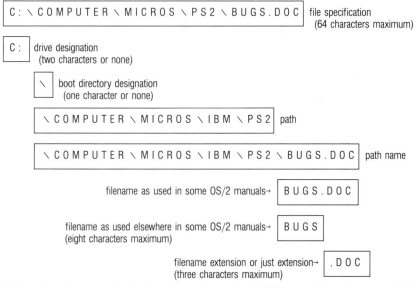

C : \ C O M P U T E R \ M I C R O S \ P S 2 \ B U G S . D O C   file specification
(64 characters maximum)

C :   drive designation
(two characters or none)

\   boot directory designation
(one character or none)

\ C O M P U T E R \ M I C R O S \ I B M \ P S 2   path

\ C O M P U T E R \ M I C R O S \ I B M \ P S 2 \ B U G S . D O C   path name

filename as used in some OS/2 manuals→ B U G S . D O C

filename as used elsewhere in some OS/2 manuals→ B U G S
(eight characters maximum)

filename extension or just extension→ . D O C
(three characters maximum)

(Don't confuse the terms path and path name used here with the PATH command or environment variable.)

Table A-3. Types of File Specifications as Mentioned in OS/2 Manuals

File Specification	Term	Explanation
DOCS??.*	Filename pattern	A filename matching pattern * or ? but containing no path.
C: \ COMPUTER \ DOCS??.*	Ambiguous filename	*Ambiguous* because it includes a filename pattern (wildcard characters * and ?).
C:COMPUTER \ DOCS??.*	Relative filename	*Relative* because the path starts at the default directory for drive C: rather than the root directory.
C: \ COMPUTER \ DOCS??.*	Absolute filename	*Absolute* because the first \ causes the path to start at the root directory (but it's still ambiguous because of the use of wildcard characters).
C:COMPUTER \ DOCS.NEW	Unambiguous filename	*Unambiguous* because it contains no wildcard characters (but it's still relative).

How File Specifications and Names Work

Nearly all commands and programs that deal with files require the operator to specify the file or files to be acted upon. Most commands allow for more than a simple filename. They allow you to specify a file or group of files which are stored in a specified region in the file system and which match certain criteria. You communicate this to the command or program with a file specification.

OS/2 goes through three steps in deciphering a file specification. In the first step, OS/2 sets up default values for these three variables:

Subject Drive   The real or assigned or substituted drive to search for the specified files.

Search Directory   The directory of the subject drive to search for the specified files.

Filename Template   A pro forma filename against which to match real filenames when selecting files from the search directory.

In the second step, OS/2 reads and processes the file specification you provide and alters the values of these three variables. Finally, in the third step, OS/2 examines the files in the search directory of the subject drive and matches them against the template to find those which meet the file specification you provided.

The third and final step can vary. If you supply a specification that is the name of an existing directory rather than a file or filename pattern, most commands and programs take this to refer to all files in that directory.

The following is an example using a filename pattern. If, instead, you wanted to specify all files in the directory C: \ COMPUTER \ MICROS \ IBM, you would supply just that directory name and not add the \ M?D*.B* used in the example.

Table A-4. Step 1 of File-Specification Processing

Assume

Current Default Drive is D:
Current Default Directory of D: is \ USR \ YOU \
Current Default Directory of C: is \ OS2 \ BIN \
Specification to Process: C: \ COMPUTER \ MICROS \ IBM \ M?D*.B*
Contents of C: \ COMPUTER \ MICROS \ IBM \:
M10DOC.BAK
M2DUP.B1
M1DOCS.SML

M1DOCS.BIG

M2DUP

M1DOCS \ (a subdirectory)

Step 1. OS/2's Initial Setting of Variables

Subject Drive = D: (the current default drive)

Search Directory = \USR \YOU (the current default directory of the subject drive)

Template = _____ (eight spaces with an extension of three spaces)

Table A-5. Step 2 of File-Specification Processing

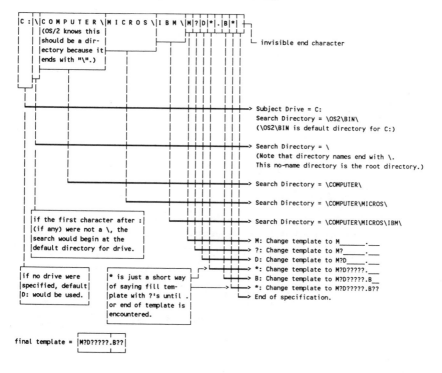

Appendix

Table A-6. Step 3 of File-Specification Processing
Matching Files in C: \COMPUTER \MICROS \IBM \ to Template

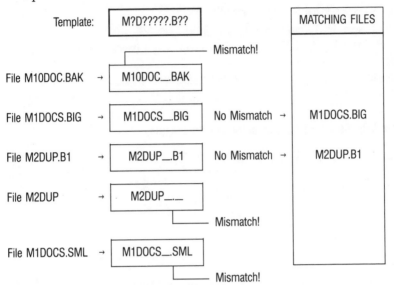

Subdirectory M1DOCS is rejected because it is not a file.

Details of Template Matching

In matching the file template against filenames, OS/2 splits the filename into its main and extension parts. The main part, if necessary, is padded out to eight characters with spaces. The extension is padded with spaces as necessary to form three characters. After padding, filenames that match character for character to the template are included in the file specification, and those that don't are rejected. Where a question mark appears in the template, any filename character is considered a match.

In general, template matching is only performed against filenames, not the names of subdirectories in the ending search directory. Usually if a file specification contains no question marks or asterisks and the last name in the path is a directory rather than a file, the specification refers to all files in the named directory. When a question mark or asterisk is used, it normally tells OS/2 to match only files, and, even if a subdirectory matches, it won't be included in the specification.

288

Dot and Dot-Dot

Where you would normally specify a directory name for OS/2, you can instead use the names . (dot) or .. (dot-dot). Dot refers to the current search directory and dot-dot refers to the directory that contains the current search directory (that is, the parent of the current search directory). Dot-dot is handy when the current directory is deeply nested and you want a branch off the tree above it. For example:

Current directory:	\ USR \ YOU \ IDEAS \ NEW
You want to see the file:	\ USR \ YOU \ IDEAS \ OLD \ WIDGET
Command:	MORE < .. \ OLD \ WIDGET
You want to search the file:	\ USR \ YOU \ PHONES
Command:	FIND "mom" .. \ .. \ PHONES

Dot is only useful by itself. The command COPY . B: is the same as COPY *.* B: because dot means *all the files in the current directory* and *.* means *all files in the current directory that match a template which matches any file.* The net result is the same. Specifications like \ USR \ . \ YOU \ IDEAS \ . \ NEW work but are silly, the dots only change the current search directory to be itself and have no net effect.

Command Peculiarities

File template matching is slightly different from the DIR command. In using DIR, if no extension is supplied, the extension portion of the template is filled with question marks. Also, a file specification that ends in a directory name gives a listing for that directory, but a file specification that includes ? or * and matches a directory name lists only the directory name itself (most commands will not include the directory when * or ? is used).

Some commands expect file specifications to give only a directory name or only filenames. Others (like ATTRIB) only find files if an individual filename or a ? or * pattern is used. They don't automatically expand a matching directory name to its constituent files.

The COPY command is a model of predictable handling of file specifications, except when a file pattern using ? or * is used in the destination file specification. In this case, the ? or * in the specification is placed in the template not as the usual one or more question marks, but as the corresponding characters from the source name. For example:

copy abcdefgh 1?34?6*

is the same as:

copy abcdefgh 1b34e6gh.

Handy Filenames and Specifications

DEL .   Deletes all files in the current directory (if you say *yes* when asked if you're sure).

COPY A:.   Copies all files in current directory of floppy drive A: to current default drive and directory.

COPY A:*   Copies only those files in default directory of A: that have no extension.

COPY A:*.?   Copies only those files with no extension and those with a one-character extension.

COPY A:*.??   Copies all files except those with a three-character extension.

COPY A:???.* Copies only files with three or fewer characters in first part of name.

COPY . ..   Copies all files in current directory to its parent (useful when you want to merge child to parent).

COPY .
.. \BROTHER Copies all files in current directory to the directory BROTHER, which has the same parent directory as the current directory. This is useful when you want to merge sibling directories.

Index

291